Whole-Systems Shared Governance

Architecture for Integration

Tim Porter-O'Grady, EdD, PhD, FAAN
Senior Partner
Tim Porter-O'Grady Associates
Atlanta, Georgia

Marilyn A. Hawkins, RN, MSN
Service Leader
Community Health System
Fresno, California

Marsha L. Parker, RN, MBA
Senior Vice President and Chief Operating Officer
Santa Rosa Memorial Hospital
Santa Rosa, California

AN ASPEN PUBLICATION®
Aspen Publishers, Inc.
Gaithersburg, Maryland
1997

Library of Congress Cataloging-in-Publication Data

Porter-O'Grady, Timothy.
Whole-systems shared governance : architecture for
integration/Tim Porter-O'Grady, Marilyn Hawkins, Marsha Parker.
p.   cm.
Includes bibliographical reference and index.
ISBN 0-8342-0951-9
1. Integrated delivery of health care.   2. Health services
administration.   I. Hawkins, Marilyn.   II. Parker, Marsha, RN, MBA.
III. Title.
RA971.P57   1997
362.1—dc21
97-10153
CIP

Orders: (800) 638-8437
Customer Service: (800) 234-1660

About Aspen Publishers • For more than 35 years, Aspen has been a leading professional publisher in a variety of disciplines. Aspen's vast information resources are
available in both print and electronic formats. We are committed to providing the
highest quality information available in the most appropriate format for our customers.
Visit Aspen's Internet site for more information resources, directories, articles, and a
searchable version of Aspen's full catalog, including the most recent publications:
http://www.aspenpublishers.com
    Aspen Publishers, Inc. • The hallmark of quality in publishing
Member of the worldwide Wolters Kluwer group.

Editorial Resources: David A. Uffelman
Library of Congress Catalog Card Number: 97-10153
ISBN: 0-8342-0951-9

Printed in the United States of America

1   2   3   4   5

Table of Contents

About the Editors

Tim Porter-O'Grady, EdD, PhD, FAAN, has been in health care for 27 years and has provided both administrative and consulting services to a wide variety of health care agencies internationally. He has written over 130 professional journal articles and has published 10 books. He resides in Atlanta, Georgia, and enjoys reading and tennis.

Marilyn A. Hawkins, RN, MSN, has provided health care leadership for over 20 years in roles ranging from staff nurse to service executive. She is currently Corporate Service Leader at Community Health System in Fresno, California. She has provided the leadership for much of the operational and structural changes necessitated by its switch to whole-systems shared governance and integration. She lives in Fresno and enjoys music, travel, and time with her family.

Marsha L. Parker, RN, MBA, has provided leadership in a variety of roles in both military and civilian life. She provided leadership support for both structural and information infrastructure changes at Community Health System in Fresno, California. She is currently Senior Vice President and Chief Operating Officer for Santa Rosa Memorial Hospital in Santa Rosa, California. She lives in Santa Rosa and enjoys her family, home, and travel.

About the Contributors

Kami English, RN, BSN, was a Shared Governance Coordinator at Community Health System at the time of this writing. She is currently Surgical Services Integrator and is pursing a master's degree in business administration.

Phil Hinton, MD, was Service Leader for Service Quality at Community Health System at the time of this writing. He is currently the Chief Executive Officer.

Jeff LaFors, MT, MBA, was Chair of the Operations Council at Community Health System at the time of this writing. He is currently Service Integrator for Laboratory Services.

Lynn Neimeth, MBA, is Service Integrator for Information Services at Community Health System.

Bruce Perry, MBA, was Chief Executive Officer and Chair of the Governance Council at Community Health System at the time of this writing. He is currently President and Chief Executive Officer of New Management Strategies, a health care consulting firm, and Chief Executive Officer of HealthPlan Management Advantage, a managed care management company—both located in Washington, D.C.

Curtis Takamoto, RPh, was Chair of the Service Council at Community Health System at the time of this writing. He is currently a clinical pharmacist.

Preface

There is not an enterprise in the United States that is not going through some form of renewal. No matter how small the activities related to renewal, the demand for efficiency and effectiveness has pushed all organizations to reassess their functions and work. Much redesign has already been initiated in the business arena and has served as the prototype or template for much of the re-engineering efforts underway in a broad diversity of product and service industries throughout the country—and indeed the world.

Much has been accomplished in the past decade. The United States has reasserted itself as the pre-eminent economy on the global stage once again, and the quality initiative, recently lost to Japan, has again been substantially reclaimed by the vast majority of American companies. Those that are most transformed have recognized that the rules are significantly different from those upon which their initial fortunes were built. It is no longer possible to simply produce goods and services in great quantities and expect that they will market and sell themselves. In addition, the products of the new enterprises depend on a level of knowledge and skill unparalleled in the history of this country.

The coming age will be fundamentally different from the age we are moving out of. Science and technology have changed the circumstances and conditions of life and have made it possible to link distant parts of the globe economically and socially in ways only the most prophetic could have predicted. And the process has only just begun.

Health care could not long remain unaffected by the realities addressed earlier by the business community. Because of the finiteness of resources, the goal of providing unlimited access and use is simply untenable. This at a time when quantum mechanics and whole-systems research have shown the interconnectedness of all things and validated the interdependence that governs sustainability.

The response to this reality has been reflected in sometimes rabid and radical efforts to uncover unnecessary costs in health care and eliminate them whenever and wherever possible. Even when such efforts affect the long-term viability of the system, many players are not slowing their attempts to reduce costs or maximize margins. While this is exceptionally shortsighted behavior, it has had its impact, as evidenced in the reactions of patients, professionals, and buyers of health care.

At the same time, major work at restructuring how care is provided has been initiated in an effort to reduce duplication, inefficiencies, and cost. Tearing down the vertical barriers between departments and disciplines has created a new construct for service. This has reflected a stronger orientation to the continuum of services across a horizontal pathway that models the health needs of subscribers rather than simply provide illness interventions. Using team-based approaches, newer interdisciplinary models of care have changed the location and relationship between all providers in a substantial way. Out of this process, however, has come even more challenge and work.

Simply pulling people together in a new relationship does not mean they want it or know what to do with it once it has occurred. All kinds of new opportunities have emerged to address the changing milieu and create a framework for learning (e.g., development of the so-called learning organization). In the usual incremental way, pieces of the transformation have been addressed, but very few organizations have taken on the task of addressing health care as an interactive system, with all that implies. Sustainability is inexorably bound together with comprehensiveness. According to systems thinking, no one part of a system can be altered without affecting all parts of the system. Simply taking on the mechanics of patient care will not effectively create a more viable patient care service. If the structures, relationships, interactions, and dependencies between parts of the system are not included in the change, it will not be sustainable.

It is fascinating to see the same mistakes made with regard to change. There is a consistently flagrant disregard of the wide variety of "fits" that have to be achieved to make an organization effective. Simply adjusting one service, component, or resource will not create the conditions necessary for sustainable change. The approach to any adjustment in an organization depends on how comprehensive the view from the center of the system is and how well the impact of any change has been considered in the context of the whole system prior to its implementation. Indeed, it is this very problem that keeps so many consultants employed today, even some who should not be.

This book focuses on whole-system change using a template as a model for transforming health care services. The authors learned early that it is necessary to start at the drawing board and completely assess the whole system and the conditions and circumstances driving change. Through systematic planning and the engagement of all the key stakeholders, a model for comprehensive redesign will emerge. Using a set of principles as the foundation for change, the leadership must ground their efforts in a detailed understanding of the need for congruence. They must exhibit a willingness to allow the context of the emerging quantum age and sociotechnological framework to drive the formation of new form and structure.

For effective renewal to occur, a new model of service and relationship must ultimately emerge. The principles of partnership, equity, accountability, and ownership define the foundations for work. These core themes form the centerpiece for all the activities of redesign outlined in this text. Every component of the point-of-service design focuses on a new construct for the organization of health care work. A conception of a continuum of care driven essentially by a focus on health service rather than sickness care forms the foundation for all system design. Recognizing that a subscriber-driven, price-controlled continuum of care will define health service for the foreseeable future ensures that all service formats will be grounded in the desire to create a truly healthy community.

The reader is advised that the models described in this book are simply that: models. While they represent a commitment to sound principle and good theoretical foundations, they reflect the unique application of thinking about service around which structure can be built. It is not recommended that any particular one be replicated as the pre-eminent model for all localities. The editors and authors hope that this book will serve as a template for the principles that guide renewal. Further, they hope that the constructs herein serve to raise questions about the appropriate application of transformational and transitional form and structure in a wide variety of settings.

This book focuses on a range of pertinent issues related to preparedness for future demands for health service delivery. However, the editors recognize that it is not an exhaustive treatment of the topic of whole-systems design for the future of health care service. All transformation is a journey. This book outlines the character and content of the journey toward a truly effective integrated health–based delivery system, but it is recommended that a host of other works intended to guide change agents toward more creative, substantive, and sustainable change strategies be consulted as well.

There is nothing fraught with more danger and difficulty than attempting to create a change in the order of things. The "noise" in the system that results is at times unbearable. Everyone's role is affected at every place in the organization. True renewal addresses the boardroom with the same intensity as the patient's room. The political, interactional, and structural challenges are impossible to conceive at the outset. The effort on the part of leaders from every place in the system is, at a minimum, Herculean. It demands a level of commitment that many are unfamiliar with and calls for a faithfulness to the process bordering on the spiritual. The results are as inspiring as the process is challenging. The ability to participate in the creation of a truly functional health system brings forth leaders and gifts where there was no expectation of them. The investment of the stakeholders in every place in the system bears much fruit in the effective design of a real service-driven system.

Of course, time will tell how successful the strategies and structures outlined in this book will prove to be. The past six years of building toward whole-systems designs has resulted in some viable service processes that could not have thrived in the Industrial Age. Regardless of the next stages of the journey, the foundations already laid will serve as a firm base for the work that lies ahead. It is in the spirit of sharing experiences and insights that this book has been written.

Tim Porter-O'Grady
Marilyn Hawkins
Marsha Parker

Acknowledgments

No work of this kind can be put together without the assistance of numerous participants. The editors wish to thank all who provided help in the creation of this book, especially Mark Ponder, whose editorial guidance singularly contributed to the final product; Hope Donaho, whose relentless attention, insight, and support helped raise the quality of the text; our families and colleagues, who supported and sustained us during the design, implementation, and documentation of this new model for health care; and our colleagues in change, whose struggles make possible every day the realization of a truly effective community health care system.

Chapter 1

Into the New Age of Health Care

Tim Porter-O'Grady

The future is like heaven;
everyone exults it
but no one wants to go there now.

James Baldwin

The health care system is changing in ways that we are only beginning to imagine, and it is essential to see the changes in a much broader context than that usually presented in health care literature. The very foundations of society are being shaken by a major shift in reality.

The globe is undergoing a change in eras. We are moving into an age whose constructs and parameters are not yet clear to us. The journey will require a great deal of adjustment—an "unbundling" of old behaviors and ways of thinking—and will challenge our understanding of what the journey means and what it requires of us.

There are broad indicators of the significance of the change in eras:

- A communication explosion is allowing all segments of the globe to be linked to each other in ways never before seen.
- The globalization of the economy is creating relationships between international regions and nations that are redefining their boundaries.
- Newtonian thinking and "reductionism" (i.e., a focus on the parts instead of the whole) is being replaced by the recognition that the globe is unified and that all issues are structurally integrated (i.e., a change in one place ripples through and impacts all the places with which it is related).
- The universal "generativity" of information is becoming fully understood, and it is increasingly recognized that information, rather than a thing, is a

dynamic through which allied process relationships are built and sustained decisions are made in ways that affect everyone's life.

A NEW UNDERSTANDING

In the context of this change, a new understanding of relationships and intersections and structures is forming, challenging the foundations of much of our social, political, business, and service organizations. At every level of human relationship and interaction, the principles that once defined who we were and gave form to our actions are now shifting and expanding into a broader set of notions affecting the very foundations of what we believe and how we behave.

THE EMERGING VALUE OF KNOWLEDGE

As knowledge becomes the foundation for economic and productive viability, it also becomes a medium of exchange. Those with specific knowledge that is necessary to an enterprise can partly determine what the future of the enterprise will be, and indeed those with such knowledge themselves become a medium of exchange. The power relationships in organizations and systems are altered as a result of the recognition that those who have knowledge also have a great deal of influence over how that knowledge is applied. Indeed, the very value of that knowledge is moderated and managed by those who have it.

Knowledge is the newest form of capital and now plays as great a role as finances in the sustainability of systems.

The recognition of this unfolding reality alone is sufficient to create a new shift in the power and relational equation in social and work systems. The application of knowledge can impact whole industries, increasing their social and financial and political stock and at the same time diminishing and even eliminating the value of that knowledge, since it might eventually cease to be applicable because of the changes wrought.

Whether intended or not, the emerging information and knowledge society is altering the circumstances of how we live and work. Those circumstances now require us to conceive our social constructs and work structures in entirely different ways. There are problems, however, associated with the need to conceive life in new ways:

- The knowledge society requires a shift in the locus of control and the position of power. It challenges those who currently hold power and requires them to locate it differently from the ways it has traditionally been distributed in organizations.
- Knowledge workers historically unfamiliar with the use of power have a difficult time understanding how to obtain it and utilize it appropriately.
- The move toward knowledge-based organizations requires a stronger focus on outcomes and results. Workers' attachment to process, functions, and activities impedes their ability to adjust as outcomes and results demand.
- Structures of organizations shift dramatically in knowledge-based organizations. Systems must make it easy for new knowledge to be applied and therefore must connect decision making and knowledge application as tightly as possible. Having many hierarchical levels of decision making impedes the speed and fluidity with which knowledge and decision making are able to interact.

These circumstances are converging to create a critical series of events both globally and locally. What is occurring in health care is simply a subset of much of what is driving change across all systems, creating the same set of challenges that every segment of society must confront. What is important for health care professionals is to realize that much of what is unfolding in health care falls within the broad parameters discussed above and to give meaning and context to many of the changes that must occur in the health care delivery system in order to make it more effective.

Knowledge is more than power; it is a medium of exchange as important as any other commodity in the workplace.

A NEW CONTEXT FOR A NEW AGE

It is to this end that whole-systems shared governance is directed. Many of the demands in the health care system, as in many other parts of society, require a different organizational construct, a different set of relationships and interactions, and different ways of making decisions if effectiveness is to be sustained. Whatever the change process, it will be a complex and high-intensity experience (see Table 1-1). Shared governance is a structural model that reflects a response to the changing paradigm, operates outward from the point of service, and gives

Table 1-1 The Changing Health Care Marketplace

Old	New
Single payments	Contracts
Physician manages care	Third party manages care
Do more, make more	Do more, make less
High hospital occupancy	Low hospital occupancy
Referrals, money maker	Referrals, money loser
Primary care, low status	Primary care, high status
Treat disease	Improve health status
Institution centered	Community centered
Free-standing facility	Integrated facility
Physicians and hospital separate	Physician–hospital organization
Patients one by one	Patients in groups
Solo practice	Group practice
Tertiary care, money maker	Tertiary care, money loser
Physician centered	Patient and family centered
Curing	Healing
Patients come to providers	Providers go to patients
High profit margins	Low profit margins
Physicians	Physicians and physician extenders
Traditional medicine	Alternative medicine
Providers as revenue generators	Providers as cost centers
Reactive medical care	Health needs assessment
Emphasis on treatment	Emphasis on prevention
Vertical organizations	Horizontal organizations
Inpatient care	Outpatient and home health care
Ignoring waste	Designing out waste
Assumption of provider competency	Competency report cards
Community practice	Critical pathway standards
Assumed outcomes	Outcome measurement
Patient as recipient	Patient as participant
National reform	State and local reform

form and structure to support function and outcome in integrated health care organizations. While it is unique to the health care system, it is based on sound systems thinking and emerging principles that are indicative of the characteristics of the age into which we are moving. Shared governance takes the characteristics and principles that reflect the age, gives them form, and builds structures that promulgate and support the newer relationships, intersections, functions, and activities of the health care system.

The health care system is made up predominately of knowledge workers who have historically applied their skills and talents in a vertically defined, compartmentalized structure. As health care changes, a much broader format is needed to view the breadth of services emerging along a continuum of care. Leadership can no longer look at health care services within a narrow, vertical, institutional format. In order to create sustainable outcomes, it is now necessary to bring together many diverse players. A wide range of

> *Leadership is no longer managership. The whole role of leader is to facilitate the growth of leadership in all roles in the system.*

providers promulgate and facilitate these outcomes in the same frame of reference, linking activities, functions, relationships, and intersections as they effect sustainable clinical outcomes. Achieving all of this requires an entirely different way of thinking and an organization designed in a meaningful way. All kinds of activities are exemplifying this emerging mandate in health care organizations.

A NEW REALITY FOR ORGANIZATIONS

In health care, a reallocation of power is paralleling the reallocation underway in other parts of American society, such as business and the service industry. There is a host of changes currently affecting the design of health care organizations (see Figure 1-1). As these organizations change from being hierarchical and management driven to being knowledge based and having a whole systems design, their operations, services, and governance functions must be reconfigured so that policy, direction, and point-of-service deci-

> *Building a point-of-service system means reallocating power in the organization to those who do the work of health care.*

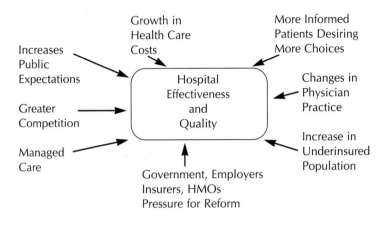

Figure 1-1 Developments in Health Care that Are Influencing Quality and Effectiveness

sion making intersect in a much more meaningful way. Also, the increasing focus on decisions made by those at the point of service requires an entirely different construct for the function and operation of health care organizations. Service integration along the continuum of care is forcing them to revise their structures and think in new ways about how health care is delivered; how worker relationships unfold; and how environments, structures, and processes affect the delivery of meaningful, value-based service.

The changes in the understanding of organizational relationships are having an impact on the design of health care systems. New rules and circumstances are affecting just how health services are being offered and will be offered in the future. For example, many hospitals are moving from unit-based department models with vertical lines of authority that are fragmented and unlinked to other parts of the system toward models founded on collaboration, shared decision making, and point-of-service function. The kinds of services provided in the new marketplace emphasize different clinical activities than in the past. Furthermore, self-directed team–based structures are emerging within the context of a much more seamless and horizontal continuum of integrated health services for a better defined population. The creation of these structures means that the organizations cannot be managed in the same way as they were in the past.

CHANGING CONTEXT FOR HEALTH CARE SERVICES

It is important, therefore, for leaders to be clear about the environmental factors that suggest workplace readiness to explore self-directed, seamless, and integrated structures in a delivery system that integrates every point of decision making along a continuum of services and must measure its results and value all along the way. The primary role of the leader is to determine the ways in which the old frameworks and behaviors (parental management style, for example) must give way to more contemporary notions about operations and the application of systems models. And we must break the old rules (see Figure 1-2).

> *The role of leadership is primarily directed toward breaking down old frameworks and practices, making organizations and people ready for newer configurations.*

This chapter outlines primary principles that exemplify the new age and must constitute the foundation for any sustainable change in structure (partnership, accountability, equity, and ownership). Without these principles or their application, structure will be built on shaky ground and will collapse quickly with the next major shift in direction and function. Furthermore, leaders need to be challenged to redesign and renew organizations in ways that reflect a much more point-of-service–driven, empowered, and information-based system.

THE EVOLVING NATURE OF WORK

As part of the health care revolution, the traditional delivery infrastructure must be reinvented to support a new understanding of work, health, information,

---

For every dollar spent on direct patient care, we spend three to four dollars

- waiting for it to happen
- arranging to do it
- writing it down

Figure 1-2 The Old Way

quality, outcomes, relationships, and intersections within an organized delivery system (see Exhibit 1-1). These changes will result in fewer managers and will alter their roles and functions as well as the expectations and functions of those who provide services. They will challenge current practices and will generally turn organizations and perceptions of work upside down and force us to think about meaning and purpose in relationship to function and activity. There are a number of shifts that are already underway:

- Hospitals are being deconstructed to do two things: diminish the focus on bed-based activities and create efficiencies in the organization.
- Health care services, traditionally scattered throughout different settings, are now being reconfigured into an integrated service pathway, some of which is hospital based and some of which is not.
- Linear administrative hierarchies are diminishing in value as more effective point-of-service designs are created. They are being transformed into equity-based models characterized by collaborative decision making, management support, and consultative roles as more decentralized point-of-service decision making arises and knowledge-based ownership of work processes emerges at the point of service.
- Competition is now moving to the systems level. Systems are competing with each other to provide a broad range of services to as broad a population as can be served. Each system, in a sense, is also competing with itself in trying to increase its ability to provide cost-effective high-quality services and maintain the satisfaction of its patients and providers.
- A short-term, fix-it mindset is not appropriate for addressing constant change. Fad surfing and fashion shifts in health care, so often seen in the past, must be replaced by a willingness to consider the contribution fads or fashions can make to the whole and their ability to facilitate sustainable cost-effective service relationships.

Exhibit 1-1 Problems with the Traditional Structure

- Fragmentation of care
- Turf issues and duplication
- Nonproductive downtime
- No coordination of care
- Task orientation versus outcomes orientation
- No accountability for big picture
- Cost management

Besides the immediate signs of a shift in practices and processes in health care, there are other key influences that define a comprehensive scope of change accompanying the above challenges. These external and internal environmental factors create the conditions that require sustainable shifts:

- the local impact of global forces of change
- contemporary systems theory (quantum versus Newtonian thinking)
- the emergence of capitated payment schemes
- the movement toward a focus on creating health
- the growing competence and decision-making role of subscribers (patients)
- the demand for change and the organizational readiness to respond

> *Most restructuring must occur between people's ears.*

Furthermore, three major forces are converging to create conditions that have made avoidance of significant change no longer a viable option: technology, social reengineering, and economic reconfiguration.

TECHNOLOGY

The computer chip has become the new vehicle upon which we are traveling into the new age. Indeed, its applications affect almost every aspect of life, from the minute our digital alarm clocks wake us up in the morning to the arming of our home security systems when we go to bed at night. Information and communications technology will link all service components and all stakeholders at the point of service, making it both possible and necessary to locate most decisions where the providers and consumers meet.

Technology has created mobility in health care. One of the effects of technology is to reduce the demand on once-necessary functions and activities. Examples include procedures such as cholecystectomy, laser surgery, chemotherapy, and monoclonal antibody therapy. All of these reduce the intensity of interventions, the lengths of stay in hospitals, and the need for beds. Each also significantly reduces the activities of one or another health care provider. Many applications of technology make care

> *Technology is not simply changing how we work; it is changing how we live.*

more portable and less invasive, thus radically altering the service structure. The impact of the techno-infrastructure is exemplified in almost every area of health care delivery.

SOCIAL REENGINEERING

The shift from national to regional and global power relationships is forcing social and work institutions to look critically at their own structures, relationships, functions, and purposes and to reconstruct them within a broader context. Politics is now about international relationships, and economics is now about international interfaces on a global business, manufacturing, and service stage. Increasingly, decisions about competition, products, services, profits, trade, boundaries, and politics are being radically influenced by an emerging set of variables that are international in character. No nation from this time forward can make decisions for itself without taking into account the context of its relationship to other parts of the global community and hope to have a sustainable future. The intersections between regions and nations on the international stage are now as critical as the activities that occur within any one nation.

> *The transformation we are experiencing is affecting every place on the globe. No one is exempt from the impact of this change, and our world is altered forever.*

At the social level, service structures that promote the future of society are also shifting and adjusting. Immigration, education, employment, entitlement programs, crime, and social health are all arenas where radical adjustments in scope, social process, and community construction have emerged, with significant implications.

For example, the increased role of computer technology in the education of children has created a conflict in the framework and structure of education in American society. Through the use of interactive technology and computer systems, children can learn in 5 to 15 minutes what it takes 5 hours of didactic, one-to-group teaching activities to instill. However, to fully implement the

> *Learning is altered by technology. We now have an educational system that is no longer adequate for the needs of those it is intended to instruct.*

technology already present would require a shift in the kinds and numbers of teachers, the design and format of the classroom, and the design and structuring of education in America.

The complex, critical issues of role, outcome, employment, and relevance all influence the viability of the response to the educational crisis created by the possibilities of technology and the emerging need for its socially relevant use. This, joined with the other issues identified above, creates a major social challenge influencing the reconstruction of the social paradigm both in America and other nations across the globe.

INSTANT ACCESS

The key components of the technological revolution are to a great extent driving the underpinnings of the transformation of society and the emergence of a new age. Communication technology alone is connecting humanity in ways that could never have been anticipated in the past. Boundaries and borders no longer have significance or meaning now that technology integrates people across artificial barriers of any kind. People of every culture and circumstance can now connect and communicate with each other across national boundaries. Further, they can generate unlimited volumes of information and almost instantly send them over phone lines to any part of the globe.

Technology in the world of commerce has already altered forever the way in which business is conducted. Companies have created so many useful technological products that we can simply not survive without them. While we might take them for granted (our generation is still suspicious of technology), we can watch them transform every part of human experience in many subtle and not so subtle ways.

> *Technology has created an opportunity to connect the world in ways only dreamt of in past generations. As a result, we have become a global community— and are confronted with all the attendant options and problems.*

Technology means instantaneous access to anything that any person might want or need. Very little information is out of the reach of individuals who know how to use computers. Not only can most information be accessed, it can be integrated in ways that permit a breadth and depth of view only previously imagined. Information provides a framework for flexibility and gives everyone the opportunity to link with others in the time it takes to dial a number. In the past 100 years we have gone from train travel to fiber-optic travel, and we can now connect with others across the globe without ever leaving home.

ECONOMIC AND FINANCIAL SHIFTS

There is clearly nothing having a greater impact on the American health care system and culture than the changes in economics and finance that are currently occurring. While the economics of health care is complex, simple conditions are converging to create the need for a major shift in the orientation and structuring of the health care system. What is currently happening in the United States is the direct result of a lack of control in spending over the last 30 years. We are simply expending too much for the health care that we are getting in return. In fact, health care expenditures are outstripping other social expenditures by a factor of three to four. Without experiencing a net improvement in the health of the nation, we continue to watch health care costs spiral above every other economic indicator.

> *The prevailing reality affecting all parts of the economy is that resources are finite. Therefore, good stewardship means careful allocation and use of resources.*

GROWING COSTS

Health care in the United States has grown from a $100-billion industry in 1965 into a $1.2-trillion industry in 1996. Despite increases in technology and the availability of services, we still have not conclusively addressed the basic health issues of the nation. It is suggested that the improved health many Americans enjoy is due mostly to improvements in public health (e.g., excellent sewage systems, immunization campaigns, and other community services), not to the services provided by our "illness care" system.

A good portion of our economy is tied up in providing or paying for health care services. Health care leadership has a powerful influence on what happens to the system and the political and economic decisions that are made about it. If there is no generalized commitment to renewal and reformation, the chances are that costs will continue to grow at or about the same rate they have in the past, creating an overwhelming demand for economic and financial retooling of the system. A new way of looking at service provision—accounting for health care, paying for it, and costing out the expense and financial outlays for service—becomes a critical focus for the health care system. While Americans seem generally opposed to creating an integrated, federally designed plan to address the issues of economics and finance in health care, those issues must still be addressed, even if it means addressing them at local, regional, and state levels throughout the nation.

> *Health care–related activities eat up a large share of the gross domestic product in a way that negatively affects the economic balance of the country. We cannot ignore the consequences of overspending on health care and thrive as a nation.*

Fortunately, much of the health care leadership is already involved in the retooling and restructuring of the delivery system in a way that is increasing the cost-effectiveness and efficiency of service provision and changing the character of the relationship between cost and value. Controlling costs and capping expenditures requires that every system and institution that provides health care services tighten its belt and begin addressing the following questions regarding the appropriate delivery of health care: What do we provide? How much will it cost? What will our work be? And what are the cost-benefit trade-offs of the initiatives that we undertake in creating meaningful health care? Much of the

> *Changing the structure means changing the way health care services are provided. This has an impact on both behaviors and expectations.*

work of redesigning health care can be seen as an attempt to respond to these questions.

CHANGING HEALTH CARE STRUCTURES AND MODELS

The medical model of health care is fraught with serious problems and issues. Medical intervention is clearly "situational" and dependent on the identification of illness for the generation of services and payment. The historic problem with the medical model is that it offers too little too late and that the treatment activities are reactive rather than proactive. Since technology makes it possible to intervene earlier and to reduce the intensity of interventions, it begins to alter the character of practice and create the conditions that provide a different framework for valuing health care delivery.

> *The American model of health care is dying on the vine. A new more fluid and integrated approach to providing health care services is essential if an effective and efficient system is to be created.*

MANAGING DEMAND

In the future of the health care delivery system, there will be a growing dependence on primary and preventive services. Accessing the consumer earlier in the cycle of life, before high-intensity and costly illnesses appear, will be an important part of the design of the system (see Exhibit 1-2). This means, however, retooling every element of the system in a fundamental way to permit early service provision. This retooling serves as the underpinning for redesigning the structure, administration, and integration of health care organizations (including the formation of shared governance structures).

CAPITATION

The goal of capping costs can lead to the creation of a subscriber-based health care system. In a subscriber-based system, individuals pay in advance for services that address their health and illness care needs. Fixing the price of health care means that health care providers must adjust services to respond to an increase in the cost of doing business. In other words, they will have to learn to develop services and offer them in a way that is ever attendant to the cost of those services yet flexible enough to ensure patient satisfaction and good medical outcomes.

Exhibit 1-2 Managing Demand

- Who will get sick?
- When do people seek health service?
- What are the subscriber characteristics?
- What do we need to do to address early demand?

OVERCOMING MEDICAL SEPARATISM

Historically, in the United States the practice of medicine has remained relatively free of broad-based and integrated accountability. Shrouded in the mystery of incomprehensible quackery, then Newtonian-based science, the practice of medicine has developed without having to provide much evidence of its efficacy for achieving desired outcomes. The individual rights of physicians have been protected by broadly permissive state practice acts and a legally protectionist physician–patient relationship. Indeed, a whole range of laws and regulations has emerged that insulate physicians and shield them from the consequences of poor practice. The only way to break through this shield has been to use the legal system (i.e., to sue physicians and other health care providers based on evidence of incompetence or gross neglect).

> *We are watching the end of the practice of medical care as we know it in the United States. The independent, nonaligned adversarial practice of medicine is dead.*

Physician practice has remained relatively independent thus far, but now that outcomes have become the driving factor and value has become the measure of viability, physicians can no longer remain outside of the circle of accountability. Increasingly, physicians are becoming partners in a number of different arrangements, either through shared risk, ownership, or other kinds of contractual or service relationships between service providers and across the continuum of care. The growth in such arrangements changes physicians and their relationship to the health care system. While there is much noise involved in this shift, it is essential for fully establishing a cost-effective and service-based system. Integrating physicians as partners in the organizational system places special demands on the design of the system. Shared governance becomes a requisite structural design that integrates physicians, creates decision-making partnerships, and provides a framework for continuously facilitating and managing these partnerships.

MANAGED CARE

As part of the effort to get control over both care and cost and to create a care delivery system that integrates cost, service, and outcome, newer managed care approaches to organizing care delivery and health services are quickly emerging as the favored models for delivery in the United States. The prepaid subscriber-based delivery approach has grown significantly in response to the belief that it improves services and reduces the costs of delivering those services. While there is still much work to do to produce sufficient evidence, it appears that pooling physicians and other providers together and contracting with buyers creates a framework for obtaining reasonable relationships, appropriate services, and manageable cost.

> *Managing lives is different from treating sickness—you must know the person before you can be successful in keeping him or her healthy.*

It is equally important that consumers be incorporated into the decision-making framework. Consumers must have access to the same range of services in managed care that they might in any other model. However, the delivery of services must reduce the total amount of cost yet provide a continuous linkage of services in such a way that consumers can access the system early on, before they need major interventions. In order to ensure attractiveness and draw appropriate consumers into the market, managed care providers are therefore forced to offer high-quality competitive services that meet the demand for cost efficiency, consumer satisfaction, and positive outcome measures.

> *We can never again make decisions for consumers; instead we must make decisions with them—they "own" their health and must be accountable for it.*

THE QUALITY MOVEMENT

There has been nothing in the United States that has had a greater impact on work, business, and health care in the past decade than the introduction of the quality movement. Deming and his associates have made Americans aware of the fact that, in the global community, competition is not just a matter of price but also of quality. And since health care professionals do not live their lives in isolation and are dependent upon the satisfaction of those they serve, quality is an essential component of health services.

Americans have jumped on the quality movement bandwagon and have achieved some remarkable results. However, we are early in the process. What we do and what we produce and how we manage costs are all now thrown together into a focus on process that is dramatic in its detail and an inspiration with regard to its impact on outcomes. Those who have taken on the task of achieving real customer orientation, process engineering, quality delineation, quality improvement, and team-based systems have shown dramatic results in terms of quality and marketability (see Table 1-2). Indeed, these results have set the level for organizational expectations.

> *Quality is about achieving sustainable outcomes. Outcomes are what we use to measure the value of processes. Our actions have no meaning separated from the ends to which they are directed.*

The quality imperative also leads to the conditions that create a demand for a shared governance structure. Quality cannot be sustained or even obtained except at the point of service, where an organization lives out its service life. Therefore, quality must be an ongoing construct of any work. That being so, the organizational structure must be one that empowers those accountable for quality to make effective meaningful decisions

Table 1-2 Transition to a Customer Focus

Traditional Focus	Customer Focus
Professional teams	Multidisciplinary customer-focused teams
Clinical standards	Customer satisfaction, priorities, and outcomes
Manage customers around department's routine	Manage resources for customer
Task oriented	Outcome oriented
Call appropriate personnel	Do not pass off work one can do oneself
Complicated organizational structure	Simplified organizational structure
Multiple customer contacts	Limited customer contacts
Documentation by profession	Multidisciplinary patient record
Point finger	Fix process
Work faster	Work smarter
Narrow job scope	Broad job scope

interdependently and free of the supervising, controlling, and approval levels of past organizational structures.

Furthermore, the quality imperative includes all of the stakeholders, and getting board members, physicians, administrators, nurses, and other providers in the same room to delineate issues of quality and service, indeed to "sing from the same sheet of music" with regard to service and quality, requires a new type of organizational structure. Shared governance creates a framework for ensuring that the right players are in the right place and make the right decisions about what they do and the impact of what they do—in short, are able to control the quality of their work.

REENGINEERING CARE DELIVERY

Finally, the reengineering movement has created the conditions for redesigning the point of service in a much more functional, cost-effective, and cost-efficient manner. The demand for outcomes ultimately focuses on the performance of those upon whom outcomes depend. Building team-based relationships, integrat-

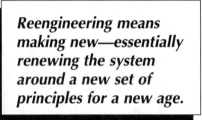

Reengineering means making new—essentially renewing the system around a new set of principles for a new age.

ing the disciplines, creating equity at the point of service, designing around the patient population, and creating continuums of relationship, linkage, and integration across the system are all fundamental ways of reengineering a health care organization to be more tightly fitted and to be able to answer the value question.

It is becoming increasingly clear that old structures no longer serve the needs of patients or providers, nor are they appropriate for providing care in a service-based organization. As a result, in health care there has been much exploration of alternative designs for patient-focused activities. Designs are emerging that better support the provision of satisfying service and the achievement of meaningful and cost-efficient outcomes.

This means, however, that old departmental, functional, "silo-based" approaches to the work must be let go. Old rituals and routines will be challenged and people's work relationships and attachment to activities and functions of the past will be severely tested. The result will be structural and political "noise" (see Exhibit 1-3). New roles will be developed, interactions and functions will be closely examined, and processes and relationships will be assessed to determine their contribution to the achievement of patient outcomes and specific cost outcomes.

Certain roles will not survive the analysis or the change, and the integration of roles will call for new kinds of players and practitioners.

Required is a new focus—a focus on discovering where service is best provided and how integration can create linkage that has imbedded in it the necessary cost and service efficiencies. Compression of the organization creates a leaner system with fewer managers, better prepared practitioners, and a clearer delineation of functions and expectations around the organization's core of clinical activities. This creates a demand for a new administrative service and organizational structure, one that can act as a vehicle for linking the stakeholders together, and can provide a decision-making framework that produces desired outcomes without sacrificing equity, investment, empowerment, and ownership at the point of service. Shared governance is one such structure.

> *Structure in systems now must be fluid and flexible in order to respond quickly to new relationships and services in the continuum of care.*

> *Shared governance is about shared decision making and building equity into the system.*

PRINCIPLES FOR A NEW AGE

It should be apparent to the reader that the constructs and foundations of the age into which we are moving are fundamentally different from those of the age

Exhibit 1-3 Structural and Political Considerations

- Team attitudes
- Turf battles
- Career goals
- Manager versus leadership roles
- Corporate culture
- Change quotient
- "Risk" quotient
- Current and future performance
- Current and future external environment

from which we are passing. One of the obstacles to progress when we move into a new age is what we think we know and understand. The constructs we have in place—the current organizational designs and structures and even the tools of our mindset—are inadequate for conceiving how we might behave or develop in the emerging new age. As we watch technology alter our conditions and circumstances, we see it create the need for a new script. Many of the constructs that carried us to this point are not adequate to carry us to the next point.

As a result of these realities, a new set of principles is being forged, and these principles will constitute the basis for new forms and structures, such as shared governance. The movement away from the Newtonian underpinning that characterized the Industrial Age and the linear understandings that represent it is creating the foundation for new ways of thinking and conceiving and doing.

The emergence in the last 40 to 60 years of quantum mechanics and the recent understanding of its impact on structures, organizations, and human systems creates a different foundation for the emerging age. A focus on whole systems and the ability to integrate across them (versus a focus on parts) requires a method of application that is fundamentally different from that used to date. Thinking about "wholes" is

> *Quantum thinking replaces vertical and linear thinking about work and relationships. It dramatically alters the way we see reality and build partnerships.*

characteristic of the new age; thinking about "parts" is characteristic of the Industrial Age. Our entire framework for thinking about organizations is changing dramatically, and questions about how they will function in the future and what they will actually become with the emergence of a global culture are being raised.

> *Principles guide our thinking about the foundations for our action and serve as a baseline, a template for measuring the consistency of our actions with our beliefs.*

The new age is represented by a set of principles that exemplify it rather than simply define it. Since the new age is unfolding, in essence being born as we live through it, it is very difficult to establish parameters that define it clearly. And in fact it is not necessarily appropriate to do so. In the midst of a move into a new age of understanding and application, the ability to "see" is better than the ability to "define." In addition, the leader can put form to what is seen only when discernment is a part of his or her skill set. However, in reading the emerging signposts, there are certain principles that can give us a clearer indication of what the underpinnings of the new age might be and what form some of the responses to it might take. These are the same principles that support the concepts of shared governance—the principles of partnership, equity, accountability, and ownership.

PARTNERSHIP

It certainly does not take much effort to realize that partnership will become an increasingly prevalent organizational model. Older nationalistic and dividing line models of social and political organization are quickly disappearing as the globe reorganizes itself into far broader and more regional relationships. However, even in the midst of the growth of regional entities, compartmentalized national and ethnic groups are attempting to hold back the future in protecting their own narrow interests at the expense of their relationships with other groups. Bosnia serves as a most recent example of this dynamic.

As globalization moves forward, it provides a motivation for nations to form economic, social, and political coalitions that strengthen their global economic viability. Isolationism and exclusivism are simply nontenable in a world characterized by an entirely different set of constructs, but the effort to create broad-based partnerships is filled with risks and some danger. Overcoming old barriers; dealing with old relationships; and working through discordant experiences, the judgments of history,

Partnership is essential to relationship building and is the foundation for constructing the future of organizations.

the circumstances of war, and a host of other regional and national issues require painstaking effort and mind-bending patience. The rewards of doing all these things are significant, of course. Broader economies show greater strength, greater potential, and longer term viability.

Partnerships are clearly arising at every level of society. The principle of partnership applies to small local communities and to large nation states. Small companies and major enterprises are forming alliances, networks, and other new types of conglomerates. Many are now becoming partners in an effort to consolidate around a certain group of products or services through which they can excel. Larger entities are designing themselves to become lean and effective and there-

> *The principle of partnership is driving changes at every level of the social order. Political, social, economic partnerships are necessary for thriving on the global stage and building sustainable relationships.*

by increase their competitiveness on the global stage. Smaller entities, on the other hand, are amalgamating to extend their power base and be able to challenge larger entities.

Partnership will clearly require the dismantling of old approaches and models of hierarchical isolationism and vertical integration. Obviously, more horizontal linkages between companies, services, structures, and systems will be required to sustain the networks necessary to compete on a broader stage. Increasingly, the work structures that develop in complex multifocal organizations must be more centered around the point of service so that the issues of service and product can be more clearly defined by those who produce the outcomes.

The growth in the role of partnership is evident in the increased use of work teams, integrative work arrangements, interdisciplinary models of organization, and multifocal service structures. As organizations form partnerships, they must increase their effectiveness in order to thrive. Lean design, more efficient functions, stronger networks and relationships, and clearer delineation of quality and outcomes become the foundation for achieving successful outcomes.

NEEDED: A NEW KIND OF LEADER

The work of building partnerships and making them sustainable offers a new challenge for leaders. The new processes of integration and organization and the shift in work structures support new models of leadership responsibility. The content of the leadership role is altered forever, and the tolerance and talents of persons making the journey toward the revised role will be sorely tested. Partnership demands dialogue about the relationship between players and the way in which work gets structured and completed. Because of the problems likely to occur in the journey from one construct of organization to

> *Leadership is an adult-to-adult interaction, not a parental role. New skills will be necessary to extinguish old "boss" behaviors.*

another, leaders must show a willingness to lay the issues on the table before the stakeholders, gather them around those issues, and facilitate their attempts to find solutions to those issues.

> **The locus of control in empowered organizations is at the point of service where most of the decisions are made.**

Old constructs and structures in an organization do not support the transfer of the locus of control to the point of service unless the structures themselves shift (see Exhibit 1-4). One of the greatest challenges in reengineering is to restructure the point of service or productivity and at the same time alter the decision-making framework, administrative structure, and governance structure in ways that increase the organization's ability to support the reengineering changes. The demand for shared governance grows because the old structures are inconsistent with an organizational format in which leadership is mainly located at the point of service.

CREATING A LEARNING ORGANIZATION

In moving toward partnership, an organization must become a learning center in which creativity, problem solving, solution seeking, integration, functional proficiency, quality improvement, relationship building, process enhancement, and outcome determination are the fundamental elements. A learning organization is continuously and dynamically shifting and adjusting what its members know and evaluating what they apply. The structures of such an organization must be as fluid as the ebb and flow of relationships necessitated by changes in the work and the organization's economic situation. New models require shared risk, shared leadership, and shared governance.

The application of the concept of partnership can create a different context for operating and functioning in the organization and can alter its relational milieu

---

Exhibit 1-4 New Rules

- Patients first, departments second
- Simplify, simplify, simplify
- Create relationships where they do not already exist
- Combine units and departments that it makes sense to combine
- No budgetary increases
- No decrease in quality

and its service structure. Command and control systems will no longer facilitate functioning, especially if the majority of decisions are moved to the point of service. Empowerment becomes not simply a concept but a modus operandi in a point-of-service organization. Furthermore, partnership demands that all of the members of the system, defined by their relationship, be linked in a way that facilitates their common commitment to achieve desired outcomes. There can be no role ascendance, no vertical integration that allows a single person or unit to captain every effort along the continuum of relationships. In health care especially, provider relationships contribute greatly to the char-

> *Command and control systems are the vestiges of a system long since past. Unilateral decision making is not the most effective or sustainable approach to good decision making.*

acter and quality of the care. No one player can know about or control all of the elements of the relationships necessary to consistently achieve desired outcomes along the service continuum. Sustained achievement of desired outcomes requires interdependency—a web of complex relationships between players that facilitates their identification with each other. Again, history and previous expectations and relationships ensure that the transition to real partnerships will be challenging. Such a shift will require the leadership to act increasingly as facilitators of the efforts of others as well as exhibit exceptional skill and patience in creating the required structures and support systems.

> *Health systems must now build a host of noncompetitive relationships. The health of an organization depends on the strengths of its horizontal relationships with partners along the continuum of care.*

Partnership in these new organizations calls for a level of openness and honesty not formerly evident in most workplaces. The quality movement has already forced organizations to look critically at their work. The next step—the revising of structures and service systems—will demand that the relationship between work and the outcome of work become increasingly more important. Ameliorating the relationships imbedded in work will require a commitment to build the intersections needed to overcome the powerful barriers to true partnership.

EQUITY

Equity is more than a measure of equality. Equity assumes equality. The foundation of equity is value. Indeed, equity is an indicator of the presence of value. It demonstrates that there is an effective and meaningful relationship between parties—a relationship from which value is obtained by all parties. Equity further involves a recognition of the contribution of each role necessary to an outcome. Equity assumes that all outcomes are dependent on the integration of the roles directed toward achieving them. Rarely are outcomes sustained through the activities of any one individual. In systems thinking, equity is a measure of the integration of all players' contributions to outcomes.

> *Equity is not a measure of equality but instead is an indicator of value. Every role has value to the extent that it contributes to the purposes and work of the organization.*

To be effective, every effort in a health care organization must be devoted to restructuring, renewing, and redesigning the structures and services of the organization to better define health and produce health through the efficient delivery of health care services. Currently, health care is being driven more by cost issues than by any other factor. However, quality and sustainable outcomes are emerging as clear elements of the value equation. It is important to recognize that each contributes to long-term viability and to understand what needs to be in place in order to achieve a healthy future.

> *Equity demands a commitment on the part of all partners in the organization and a recognition of the contribution each makes to the success of the system. No outcome is sustained through the activities of any one person.*

Equity assumes that there is commitment to effectiveness on the part of all players. Furthermore, equity validates the belief that different roles contribute in different ways to outcomes but that no role is clearly more important than another. In the past, roles were defined by their location in the hierarchy and by their job content. In an integrated whole systems approach, roles are merely distinguished by the activities of the individuals who are acting within the roles.

Clearly, different roles are necessary to sustain an organization. There are those who must administer and those who must provide services. Further, there is a need to delineate the different contributions of those who provide services and those who manage. It should be assumed by anyone reviewing an organization that roles that have no clear account-ability and no specified relationship to the desired outcomes should simply not exist. This principle provides a realistic basis upon which to look at roles along a continuum of services in a nonhierarchical and integrated sys-tem with a point-of-service design. Because control, leadership, function, activity, determination of quality, and value are mainly located at the point of service, the relationship between the players there becomes more important.

> *The knowledge worker at the point of service is as important to the success of an organization as anyone else and must be included in decisions that affect the work he or she does and the outcome of that work.*

In a point-of-service organization, the success of the organization depends on the judgment and activities of those who live at the point of service. Toffler, Drucker, and others have pointed out that over this next decade leaders must increasingly realize that an organization's human capital—the persons who do the work of the organization—actually determines its level of performance. As Drucker succinctly puts it, it is not only financial capital that ensures the ability of an organization to thrive over the next millennium, it is the understanding that human capital is the vital variable that ensures continuing ability to thrive over the long term. This growing notion of check and balance between fiscal and human capital creates a new equation in the workplace that requires a distribution of emphasis and value in creating effective constructs and structures for work. It is upon this premise, as well as that of partnership, that shared governance begins to take more legitimate and specific form.

Inevitably, providers and their partners will function in a more decentralized interdependent continuum of services across a broad-based service structure. That will demand empowerment, independence, and interdependence and an abil-ity to understand the application of value at the point of service and between and among the players. The viability of the organization, its cost-effectiveness, and the efficacy of service provided will depend on the competence of the worker. This concerns not only technical proficiency but also the integrity of the provider relationship. Also important is the interdependence between the providers and other professionals as well as the effectiveness of their decisions without the kind of supervision so evident in the past. A decentralized broad-based delivery system unfolding in a number of different sites, highly mobile and consumer driven, simply cannot afford or sustain enough managers to supervise and approve the activities of these workers. They therefore must become interdependent and independent in their activities and relationships. The question that arises is, how does one build a structure that (1) makes that possible and (2) creates sufficient checks and balances to ensure that defined outcomes are obtained and sustained?

> *Decentralizing the structure of an organization does nothing if the decisions are not decentralized to the point of service. Unilateral control at any place in the system is just as destructive as it is at the top of the system.*

Equity therefore is more than simply a concept or a belief. It is the best mechanism for integrating relationships at the point of service in a service-based organization. It forces the organization to stay focused on its services and customers. It is represented in the organizational structures, processes, and mechanisms. Equity is evidenced, among other ways, by a strong organizational commitment to supporting people's involvement and investment in the point of service.

Equity is clearly enhanced through inclusive processes at every place decisions are made. It also demands accountability and ownership. And as already mentioned, organizational and administrative constructs must exhibit commitment to equity as a fundamental principle.

> *Integrating relationships means committing to the linking of all persons around the roles and intersections necessary to build the system.*

ACCOUNTABILITY

The most significant transition occurring in organizational systems is from responsibility to accountability. In the industrial model, command and control strategies define the decision-making construct for the organization. Subordinating relationships were essential to the character of the system.

Indeed, satisfaction of the "boss" was the paramount consideration in the work relationship, no matter how it was characterized. If the boss was satisfied with the employee's work, the employee was well rewarded (and ostensibly also satisfied). If the boss continued to be satisfied, the employee could thrive and advance up the organizational ladder.

> *Accountability is generated from within a role, not delegated from one role to another.*

The main problem with the worker–manager relationship, besides the fact that it does not much benefit the organization, is that it rarely creates ownership, investment, and commitment on the part of the worker—except in regard to the worker's own purposes. It tended to polarize workers and managers and was a major cause of the labor movement in the United States.

Organizational parentalism became the essential model for human relationships in an organizational system, but the increasing availability of outcomes data, which gave everyone access to information about work and its products, put a strain on this model. Eventually the constructs of the "work environment," advanced information technology, and systems understanding converged to create the demand for a different context for the relationship between people and systems.

> *Accountability is about outcomes. Rather than being accountable to someone else, an individual is accountable for performing to a level of expectation clear to all the stakeholders who shared in defining it.*

Further affecting work relationships is the fact that organizations are steadily becoming more dependent upon the knowledge of workers at the point of service. As already mentioned, the knowledge possessed by workers is now one of the mediums of exchange in the workplace. In the old industrial model, organizations owned the means of production. As organizations become more technologically and knowledge dependent, the means of production and the mediums of exchange are passing into the hands of those who do the work. A different kind of work relationship must exist when the tools of work and the mediums of exchange are no longer owned solely by the organization. The conditions for real partnership are created and produce a demand for increasing levels of accountability.

Accountability, rather than being delegated (as is responsibility), is specifically imbedded in roles. Indeed, accountability cannot be delegated away. People are always accountable for something, not accountable to someone. Accountability must be self-described. It is owned by those who express it and is defined not by processes or activities but by the outcomes (i.e., people are accountable for achieving specific results and not for following certain routines or procedures).

> *In the case of accountability, all stakeholders share a role in evaluating the performance of others upon which their roles depend. Accountability creates the need for a real 360° evaluation.*

Accountability demands an understanding of its contribution and the activities necessary for that contribution, and each individual in a given role has an obligation to know and to give evidence through both performance and contribution that there is value in the work.

Accountability focuses the organization and all of its resources on the purposes and the outcomes of collective activities. Accountability reflects relationship. In accountability-based systems, there is a fundamental understanding that it is the intersection of roles and functions that leads to accountability (as defined by outcomes). The relationship and interaction between and integration of processes have a much larger impact on the success of the activities and the quality of results when they are viewed within the context of those results. Systems thinking teaches that the effectiveness of an enterprise depends on the contribution of every member of that enterprise. Brokenness in any one place in the system affects the whole system.

> *Broken accountability in any one place in a system is brokenness in all parts of the system. Integrity requires the linkage between all the places where essential decisions are made.*

Accountability-based models take into account the essential relationships between the elements of the system, especially between its members. They are founded on an understanding that the results of work depend on the intensity of the relationships of those who do it.

Accountability directly intersects with partnership. Since any partnership demands a clarity of role, function, and contribution and a mutual understanding of its purpose and direction, the accountability of the players is critical to its success and the achievement of its purpose. Dialogue, negotiation, and clarification of role and function are built on a strong core of relationship and are part of the foundation of any successful organization. In the case of accountability, clarity demands that there is nothing left to guess or assume so that all elements of a role are focused on the outcomes to which it is directed and validated by its relationships. Evaluation of the results of partnership is evidenced in performance outcomes. Functions, activities, relationships, and experiences form the process foundations leading to good outcomes.

Accountability-based systems always demand clarity. Clarity is essential for delineating the contribution of a role to outcomes. Without clarity, processes and activities have uncertain significance and in fact have only limited value. Role definition is basically valuable because of the outcomes to which the role contributes. The full meaning of accountability can only be understood in this context.

Accountability is a fundamental construct of shared governance. Indeed, the structures and relationships and elements articulated in a shared governance framework are evidence of the presence of accountability and its necessary foundations.

OWNERSHIP

In the journey into a new age of work and work design, it is simply not possible to stop the process of change. The particular journey we are on is a collective one, requiring the engagement of societies, organizations, and individuals. Regardless of how individuals respond, the journey of change will continue relentlessly and will require the ownership and investment of all players that make up a system. All players must realize that the essential characteristics of the changes occurring depend on the contribution each player makes.

A commitment to change carries with it some risk. This risk has to do with one's sense of value in making a contribution to the journey. Individual value during a time of transformation is always driven by circumstances beyond the control of any single person. Change can never be designed to satisfy all of the needs and interests of one person. Much of the impact of change is random and serendipitous at best. Adjustments and transformations in

> *Ownership means investment on the part of every person in the system.*

role and function are simply reflective of the perceived impact of change on the organization as a whole.

Because of this, it is necessary for an organization to restructure itself in a way that reflects the emerging paradigm. To do this, the organization and its members must commit to the activity of moving roles, functions, activities, processes, and structures into a new context for shaping a new framework for success.

Questions that often get raised these days include, who will survive the craziness and uncertainty associated with the journey into the new age? Who will make it and who will not? Who should go and who should not? What size should the organization be and who should be left when the organization is retooled? These questions are simply examples of the kinds of issues that are confronted by all social systems in a time of great change. Processes of restructuring can cause players to recall a naked truth that is often forgotten: one's ability to thrive depends entirely on the tightness of fit between what one has to offer and the needs of the organization. As the demand for work changes, so do worker requirements. In an era of change, the focus is no longer simply on a job or work but on career fit. That causes pressures that, for most, are unfamiliar and requires a level of role fluidity and flexibility not typically expected.

> *An organization simply cannot afford to have on board people who cannot clearly articulate their individual contribution to its purposes and outcomes.*

The change of focus demands commitment and investment throughout the organizational system. The fit between the roles of individuals and the needs of the organization becomes crucial to its ability to sustain and thrive. The organization has an obligation to ensure a tightness of fit between what it does and what it is. The individual has an obligation to ensure that his or her skills will make a broad-based contribution to the organization and the changes it is undergoing. The level of energy and commitment demanded from everyone in the organization sometimes goes beyond basic expectations. This level of commitment is a sign of people's willingness to recognize the relationship they have to the organization and how much the organization depends on them for its success.

THE INTERDEPENDENCE OF EVERYTHING

The level of commitment demanded from everyone also shows the organization how dependent it is on all of its resources. Not only are its stock values or fiscal strength essential for organizational survival, but so are its human and knowledge resources. The balance between its objective and subjective resources creates the ebb and flow necessary to facilitate the life of the organization and ensure its ability to thrive (see Exhibit 1-5).

> *A system is always self-organizing and, given the appropriate support, will be self-sustaining and oriented toward thriving.*

In shared governance, ownership is required because it enables the stakeholders in every part of the system to participate fully in decisions that will affect the outcomes of their activities. Structures of shared governance ensure that all players have a forum and a role to play in creating a seamless system.

Fostering stakeholders and investors—people committed to the organization and its purposes—is critical work in a time of great change. The ownership and the investment of all players must be built into the fabric of the organization, not simply encouraged by the words of its leaders. It does not take staff long to find out whether true investment and commitment exist in an organization or whether expressions of commitment by its leaders constitute mere rhetoric. The language, structures, processes, and outcomes must be congruent if true ownership of an investment in the sys-

> *Every member of a system has both a right to membership and the obligations that brings. Both must be clear to all who contribute to the system's work.*

Exhibit 1-5 Building Interdependence

- Use single focused strategy
- Engage in planned corporatewide effort
- Consistently apply organization's philosophy
- Simplify
- Support the strategic plan
- Work together, do not compete within
- Focus on the patient
- Lower costs
- Grow by design, not accident

tem are to be engendered. Shared governance requires the application of this principle to the work of building new structures. Shared governance should recognize the key role of every player in the system and facilitate the creation of a truly effective organization based on a new health system paradigm.

CREATING A REAL SYSTEM

The foundations and principles discussed in this chapter create the conditions out of which the need for a shared governance structure emerges. The coming of the new age and the changing character of organizations necessitate a shift to a new organizational format and a supporting structure.

Shared governance is simply a framework for whole-systems effectiveness providing a context for partnership, equity, accountability, and ownership.

Shared governance is an organizational model that utilizes systems principles to integrate stakeholders along a continuum of care and create an organization that exemplifies the principles of partnership, equity, accountability, and ownership. All of these principles have direct and immediate applications in a shared governance system. Together they serve as an indicator of the presence of shared governance and foster the type of implementation of processes and structures that ensures its appropriate operation.

In perusing later chapters, where the structures and elements of the model of shared governance are discussed in greater detail, the reader should remember that the principles are what guide the building of all structures. The principles should also be used as a template to assess the integrity of any structure and to evaluate the implementation of shared governance. Dissonance—a lack of harmony between the structure and the principles it reflects—indicates a challenge, difficulty, or noncongruence and requires the leaders to be called back to the table to talk about what is missing or has not been done to ensure integrity and effectiveness.

SUGGESTED READING

Argyris, C. 1993. *Knowledge for action.* San Francisco: Jossey-Bass.
Baig, E. 1994. The information society. In: The information revolution. (Special issue of *Business Week*), pp. 122–133.

Bennis, W. 1990. *Why leaders can't lead.* San Francisco: Jossey-Bass.

Block, P. 1991. *The empowered manager.* San Francisco: Jossey-Bass.

Byham, W. 1991. *Zapp! The lightening of empowerment.* New York: Harmony Books.

Byrne, J. 1993. The horizontal corporation. *Business Week,* 20 December, pp. 76–81.

Coeling, H., and J. Wilcox. 1994. Steps to collaboration. *Nursing Administration Quarterly* 18, no. 4:44–55.

Delavigne, K., and D. Robertson. 1994. *Deming's profound changes.* New York: Prentice-Hall.

Devereaux, M., and R. Johansen. 1994. *Globalwork.* San Francisco: Jossey-Bass.

Gordon, S. 1991. *Prisoners of men's dreams.* Boston: Little, Brown.

Hammer, M., and S. Stanton. 1995. *The reengineering revolution.* New York: Harper Business.

Kaluzny, A., H. Zuckerman, and T. Ricketts. 1995. *Partners for the dance: Forming strategic alliances in health care.* Chicago: Health Administration Press.

Kanter, R. 1994. Collaborative advantage: The art of alliances. *Harvard Business Review* 72, no. 4: 96–108.

Kodama, F. 1995. *Emerging patterns of innovation.* Boston: Harvard Business School Press.

Kritek, P. 1994. *Negotiating at an uneven table.* San Francisco: Berrett-Koehler.

Luthans, F., R. Hodgetts, and S. Lee. 1994. New paradigm organizations. *Organizational Dynamics* 22, no. 3:5–19.

Maynard, H., and S. Mehrtens. 1993. *The fourth wave: Business in the 21st century.* San Francisco: Berrett-Koehler.

Negroponte, N. 1995. *Being digital.* New York: Knopf.

Pelletier, K. 1993. Healthy people, healthy worksites. *Healthcare Forum Journal* 36, no. 6: 34–39.

Peters, T. 1992. *Liberation management.* New York: Harper and Row.

Porter-O'Grady, T. 1992. *Implementing shared governance.* Baltimore: Mosby.

Porter-O'Grady, T. 1994. Building partnerships in health care: Creating whole systems change. *Nursing and Health Care* 15, no. 1:34–38.

Porter-O'Grady, T., and C. Krueger-Wilson. 1995. *The leadership revolution in health care: Altering systems, changing behaviors.* Gaithersburg, MD: Aspen Publishers.

Schaaf, D. 1993. Is quality dead? *Training* (Supplement): 7–11.

Senge, P., et al. 1994. *The fifth discipline fieldbook: Strategies and tools for building a learning organization.* New York: Currency Doubleday.

Taguchi, G. 1990. Quality imperatives. *Harvard Business Review* 70, no. 1:65–71.

Toffler, A. 1990. *Powershift.* New York: Bantam Books.

Weisbord, M. 1993. *Building common ground.* San Francisco: Berrett-Koehler.

Wheatley, M. 1992. *Leadership and the new science.* San Francisco: Berrett-Koehler.

Chapter 2

Whole-Systems Shared Governance: A Model for Integrated Health Care Systems

Tim Porter-O'Grady, Marilyn Hawkins, and Marsha Parker

Civilization is a movement, not a condition;
a voyage and not a harbor.

Arnold Toynbee

T he foundations for change established in Chapter 1 create new conditions for the design and structuring of health care organizations. The old hierarchical, linear, and vertical models of decision making no longer fit the character and content of the decisions necessary at the point of care in the new health care environment. The emerging continuum of services, the reengineering of health care organizations, and the integration of the health care system require partnerships to replace other kinds of relationships, changing the framework for decisions forever.

In the old system, decisions were often compartmentalized based on the authority of the individual (the physician) or the location of the service (radiology, laboratory, nursing, etc.). As discipline- and function-specific walls get broken down and partnerships increasingly form the foundation for functional clinical activity, integrating decision making and structures that support it becomes a critical task for the organization (see Figure 2-1).

BUILDING ON FOUNDATIONS

In an integrated organization, it is essential to create structures that support it, especially at the point of service, and sustain the work processes of the organization. As the organization builds partnerships between its providers, creates a continuum of care, and integrates health care services along a horizontal pathway, the structures that support these processes represent a different set of beliefs than those historically present in health care.

   Whole-systems shared governance, (i.e., shared governance that addresses every component of the organization) requires that some measure of integration, reengineering, and continuity of care be established in the organizational system. The shared governance

> ***Integration is evidence of the attempt to configure services around the point of care and to bring providers together in a service partnership.***

structure reflects the processes and relationships that exist in the system, and, as Chapter 3 makes clear, the activities of renewal and restructuring can create conditions that will undergird the formation of a shared governance structure.

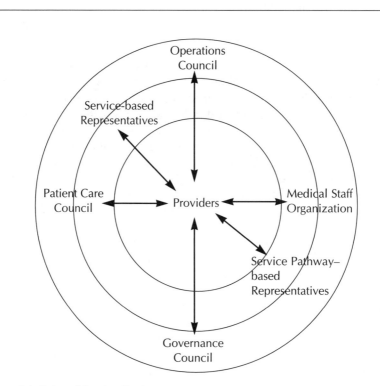

Figure 2-1 Point-of-Service Design

These new health care service constructs create a demand for a context that will support them. Shared governance structuring reflects what Deming has defined as the minimum amount of structure needed to maintain the integrity and form of the organization. He suggests that any more structure than the minimum often ends up serving itself in place of providing support and service to the organization's work. It is the need to find the line between sufficient structure for organizational integrity and too much structure that should motivate the leadership to look for a structural model that supports the delivery of patient services—and to be cautious in choosing one.

WHY SHARED GOVERNANCE?

There are three specific reasons why shared governance is an appropriate model for restructuring a health care organization. First, the sustainability of health care greatly depends on how point-of-service (point-of-care) health care providers will function. In a subscriber-driven, capitated, continuum-based health care organization, an entirely different organizational structure is necessary. The old model of a compartmentalized, centralized, vertically integrated, free-standing, institution is simply no longer workable in its current form. The organizational framework necessary to support health care in the new environment requires a different set of constructs. It is this set of constructs that shared governance specifically addresses (see Exhibit 2-1).

> *Shared governance requires a commitment to partnership in order to work effectively.*

> *Managing knowledge workers requires getting them to invest in decision making and express a sense of ownership over the decisions they must make.*

Second, the emergence of the knowledge organization, as Peter Drucker calls it, has occurred. Over the years, higher levels of knowledge have been required to provide health care services. As a result, there has been accelerating dissonance between the needs of knowledge workers and the design of organizations. Hospitals and other health care organizations have sought to revise in their narrowly controlled structures to accommodate the growing need for independence of the judgment on the part of the knowledge workers, the changing needs of the professions, and the increasing complexity of health care delivery; but although each sector has agreed to some compromises, the fundamental issues that created the conflict have been left essentially unresolved.

Knowledge workers require an entirely different framework for work and professional relationships. Because of the increased dependence of health care on the aggregated comprehensive knowledge of all the various constituencies, professions, and providers, a different kind of organizational relationship must emerge to support them. With the building of the continuum of care, the community and the patients become central components of the delivery system, and a whole new frame of reference that gives form to it, sustains and nurtures it, and allows everyone in the partnership to act in concert with each other will be essential. It is partly to meet these unique needs and to facilitate the application of the knowledge workers' skills that shared governance is arguably necessary at this point in time.

> *In a continuum of services, no one person can control all the relationships and decisions necessary to make it effective.*

Third, it is vital to realize that in a continuum of care system, no health care organization can own, control, or unilaterally mandate all of the service linkages and connections necessary to serve a specific population. Fluidity and flexibility will be key to organizational survival in the emerging health care environment.

Exhibit 2-1 Whole-Systems Principles

---

1. The whole always defines the parts.
2. Each of the components of a system supports the whole system.
3. A problem in any one part of the system affects the whole system.
4. A system always "lives" where it provides its services or produces its products.
5. All roles either serve the customer or serve someone who does.
6. The design of a system must configure structure around its point of service or product, which always lies at its center.
7. Form must always follow function.
8. All members of a system are stakeholders. The structure of the system must facilitate the effectiveness of every stakeholder.
9. In a system, managers are facilitators, integrators, and coordinators of the processes that support the work and workers of the system.
10. Outcomes always define the value of process. Function is subordinate to its purpose.

Increasingly, consumer demands and subscriber requirements are setting the parameters for health services that will be offered. As subscriber populations shift, as services are adjusted to meet the needs of our aging populace, and as community priorities are modified, the organizational structure must make it possible to adjust to the changes quickly and efficiently.

In order to provide a comprehensive range of necessary services, "virtual" relationships (highly fluid and flexible) must be established between players. Bringing in new services and eliminating services requires service leaders to be involved in decision making and direction setting throughout the continuum of care. Therefore, structural boundaries must be permeable to accommodate the need for flexibility of membership in those groups that make decisions, set strategy, implement processes, delineate outcomes, and evaluate results.

> *Providers are partners in decision making. Ninety percent of all decisions made in a system should be made at the point of service.*

The three reasons presented above constitute a good argument for implementing a shared governance structure. Whether or not the term *shared governance* is used to designate the type of structure, most of the principles and processes outlined in this text will need to be implemented in order to achieve organizational and service sustainability. While the term implies all key stakeholders are involved in governance, it does not refer to a uniform set of rules that must be rigidly applied. Rather, the application of the principles of partnership, equity, accountability, and ownership and the related concepts is what characterize the type of structure appropriate for service-based, community-driven health care.

BUILDING TO SUPPORT THE POINT OF CARE

The purpose of much of the current integration and clinical restructuring of health care organizations is to better organize services and care around the point of service. Where patient and provider meet is the place where a health care organization lives its life and the fundamental construct around which all structure should be built. However, organizational structures typically must be substantially revised to support point-of-care decision making and activity throughout an integrated and broad continuum of service. Among the principles to be kept in mind in the process of revision are the following:

- The primary point of decision making in the clinical delivery system is the place where patients and providers meet.
- In an integrated approach, providers are allied to each other in a noncompartmentalized way—that is, in a broad set of linked clinical relationships.
- In service-based approaches, providers and patients need much more freedom to make clinical decisions (and patients need more involvement in such decisions) than was permitted in the past.
- A much broader range of information must be provided to the point of care to support decision making, clinical activities, and evaluation of outcomes.
- The purpose of organizational structure in health care is to help ensure that there are no impediments preventing people from making the right decisions at the point of care.
- Linkage of point-of-care activities with the system must occur in a way that engages all stakeholders and motivates them to undertake procedures that will result in meaningful outcomes.
- The effective clinical organization is constructed from the point of care outward so that all structures, activities, and support systems serve the primary purpose of the organization as exemplified at the point of care.

In the past, much lip service was given to the importance of building a structure that supported caregiving and ostensibly placed the patient at the center of the organization. However, there has been no evidence that organizational structures operated in such a way that the patient was ever at the center of anything. The traditional organization was designed to support the provider, not the patient. As a result, the patient tended to get lost. In order to obtain the efficiencies that come from integration, the organizational structure must reflect support for these new structures, which are patient- rather than provider-driven.

THE PREMISES OF SHARED GOVERNANCE

Shared governance reflects a set of beliefs (its premises, so to speak) that have arisen from research done in the past 30 years on organizational effectiveness and human dynamics in the workplace. Applying this research to health care organizations attempting to create a service continuum is the cur-

> *Shared governance is not democracy. It is an accountability-based approach to structure in which there is a clear expectation that all members of a system participate in its work.*

rent challenge of health care leaders. The overall goal is to respond to the changing health care environment by using their new understanding of effectiveness, work relationships, decision making, and human dynamics to create an organizational structure that does not replicate the limitations of past structures.

The premises of shared governance include the following:

- All structure must directly support the work of the organization. Any part of organizational structure that does not specifically support the organization's work impedes it.
- What goes on at the point of service or productivity in an organization defines the organization's life and purpose.
- In a knowledge-based system (such as a health care organization), all workers contributing to the outcomes of the system have a right and an obligation to own the decisions that relate to their work. There should be nothing in the system that arbitrarily or capriciously moderates or removes or impedes the rights and obligations of any individuals who work in the system.
- In horizontally linked organizational structures (as opposed to vertically linked structures), there is an emphasis on relationship and integration. Consequently, a horizontally linked organization must create a structure that facilitates the establishment and flourishing of relationships among its members.
- There are three major components of an organization necessary to ensure its integrity: governance, operations, and production or service. In a systems design, each of these must be linked to the other in a seamless connection of interfaces that support the needs and accountability of the others.
- A health system's main obligation is to meet the needs of the community it serves. It exists at its points of service, where the community need is met one person at a time. The provider–patient relationship has the same constituents as the community–system relationship. Therefore, the mandates, principles, and processes that govern the latter relationship are the same as those governing the former.
- An effective service system is an open system. This means that there is a seamless connection between the decisions and the decision makers at one point in the system (e.g., governance) and those at other points in the system (e.g., patient care). In an effective system, there are no artificial or structural barriers between the interdependent components of the system. Compartmentalization is the death of integration.
- Managers in a system are both stewards and servants. Their primary role is to see that the system both serves and supports what goes on at its points of service.

- Accountability (internally generated locus of control), not responsibility (delegated or externally generated locus of control), is the foundation for all performance expectations. Every member of a system (systems have members, not subordinates, superiors, employers, employees, masters, or servants) has a right and an obligation to participate fully in the activities of the system. To the extent of their ability to contribute, each member has the obligation to ensure that the system thrives.
- An effective system should provide a sustainable format for the engagement of every member of the system. A system creates a framework for ensuring that the processes of empowerment operate effectively throughout the system—at every point where work, relationships, and decisions intersect.

> *Shared governance is based on a belief about people and the nature of work in an organization: all are partners in the enterprise.*

These premises reflect the latest understanding of sustainability in organizations. They also reflect current systems and human relations research and are essential for any implementation of shared governance—or even for comprehending the shared governance model.

TEAMS: THE FOUNDATION OF ALL WORK

In the past decade, the understanding that relatedness is as critical as competence to achieving effective outcomes in work has revolutionized the design, structuring, and application of work across a wide variety of industries. It has also served as the foundation of the work team movement throughout the world. Team-based activities reflect a move away from the traditional system of compartmentalizing work into individuated tasks, functions, and activities in isolated and unilateral work constructs. In this system, preserving the integrity of one's own work became the priority rather than focusing on the needs of those the organization served. As a result, there were severe incongruities between the efforts and activities of individuals, disciplines, departments, and structures in the organization and the organization's purposes and fundamental mission. Rather than a situation in which everyone worked together to meet the needs of patients and ensure the continuity of services, competition and compartmentalized, discipline-driven care brought accelerating levels of cost, created gaps in services, and fractured relationships between disciplines and between patients and providers.

Use of teams is neither new nor revolutionary. However, a full understanding of how teams work, how to apply them to the work system, and how to ensure their viability has only recently been achieved. The notion that each outcome results from the joint activity of many players rather than the efforts, no matter how dedicated, of a single player has created a critical shift in the focus of organizational design and work structuring.

In a team-based approach, team members must first develop relationships with each other and then make the decisions and undertake the activities essential to the outcomes of the team's work. Shared governance reflects the essential character of team-based approaches. It takes into account the centrality of work teams and uses team concepts and formats. Further, there is an assumption that as team-based approaches become the preeminent frame of reference for work in health care organizations, the shared governance structure will predominate. It will serve as a means for integrating teams within an organizational construct and linking them along the continuum of essential relationships and services in an increasingly horizontally linked system.

> *Teams, not individuals, are the basic unit of work in a whole-systems organization.*

Any team-based approach requires a change in structure that allows teams at all levels of the organization to be given responsibility for making broad-based systems decisions and for linking processes and providers across a wide range of services. It requires, in other words, teams to be self-organizing and self-directed and to act as the basic units of service (or work).

Building a structure, such as shared governance, that links teams and facilitates their function requires specific conclusions about the functions and activities of teams. In a team-based approach, many of the activities that were once controlled by the system in its parental role now become the responsibility of the team. The manager's role is no longer to control activities (acting as boss, superior, supervisor, administrator, or parent) but to facilitate the activities now placed in the team's hands. Some responsibilities that might devolve to the team include the following:

- hiring, evaluating, and terminating team members
- scheduling and assigning team members
- determining the critical activities and flow of work of team members
- evaluating the competence of and fit between team members

- assigning elements of function and activity along a critical path to individual team members
- resolving conflicts between team members and dealing with other difficulties
- planning, organizing, and designing activities in the context of the team's accountability
- defining standards and measures of team performance
- aligning team behaviors and activities with performance expectations and outcome determinations
- Establishing a framework for leadership, assignment rotation, member responsibilities, and quality enhancement

While this list is not all inclusive, it includes some of the major team responsibilities that once belonged to managers. Increasingly, organizations are recognizing that moving the majority of decisions (up to 90 percent) to the point of service and structuring work around those decisions is critical. The goal is to allow the locus of control to reside in the places where the decisions are carried out.

THE DIFFERENT KINDS OF TEAMS IN A SHARED GOVERNANCE CONTEXT

There are two kinds of teams that play a role in a shared governance framework. The first kind of team focuses on specific functions and activities that constitute the work of the organization at the point of service. Its whole purpose is to work collaboratively facilitating each patient's journey through the health care system.

> *Clinical teams are the foundation for work in an integrated system and best reflect the provider relationships necessary in a continuum of care.*

The second kind of team focuses on system and relationship issues. It looks at the structure and framework that provides the support and context for its own activities. This team's focus is the team itself, the relationships within the team, the interactions and intersections between itself and other teams, and its relationship to the services it provides and to the system it represents and is a part of.

Each kind of team has a specific role in ensuring the efficacy and success of the organization. The service team (the first kind mentioned) is designed to facilitate, improve, and advance the services provided by its members. Its services constitute its fundamental focus and purpose. The second kind of team tries to ensure that the relationships between itself and the organization, between itself and other teams, and between the system and all of the teams function effectively to support the work of each team at the point of care. It is the interface and the "connectiveness" between these kinds of teams that form the core of a shared governance structure.

> *Everyone in a system is a stakeholder and has a right to participate fully in the life of the organization.*

Clearly, if stakeholders are located everywhere in the system, there must be a mechanism for them to intersect continuously and to ensure that their decisions are mutually supportive and facilitate the achievement of desired outcomes. In fact, it is the purpose of shared governance to create a framework for supporting effective relationships between stakeholders throughout the organization.

THE SERVICE TEAM

All activities in a health care organization center around the delivery of services to the patient population (or subscriber group), and thus care teams are the primary units of service. These provider-based teams are the foundation for the delivery of all health care.

Because care teams are being used more in the provision of health care services, much is changed regarding the relationship between members and the services they provide. In a team-based format, no role is looked upon as more important than any other role. For example, while it is clear that the physician's role is to link the medical components of patient care delivery to the other essential health care services provided by other members of the team, in a team-based approach that role is looked at as no more important to the integrity and value of the team than any other team member's role. A team's effectiveness is directly determined by the ability of its members to work together to achieve common clinical and service-related goals.

> *Service is the lifeblood of all health care systems. It is to providing service that all roles must be firmly committed.*

The organization must therefore provide a system of support that ensures the integrity and viability of its care teams. The organizational framework at the service level must be designed to ensure that the care teams are available to define, perform, and evaluate their work in an effective and meaningful way. Also, the organization must provide a mechanism for the teams to correct anything that impedes their relationships or functioning. Quite simply, they need to be able to work successfully, and the resources, structure, and operational components of the organization must support their integrity and activity.

THE POPULATION-BASED CONTINUUM

Each team functions in relationship to other teams' functioning. In the redesign of patient care along a continuum of care, an organization's structure becomes centered around either patient populations, specific subscriber groups, or clinical pathways. Further, wherever the structure is centered, an interface between teams that falls within a particular category of service is needed. Some mechanism must exist in the organization to ensure that linkage occurs and to guarantee that each team is fulfilling its obligation in a way that helps achieve the outcomes all teams are committed to achieving.

> *All teams are configured around specific kinds of services. The population defines the work of the team.*

In shared governance, a collection of service or care teams centered on a specific population or service continuum is called a service or patient care pathway. These pathways can be defined in a number of ways—as centers, processes, product lines, service lines, programs, and so on. Regardless of what they are called, they share common characteristics and require an integrated structure to support them.

> *A service pathway follows the trajectory of the patient through the system, not the route of the provider.*

In a shared governance model, the teams in a given pathway must link or interface with each other in order to ensure that the standards of practice, generic service requirements, system mandates, mission, purposes, and goals to which they are committed are clearly articulated and to also ensure that each team is operating in harmony with the activities of the other teams (see Figure 2-2). System linkage occurs when an individual unit of service begins to link with other units of service. The ultimate goal is linkage of all of the components of the system, and that means confronting those places in the system where lack of linkage is most evident (see Exhibit 2-2). Everything else in the system is directed toward facilitating or supporting the work of the primary units of service, and it is at the level of the service pathway that the teams that make it up begin to converge to integrate their efforts to provide a continuum of services. The integrated service pathway is the critical point where the issues that affect both the interface of the teams and the teams' collective linkage to the system are addressed. In the shared governance model, this point of convergence creates a need for pathway-based decision making, and it is the first place where the council structure emerges. Also, as discussed in Chapter 1, all shared governance organizations apply the principles of partnership, equity, accountability, and ownership in everything they do (see Exhibit 2-3).

COUNCILS: THE BASIC UNIT OF ORGANIZED DECISION MAKING

In a shared governance model, a council is a place where authority exists for making decisions that will impact the system in a direct way. All councils have

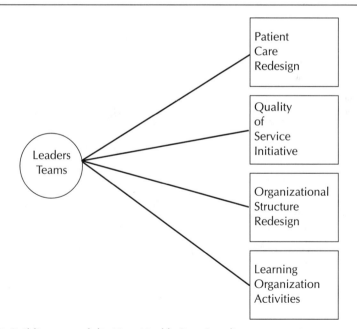

Figure 2-2 Building toward the New Health Care Paradigm

Exhibit 2-2 Outmoded Organizational Characteristics

- Separate, nonlinked institutions with their own operational processes working independently of other parts of the system
- An institutional hierarchy that maintains vertical control over the system
- A large number of senior executives and middle- and first-level management positions
- A fragmented service model where none of the providers are aware of the contribution of the other
- A centralized control structure that approves the majority of decisions made and controls most of the functions and activities of the system
- An unclear connection between health leadership and the medical staff so that decisions made by physicians and others are not linked to mutually defined outcomes
- A governance structure that does not tie the board directly to the point of service and connect providers and board leadership together in a mutually supportive decision-making process

the right to make such decisions, have accountability for the decisions that they make, and have an obligation to see that the decisions are fully implemented. There are essentially two types of councils: point-of-service (clinical pathway) councils and systems councils. The only thing that differentiates the two is the focus of their work. All councils are made up of stakeholders brought together to deal with specific kinds of issues in a way that facilitates the achievement of mutually desirable outcomes.

> *A council is a decision-making body, not a process group. It has the power to do its work without seeking approval of other sources of power.*

The clinical pathway council is the primary point of decision making in the shared governance model. One of the basic tenets of sound reengineering is that 90 percent of decisions made in the organization should be made within the context of service pathways. This ensures the appropriate point-of-service focus of the providers and the delineation of decisions around the particular patient population. It is in this council that team activities converge for the making of decisions that affect all teams within the patient pathway. It is also in this council that the managers of a particular service pathway (or in the case of self-directed work teams the leadership of the work

Exhibit 2-3 Principles of Shared Governance

Partnership
  • Role expectations are negotiated.
  • Equality exists between the players.
  • Relationships are founded upon shared risk.
  • Expectations and contributions are clear.
  • Solid measure of contribution to outcomes is established.
  • Horizontal linkages are well defined.

Equity
  • Each player's contribution is understood.
  • Payment reflects value of contribution to outcomes.
  • Role is based on relationship, not status.
  • Team defines service roles, relationships, and outcomes.
  • Methodology is defined for team conflict and service issues.
  • Evaluation assesses team's outcomes and contributions.

Accountability
  • Accountability is internally defined by person in role.
  • Accountability defines roles, not jobs.
  • Accountability is based on outcomes, not process.
  • Accountability is defined in advance of performance.
  • Accountability leads to desired and defined results.
  • Performance is validated by the results achieved.
  • Processes are generally loud and noisy.

Ownership
  • All workers are invested in the enterprise.
  • Every role has a stake in the outcome.
  • Rewards are directly related to outcomes.
  • All members are associated with a team.
  • Processes support relationships.
  • Opportunity is based on competence.

teams) meet to make essential decisions concerning the pathway's functioning, the relationship between the teams, the clinical standards and activities that are fundamental to the work of the pathway, and other issues associated with the interface between the health system and the service pathway.

SHARED GOVERNANCE AND DECISION MAKING

Shared governance is an accountability-based model. In shared governance, accountability must always be located at the place where decisions are most appropriately made. The distinctions between decisions in an organization in a shared governance model are based on the appropriate locus of control for specific areas of accountability. For example, all accountability related to patient care derives from the point of service, and therefore the decisions must be made at the point of service. Patient care decisions should not be located at any other place in the system. Placing them elsewhere would impede both the ownership and the exercise of authority at the most appropriate locus of control—the patient care environment.

> *Accountability is the principle that drives all shared governance structures.*

DECISIONS AND THE LOCUS OF CONTROL

A service pathway council should not assume authority for decisions that rest specifically with the teams. The teams, on the other hand, should not assume authority for decisions best made by the service pathway council. Indeed, decisions made by the service pathway council serve as checks and balances for decisions made by the individual teams (see Exhibit 2-4).

In shared governance structures, it is vital that clarity be achieved in advance regarding the kind and content of decisions and the exercise of decision-making authority. Each decision-making body must be fundamentally clear about its locus of control, authority, and responsibility for specific decisions. The parameters of decisions are defined by the content of the decisions themselves. For example, each team makes decisions specific to its clinical responsibilities, the clinical contribution of each of its members, and the relationships and intersections necessary to provide the team's services. Anything related to those critical functions and activities essentially belongs to the team.

> *All councils have the authority they need to make their own decisions. There are no approval structures in shared governance.*

Exhibit 2-4 Locus of Control Decision Making

Point-of-Service Provider Teams
- Work-based clinical actions
- Functions between the team members
- Patient service problems
- Provider relationship issues
- Clinical priorities
- Application of clinical protocols
- Service/care evaluation

Service Pathways
- Design of clinical protocols
- Development of clinical standards
- Definition of the content of provider relationships
- Quality improvement plan implementation
- Structural problems in the service relationship
- Conflicts and problems related to service design
- Structure, content, and processes tying together resources and service within the pathway
- Problems between providers within the pathway

Patient Care Council
- Design of delivery system
- Integration of disciplines in the system
- Service goals for the system
- Creation of continuous quality imperative
- Creation of continuous learning mechanism
- Forum for the foundations of the continuum of care
- Definition of service priorities and activities of the system

Decisions that belong to the service pathway council concern the fit between the pathway and the system, in particular, the relationships between teams along the continuum of service, the problems that arise between teams, the design of an effective and efficient continuum of service, the professional standards of service that guide the teams, and the critical interface of the service pathway with the mission, purposes, and objec-

> ***Decisions always belong at the place closest to where they are implemented.***

tives of the organizational system. Decisions of this kind simply cannot be made at the team level.

COUNCILS AND REPRESENTATION

The service pathway council is usually a representative body. That means that, through some mechanism defined by the organization, team members are represented on the service pathway council in a way that ensures that a broad cross-section of disciplines has a say in the decision-making process. However, the council should be as small as diversity permits and the work of the council demands.

> *Decision-making groups should be kept as small as the effectiveness of the decisions allows. The smaller, the better.*

There is an inverse relationship between the size of a decision-making group and the effectiveness of its decisions. Therefore, the goal of any system is to make sure that its deliberative bodies are small enough to facilitate effective decision making and large enough to be appropriately inclusive.

SERVICE PATHWAY LEADERSHIP

In shared governance, there is a distinction between the role of the service pathway leader (manager) and the role of the service pathway council. The service pathway leader has a designated set of obligations derived from the system and its expectations regarding the organization, integration, facilitation, and coordination of services and generated by the service pathway members as well. The pathway members expect the leader to make available the same information and support to all of them. They also expect the structural underpinnings necessary for the provision of health services to be appropriate to their needs. The tension between resources and need essentially defines the role of the service pathway leader. Managing the support system and the

> *Effective decisions are ensured by the use of the right information by the right people in the right place at the right time. Access to information is essential for effective decision making.*

resource linkages for the service providers is a critical undertaking and demands the highest level of leadership and management skills. (In fact, it has been said that in decentralized, reorganized, team-based systems, point-of-service leaders require the same degree of skill and competence that once existed at the highest organizational levels in the past.)

A service pathway leader becomes the focal point for integrating and linking the activities of the pathway together in a way that ensures continuing operation of the pathway and the interface of the operational processes of the pathway and the needs of the individual teams. The service pathway leader integrates, coordinates, and facilitates the activities of the pathway. He or she makes sure that linkage and cohesion are continually resonating in the work of the organization and the pathway. Issues of concern, problems, and inefficiencies are addressed and dealt with. (Service pathway leadership roles are discussed in greater detail in Chapter 4.)

THE SYSTEM COUNCILS

The interface between a system and its patient occurs at the pathway council level. The interface between the service pathway and the system occurs at the system council level. The system councils are those decision-making bodies that render decisions that impact the system as a whole. Those decisions affect individual providers, teams, service pathways—indeed whole components of the service structure.

> *In shared governance, the councils are the convergent points of decision making for all teams at the system level and the point of service.*

There are primarily three system councils in the shared governance model: the patient care council, the operations council, and the governance council. Each of the system councils has defined obligations for making decisions that affect the component of the system toward which the council's work is directed.

> *System councils address the relationship of the system and its internal and external communities.*

While each of the components of the organizational system has accountability for specific decisions, there must be a seamless linkage between those decisions and the other components of the system. Also, each system council must also link back to the point of service through its service pathways. The linkages ensure that the decisions of each council will have a direct and clear impact on the context for decision making and foster seamlessness in decision making across the various components of the health care system.

DISTINGUISHING SYSTEM ACCOUNTABILITY AND SERVICE ACCOUNTABILITY

Accountability in a shared governance framework is built on the understanding that there is shared function and obligation on the part of all stakeholders in the system and that clear contributions to the system are part of the expectations of membership in the system. One of the options not available to members is to behave as though they were not stakeholders. They must exhibit an acceptance of accountability for the outcomes toward which their roles and work are directed.

> *Accountability demands clarity in roles, functions, and outcomes. Accountability abhors ambiguity.*

Accountability abhors ambiguity, and therefore clarity of accountability and contribution must be one of the attributes of every single role that makes up the system. That clarity must also be incorporated into the team framework to ensure that every individual's relationship to the team, function on the team, and obligation for the team's outcomes have been outlined and lucidly articulated.

> *Accountability implies that different decisions are made in different places and that they are carried out independently of control located anywhere other than where the accountability is expressed.*

Further, in a shared governance model, there is no one place in the organization where "ultimate" responsibility is located. Ultimate responsibility is an Industrial Age, linear notion—the idea that there must be some one person, one location, or one function where all responsibility aggregates. Everyone has heard the phrase "The buck stops here." Effectiveness in an organization does not depend upon where the buck stops but where the decision gets carried out effectively. If it does not work there, it does not make any difference where the final point of authority is. Ultimate responsibility is an anathema to the notion of accountability and therefore is not a functional or structural component of a shared governance model.

Accountability implies that different decisions are located in different places. Clearly, the checks and balances of the system must be strong enough to ensure that goals are achieved in the places where they need to be achieved by those who are required to achieve them. Such checks and balances must be built into the system. Accountability requires that it be clear just where those points of decision making are and just what that accountability is.

There are two kinds of accountability in any organizational structure: system accountability and service accountability. System accountability relates to those activities and functions that increase the effectiveness of the system as a whole and ensure systems integrity and effectiveness within every component, function, linkage, and role in the system. The primary sources of system (or manager) accountability are the resource and stewardship requirements of the organization, namely, the human, fiscal, material, support, and system resource requirements. Each of these has imbedded within it functional activities that provide system and leadership support to the service activities undertaken at the point of service. Indeed, they have been characterized by Mintzberg and others as the core activities of the management process.

> *The language of shared governance is systems language.*
> *Understanding how whole systems work is essential to making shared governance work.*

In shared governance, decisions about human, fiscal, material, support, and system resources fall within the ambit of the system and its managers. These decisions are often referred to in systems language as "contextual decisions." They provide the context, the parameters, the framework, the "basket" (if you will) into which all management functions, activities, work, and roles must fit to support the outcomes toward which the organization's resources are directed.

On the other side of the coin is service accountability. This includes accountability for the work, functions, and activities that relate to the purposes of the organization. In all health care systems, the main purpose is to provide clinical health care services. The providers of these services are called upon to undertake the shared activities intended to produce the desired clinical outcomes.

All the activities related to providing health care services and achieving clinical goals are encompassed within service accountability. Service accountability demands the actual performance of the activities needed to meet the quality expectations of the health care system. It is a requisite for the critical interface or partnership between the providers and the system and is equally as important as system accountability.

> *Service is the central role of the health system. In it you are either providing a service to a patient or serving someone who is. There is no other orientation for the service organization.*

In an effective health care system, there must be balance between service accountability and system accountability. Each has a direct and dramatic impact on the other. The balance between the two reflects a dynamic tension that continually ebbs and flows depending on the external and internal circumstances. This ebb and flow of influences creates the dynamic that continually defines the living interface between service capabilities and outcomes and resource availability and use.

In whole systems thinking, this dynamic is the fundamental core of the system–service partnership that must be continuously facilitated, defined, and refined. It is also a reflection of the foundation of the shared governance structure. In shared governance, managing the tension between service accountability and system accountability requires a seamless intersection between system and service—a con-

> *Pathways are the routes the patient follows in accessing service from the health system. Service structures should be built around such pathways.*

nection of the partners in an inexorable and continuous relationship that is essential to the success of either partner.

THE PATIENT CARE COUNCIL

Patient care is the central activity of a health care system. The delivery of health care services provides the foundation upon which the system's purposes unfold. Therefore, at the core of effectiveness in the system are the activities that facilitate the provision of patient care services.

In a health care system, there is a diversity of patient care services. In integrated organizational structures, especially within a shared governance framework, these services are often identified as service pathways. Since there is a wide variety of patient populations that may be served by any one particular health system, there may be a wide variety of patient pathways (e.g., women's health, gerontology, mental health, acute care, etc.). Each of these pathways must be designed in a way that fits the culture of the services that

> *Patient care is the central activity of any health system. If you forget that, you soon forget what business you are in.*

make up the pathway. This truism is expressed by the saying "Culture always rules." Each pathway may have constructs, relationships, team members, functional activities, standards, measures, and performance expectations that differentiate it from other service pathways, and this diversity means there is a need to ensure that the culture of service tightly fits the population toward which the pathway is directed.

However, in an organizational system there must be a way in which each unique service pathway is integrated and linked within the system as a whole. When a system is made up of culturally specific service pathways, it is difficult to build the system's structure in a way that does not impede the cultural specificity of each service pathway and at the same time supports integration. Somewhere there must be points of convergence for service pathways so that the issues of the system as a whole can be addressed and a unified commitment to the mission and purposes of the system as a whole can be created. It is at this level that the system councils operate.

As suggested earlier, the system councils' primary role is to provide forums for making decisions that affect the direction, functioning, and activities of the system as a whole. The patient care council serves as the system council responsible for decisions regarding patient care (see Figure 2-3).

> *The patient care council is the place where staff confront model of care issues and express their partnership in making decisions that affect the entire system.*

The patient care council is where the leaders from the service pathways, by bringing to bear their diverse viewpoints on issues of general concern, help to

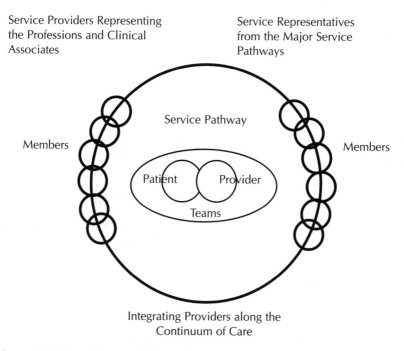

Service Providers Representing the Professions and Clinical Associates

Service Representatives from the Major Service Pathways

Service Pathway

Members

Members

Patient Provider

Teams

Integrating Providers along the Continuum of Care

Figure 2-3 Patient Care Council Structure

integrate the health care system around its main purposes—the provision of clinical services.

> *Representation on a council means taking into account the whole, not just those who sent you to the table, when making decisions. Each member represents a perspective, not a single group.*

The patient care council deals with the issues related to generic standards of practice, the relationships between the disciplines, the integration of patient care services around the community of service, the design of the patient care delivery system, all activities related to quality initiatives, and clinical performance expectations and competencies. In fact, anything related to the integrated patient care delivery process in the system as a whole falls within the ambit of authority of the patient care council.

Representation from the patient care council comes from two major constituencies: the service pathways and the major provider disciplines. The partnership between the pathways and disciplines creates the linkage between the key players at the point of service and causes them to converge around the issues that affect patient care activities at the point of service. As previously indicated, councils are authorized to make specific kinds of decisions. In a shared governance model, decisions about standards of practice, critical paths, clinical service, professional relations, functions, and activities are excluded from range of authority of the patient care council. The intent of shared governance design is to keep the majority of patient care decisions (90 percent) as close to the point of service as possible and always within the service pathways. Therefore, the patient care council is not responsible for decisions that rightly belong to and should remain within the service pathways. It is the task of the patient care council to make decisions related to the organization's patient care priorities. Adjustments in the design of service pathways as the patient population shifts; the design and construction of the model of patient care delivery; the establishment, operation, and assessment of the quality improvement initiatives throughout the organization; and

> *The leadership facilitates the council's decision making. Leaders should not make decisions that rightfully belong to someone else. Making other people's decisions for them illegitimately shifts the locus of control.*

the delineation and articulation of performance expectations for each of the disciplines involved in the delivery of patient care services all fall within the domain of the patient care council. Other focuses of the council include clinical integration; the interface of clinical services; conflicts between clinical services; issues surrounding the service continuum; and problems associated with the provision of coordinated, comprehensive services. In doing its work, the council receives organizational and staff support from patient care services, the medical staff, quality improvement services, provider education, clinical information systems, and human resources.

Since the patient care council is made up of clinical rather than management leaders (see Chapter 3), much of the control over patient- and service-related decisions remains with the providers and those who focus on the point of service. Organizational staff support is provided by those organizational functions that can best guide the work of the clinical leadership in the patient care council.

It is the responsibility of the council to deal with issues that affect the relationship between the service pathways and to provide the parameters, contexts, and foundation for the functions and activities within the service pathways. Ultimately the council must establish some degree of consistency across pathways. It must do this in a way that fosters the investment of all of the stakeholders, keeps the system focused on the point of service, deals specifically with the issues that arise with the provision of services, links key point-of-care decision makers together in dealing with comprehensive issues, and provides a seamless connection between the other components of the health care organization.

> *The system's councils make decisions across pathways in order to address issues that affect the whole. They never make decisions that belong to or within the pathways.*

In order to ensure a seamless linkage, leaders from the operations council and governance council are included in the membership of the patient care council. Decisions regarding the direction, mission, and purposes of the organization require the involvement and investment of representatives from the operations and governance decision-making forums. Also, the patient care council occasionally makes critical decisions affecting the resources of the organization. It is therefore appropriate that a linkage between leaders accountable for those decisions in patient care be provided within the shared governance structure. It is for that reason that the leaders representing operations and governance are full and active members of the patient care council.

THE OPERATIONS COUNCIL

In an effective integrated system, there must always be an ongoing mechanism for the stewardship of resources and for setting direction. The operations council is the place where management decisions centered around resources and other operational issues are made and implemented. It is in this council that the management leaders of the service pathways, the system and

> *Stewardship of resources is a critical part of the work of the leadership. It is one of the fundamental areas of accountability of system's management.*

organizational leaders, the organizational consultants (in the old system, vice-presidents of administrative departments or divisions) from finance, human resources, development and planning, administration, systems integration, and information services (and possibly other departments, depending on the design of the system) meet to make fundamental decisions about resource distribution, the integration of the system, and the direction of the system and engage in fiscal and capital resource planning (see Figure 2-4). The council also tries to resolve problems that arise regarding the structure and function of the system and the functional relationships between the service pathways and deals with all issues related to the contextual resource accountability of management. Like the patient care council, the operations council has specific goals and objectives given to it by the governance council. Also, each service pathway brings to the operations council specific resource objectives. Service pathway budget accountability, information management, and human resource requisites are examples of the issues that the service pathways present to the operations council. While it is critical that each service pathway maintain its unique culture, the operations council's obligation must see to it that each culture does not interfere with the resource priorities and obligations of the system as a whole. Dealing with the issues and conflicts related to organizational stewardship constitutes much of the work of the operations council.

> *The purpose of the operations function in a system is to provide a stable and safe context within which to make service decisions that are consistent with available resources and the needs of the customers who use them.*

Most of the activity of the operations council concerns fiscal and capital planning and performance accountability. The operations council is where the system's financial and capital plans are constructed. It is where the system converges to resolve issues related to the application of the organization's resources to achieve its goals and objectives and to provide its essential

> *The operations council is the place where leadership translates strategies into tactics for the organization as a whole and for each service pathway in the system.*

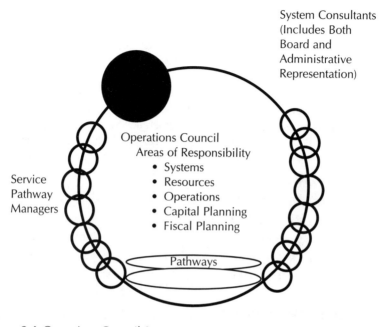

Figure 2-4 Operations Council Structure

services. Further, the council discusses and coordinates changes in the service pathway configurations, structural adjustments, design and control of the management information system, changes in the market or subscriber base, and the system's developmental plan. It also reviews the performance of the service pathways in meeting their main objectives, defines performance requisites for the service pathway leadership, articulates performance accountability, and outlines the evaluation mechanism.

Leaders from the patient care council and the governance council are included as members of the operations council. Organizational integrity requires that the implications of decisions about patient care and the mission, purposes, and strategic direction of the organization be taken into account when decisions about resource use are made. The presence of leaders from patient care and governance on the operations council exposes them to the issues that others must confront and highlights the interdependence of all components of the system. The interface of leaders from the different components around contextual and resource issues is critical to the effectiveness and sustainability of the decisions that are made.

THE GOVERNANCE COUNCIL

In systems thinking, integration is as important as function, and the ability to link the mission and activities of an entire system is critical to its effectiveness and the viability of its work. It is the purpose of the governance council to provide a locus of control whose primary focus is integration of the whole system (see Figure 2-5).

> *The governance council translates the board-defined mission, purposes, and objectives into strategies that give form to the work of the system.*

The governance council tries to ensure that the mission, purposes, and objectives of the system are translated into practical strategies that can be carried out by all of the system's components, stakeholders, and decision makers. It is the place where all the activities of the system converge. The governance council provides a place where the designated and elected leadership of the organization can meet to (1) ensure that the mission and objectives of the system are being achieved across all components of the system, (2) make the decisions necessary to connect the system to the community, and (3) ensure the integrity of the linkages between the various components of the system as they undertake their work within a shared governance framework.

> *The governance council is the place where all designated leaders meet to link activities and integrate the whole system.*

The focus of the governance council centers on the linkages between operations, practice, and governance in the system; the effectiveness of the system as a whole; system quality determinants and the measurement of their effects; and the attainment of the board-directed organizational goals. The council is accountable for the implementation of the directives for the system; the interface between the medical staff, the board, and the other disciplines and components of the system; and the development of a strategic plan for the system. The governance council deals with decisions about changes in the character, direction, and number of service pathway processes within the system and the evaluation of the interface between the strategic plan and the financial performance of the system.

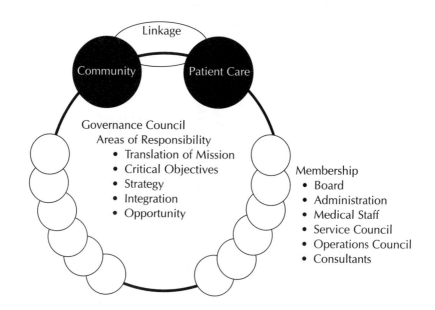

Figure 2-5 Governance Council Structure

It is the purpose of the governance council to look at the system as a whole—its integrity, efficacy, and efficiency. Further, the governance council's facilitation of linkages to the board and to the community is critical to the creation of a healthy community and thus to the long-term viability of the system.

The view from the governance council is the whole organization. The close fit of each of the components into a web of intersections and networks defines the structure as a seamless system.

The governance council receives support from components involved in the strategic activities of the system, such as marketing and planning, information systems, the administrative offices that handle the relationship between the system and the board of trustees, the medical staff leadership, the finance office, and community services.

The core membership of the governance council includes selected leaders of the patient care council and operations council, the chair of the medical staff, the

> *No one council supervises the work of another. They fulfill their individual accountability, and that serves as a check on the others. The integrity of the "fit" between one council and another is their faithfulness to their own accountability.*

chair of the board of trustees, the chief executive officer, and whoever else the council deems essential to the integrity of the system and to the performance of its decision-making duties. Consultants to the system occasionally act in a supportive role.

As with the other system councils, the governance council has the right and obligation to access whatever information, resources, individuals, and supports are necessary to do its work. The non-patient-care support services of the organization are the servants of the organization's decision makers and the patient care function. Indeed, those services can be called upon for assistance wherever key decisions are made in the system. If financial information is needed in the patient care council, it should be made available to that council. If such information is needed at the point of service within a specific service pathway, the finance office has an obligation to make that information available to the appropriate players. Support must be provided wherever it is needed.

INFORMATION SUPPORT

In shared governance, the fluidity and mobility of information are critical to the success of decision making. Increasingly, as the information system becomes more amenable to the users and provides a more comprehensive range of services and data, it allows much more decentralized and localized decision making to occur. Each one of the system councils, as well as the point-of-service decision-making bodies (from team to service pathway council), should have unencumbered access to the information necessary for their activities. The information system (see Chapter 9) is one of the essential con-

> *It is essential to the effectiveness of a system that information be easily accessed by and generously shared with every place in the system that requires it.*

stituents of an effective shared governance model, and there is no place where its importance is greater than in the governance council.

The governance council's role is to be able to look at the integrity of the system as a whole. The flexibility of the system depends on the fluidity and mobility of the information it has. In order to be able to assess the integrity of the system, the council must have ready access to critical information from finance, services, and quality improvement.

> *Every integrated system requires a different insight, skill set, and behaviors to sustain it. All systems are forever learning and adapting to continuously changing realities.*

The governance council, where key decision makers sit at the same table, is accountable for creating linkages and ensuring collective effectiveness. Exposure of the representatives to each other's frame of reference, functional roles, and leadership obligations provides a common foundation for dialogue and decision making regarding strategy delineation, conflict resolution, direction setting, system integration, community issues, and other concerns. It is in fact the place where all components of the system intersect and where the evidence of whether it is performing well or not is present for all to see.

NEW CONSTRUCTS ... NEW MINDSET

It should be clear to the reader at this stage that a whole-systems shared governance framework calls for an entirely new mindset. It essentially revolutionizes notions of workplace design, the provision of health services, and the relationship between players. It has broad legal, organizational, governance, and relational implications for the structuring of work and the design of health care (see Figure 2-6).

Many readers might suggest that the current legal and organizational context for health systems does not make the structure of shared governance as

> *When new structures are created, conflict always arises between old patterns of life and emerging requisites for new behaviors. Leadership means willingly confronting old frameworks and transforming them into new frameworks.*

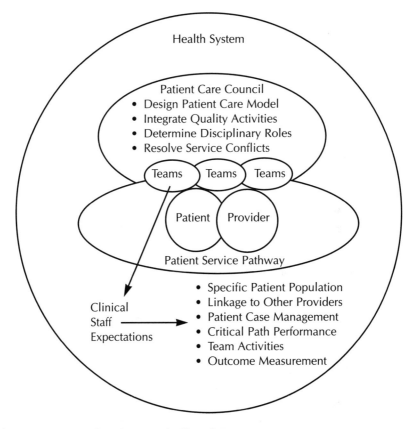

Figure 2-6 Patient Care Structure in Shared Governance

outlined in this chapter possible—and they would be right. However, if one looks over the whole scope of changes in health care, much of what is currently unfolding in health care would not have been legally or organizationally supported even 10 years ago. All change has an impact on legal, social, and relational constructs. It can be anticipated that building a shared governance system will require changing many of the social, legal, and organizational foundations that define the relationships in health care.

Creating structures that challenge past mandates, prescriptions, and regulations will necessitate the inclusion of new constructs and parameters that provide the kind of uniformity and consistency that usually results from a shared decision-making, shared leadership, or shared governance structure. In subsequent chapters, the components of the shared governance system are discussed in greater detail, from the individual and team relationships to the service pathway councils and the governance council.

While its conceptual foundations are sound and reflect a growing database on work, relationships, and organizations, the constructs, models, and applications of shared governance are a work in progress. The intent of this detailed presentation is to provide a basis for continuing discussion, development, and refinement of the structural elements and intersections that will make point-of-service whole-systems designs efficient, effective, and viable.

Creating a whole-systems framework based on point-of-service constructs is "noisy" at best. Any organization that has already undertaken this work knows the challenges, excitement, anxieties, and noise that attend the creation of a new order of things. It is the intent of this book to challenge and to stimulate the thinking and dialogue of leaders engaged in reformatting the health care system. Out of the process should come a variety of viewpoints, ideas, notions, and suggestions that will improve the foundations and functioning of shared governance systems.

SUGGESTED READING

Bergquist, W. 1993. *The postmodern organization: Mastering the art of irreversible change.* San Francisco: Jossey-Bass.

Coile, R. 1989. *The new medicine: Reshaping medical practice and health care management.* Gaithersburg, MD: Aspen Publishers.

Drucker, P. 1989. *The new realities.* New York: Harper and Row.

Handy, C. 1989. *The age of unreason.* Boston: Harvard Business School Press.

Mintzberg, H. 1990. *Mintzberg on management.* New York: The Free Press.

Morganthau, T., and M. Hager. 1993. The Clinton cure: Reinventing health care. *Newsweek*, 4 October, pp. 36–43.

Porter-O'Grady, T. 1992. *Implementing shared governance.* Baltimore: Mosby.

Relman, A. 1988. Assessment and accountability: The third revolution in medical care. *New England Journal of Medicine* 319:1220–1222.

Stayer, R. 1990. How I learned to let my workers lead. *Harvard Business Review* 46, no. 6:66–83.

Wheatley, M. 1992. *Leadership and the new science.* San Francisco: Berrett-Koehler.

Chapter 3

Transforming the Organization: Getting Started

Tim Porter-O'Grady, Marsha Parker, and Marilyn Hawkins

You cannot step twice into the same river,
the waters are forever flowing by.

Heraclitus

The initiation of a change in an organization is perhaps the most perilous and challenging component of the change process. Introducing the right activities to ensure that both the energies and the content of change are appropriate is critical to the effectiveness of any implementation, including the implementation of whole-systems shared governance.

THE INTEGRATING PROCESS

The implementation of any strategy should not be undertaken unilaterally. There are a host of shifts and adjustments in the organization that must be made in proximity to each other. Changes in the organizational structure should accompany other changes. After all, organizational structure is meant to support the fundamental functions and activities of the organization (see Figure 3-1). Structure yields no products. Rather, the purpose of structure is to provide form and format for the work of the organization. There should only be enough structure to support the activities and functions of the organization. Any

> *Structure serves no other purpose than to give format to purpose and integrity to work.*

more structure than this eventually tends to serve itself and draws resources and focus away from organizational objectives.

In today's health care organization, the main purpose of restructuring is to support the emerging point-of-service patient care delivery system. Patient care lies at the core of any health care system. Patient-centered services will require a substantial overhauling of departmental structures. This shift will integrate and facilitate the delivery of patient care over a broadening continuum of services across defined populations.

The changes in patient care design and service structure form the underpinning for the substantial changes necessary in the design of health care organizations. Building organizational structures, such as whole-systems shared governance,

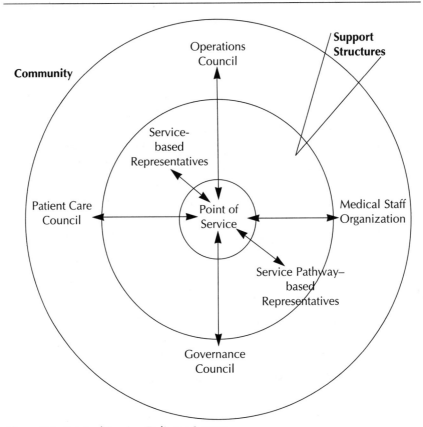

Figure 3-1 Point-of-Service Delivery System

helps sustain these fundamental changes. This is often why both are undertaken in a closely related time frame.

Many of the processes and teams used for patient care redesign also can be applied to structural redesign. Shared governance is a point-of-service, accountability-based model that supports patient care redesign strategies. There is cross-referencing of work groups, task forces, and functional activities related to patient care redesign and to the building of a new organizational structure to support it. Regardless, in designing a shared governance structure, integration becomes a critical theme in the effort to provide an appropriate structure for patient-centered service arrangements.

> *Processes have no value in and of themselves. Structure gives them form and outcome gives them value.*

THE INADEQUACY OF STRUCTURE

As hospitals and health systems begin to redesign themselves to create a continuum of services in a "capitated," price-managed patient care environment, a number of conflicts with the old organizational design emerge.

- While vertical integration is essential, the primary task of integration is horizontal linkage across the continuum of care services. There is a natural conflict between vertical thinking and structuring and horizontal planning and implementation. This conflict is exacerbated by the many levels of vertical hierarchy that remain in traditional organizations at a time when there is a need to reduce hierarchy and refine decision making at the point of service.
- Players and partners at the point of service must be increasingly accountable for making decisions and for owning the outcomes of those decisions. This requires a high degree of decentralization, local decision making, and fewer levels of hierarchical management.
- A central theme of the age and a function of transformation is the recognition that the information infrastructure is the emerging architecture for health services. Building decision making on an excellent information framework becomes a critical function of design in health care organizations.
- Relationships are the glue that holds all organizations together. Building systems to value and support essential role and decision relationships will be

critical to the flexibility and fluidity of an organization as it responds to the demands of its points of service.

The purpose of shared governance is to fundamentally change the locus of control, the decision-making process, and internal relationships in an organization. Shared governance structures take into account the need to increase the amount of decisions made at the point of service (up to 90 percent) and to ensure that the decisions made there are correct, "implementable," and do not require broad organizational approval or a long decision-making process (which might reduce the efficiency and effectiveness of the clinical delivery system). Furthermore, shared governance provides a format for creating a structure that makes it less possible for decisions to move away from their appropriate locus of control to other places in the organizational system, where they will almost certainly be less effectively made or inappropriately carried out.

> **Shared governance changes the locus of control in the system and always favors locating power at the center of a system.**

As the clinical and systems design of patient care services takes form, intersection with decision making in the operational and organizational components of the system becomes critical. It is at this place where implications for shared governance become more apparent. As patient care redesign pulls more decision making and accountability to the providers—at the points of service along the continuum of care—a structure must emerge that provides a supporting foundation for the changes in organizational and patient care design. Shared governance planning and decision making, therefore, interface directly with many of the functions and activities associated with redesign. Enumerating the impact on structure at the outset of shared governance implementation and incorporating that planning into initial patient care and service redesign can have an enormous facilitating effect on the fundamental activities associated with service redesign and patient care reengineering.

A FOCUSED WORK GROUP

In the renewal and reengineering process, focus on structural elements should begin at the outset of the process. If the organizational design and the supporting structures that underpin it are not revised, conflicts

> **The purpose of the design team is to design and then cease to exist.**

between the structure and the function of the organization will emerge very early on.

In shared governance, every leadership role, functional activity, and decision-making process is radically altered to fit integration and point-of-service decision making (see Figure 3-2). Shared governance reflects accountability-based rather than responsibility-based processes, and therefore the new design should support the emergence of accountability at every level of the organization.

Good patient care and service redesign are going to accomplish several objectives. These objectives form the framework for activities of redesign that unfold in effecting outcome determination, process activities, service efficiencies, and quality measurement. The prevailing organizational structure should support and act in harmony with the processes associated with restructuring. It should not impede the efficiencies being created in the service and patient care delivery activities of the organization. The redesign activities should achieve several outcomes:

- All professional and associated service providers should develop an orientation toward specific patient care populations.

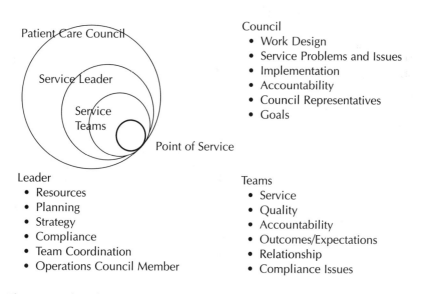

Council
- Work Design
- Service Problems and Issues
- Implementation
- Accountability
- Council Representatives
- Goals

Leader
- Resources
- Planning
- Strategy
- Compliance
- Team Coordination
- Operations Council Member

Teams
- Service
- Quality
- Accountability
- Outcomes/Expectations
- Relationship
- Compliance Issues

Figure 3-2 Shared Governance Systems Integration

- The continuum of care and the patient's journey through the health care experience should be facilitated by life and health processes, demand management, critical clinical pathways, outcome consistency, and quality measurement.
- The design of service should center on patient processes and bring all necessary health care providers into the same context so that they will be able to offer integrated care services.
- Resource management and allocation should be focused on processes associated with the point of service. As much as possible, decision making related to resources should be located as close to the point of service as possible.
- All partnerships, clinical processes, and players (physicians, nurses, allied health professionals, etc.) are brought together to form a seamless web of providers and supports configured around the patient's pathway.

These outcomes create the foundation for substantial patient care redesign and a restructuring of the organization to support that redesign. A shared governance structure provides an organizational framework within which decisions can be implemented throughout the system in support of the above redesigned activities. In order to ensure that the organization operates effectively, structures in the system must be in congruence with the expectations for decision making, relationships, and performance at the point of service. This seamlessness in concept and design must play out in the organization's operations as well as in patient care services and provider decision making.

THE SHARED GOVERNANCE STEERING GROUP

Creation of a team focused on the type of organizational structuring and design needed to support patient care is an essential step toward whole-systems shared governance. The shared governance steering group (SGSG) is the place where the activities of structural design and implementation unfold. Again, it must be emphasized that the shared governance implementation is a corollary of patient care delivery system redesign and all service-based activi-

Every key role in the system, staff or management, should be represented in the steering group. The majority of planners, however, should be from the staff, not from management.

ties related to it. It is a part of a comprehensive strategy for organizational redesign. Shared governance implementation simply reflects the organizational structure portion of that redesign (see Figure 3-3).

The initiating of the activities of the SGSG should be timed to occur simultaneously with the implementation of key components of the redesign. For example, when the service pathways get created, the structures that support decision making at the level of the service pathways must also be created. Therefore, cross-linkage between the membership of the SGSG and the redesign implementation process is essential. Not only are timing issues important for cross-referencing the work of the two processes (work redesign and shared governance implementation), but elements of fit between the two processes must be considered by both. The SGSG will want to ensure that the stages of structural change match closely the stages of redesign implementation. Each level of redesign, from the patient care pathways to the management structure, the support system, the administra-

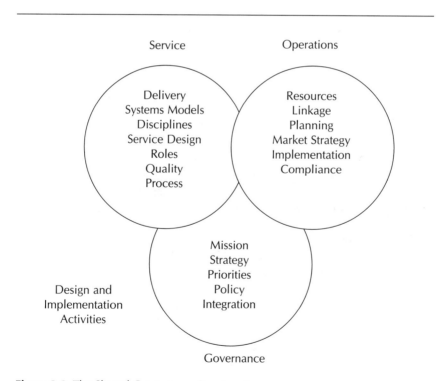

Figure 3-3 The Shared Governance Steering Group

tive configuration, and the board-organization interface, has implications related to successful construction of a good organizational structure.

The tasks of the SGSG should include the following:

- review of the existing organizational structure and its interface with current patient care system redesigning activities
- identification of the key elements of structural change supporting process shifts at the point of service
- enumeration of the structural supports necessary to underpin the patient care redesign and point-of-service focus in the organization
- delineation of the essential characteristics and accountability of emerging roles in the new structure and the articulation of those roles in position descriptions
- outlining of the team, service pathway, and system council format for decision making throughout the health system from the point of service to the policy and governance levels
- definition and implementation of the activities and change events necessary for formally reshaping the organizational structure
- institution of developmental and learning processes appropriate for the leadership changes, role shifts, performance expectations, service adjustments, and leadership outcomes associated with a shared governance design
- evaluation of the effectiveness of staged implementation of the shared governance design and the effectiveness of decision making at the various locuses of control within the organization.

Reengineering the organization and modifying the structures demands a concerted effort on the part of the leadership. The shared governance structure changes the role of leaders, alters the character and number of leaders, and shifts the locus of control for decision making to the point of service. Revising the leadership roles and functions *Timing is everything.* while simultaneously implementing the reengineering process is critical to the success of both reengineering and shared governance implementation. It must be remembered that the purpose of the shared governance structure is to support the reengineered organization and to ensure sufficient structure to sustain its activities and create linkages and efficiencies in the system, especially in decision-making arenas.

SHARED GOVERNANCE STEERING GROUP MEMBERSHIP

The criteria for selecting the SGSG members should include not only breadth of representation but also linkage of the representatives to other parts of the system. Clearly, included in the SGSG should be individuals involved in the reengineering process—in order to ensure cross-referencing and appropriate timing of changes.

> *However membership for the steering group is selected, it should draw in the best and the brightest. They will be needed to do good design.*

A decisional group like the SGSG should be as small as possible and as large as the breadth of representation requires. The preferred number of members lies between 7 and 14. A group any smaller will usually lack representativeness, and a group any larger will not be able to reach decisions efficiently. Since every major constituency in the organization is going to be affected by the decisions of the SGSG, it is critical that each component have someone serving as a member of the group.

Following is a list of staff members who should be considered for SGSG membership. The importance of empowerment and stakeholder accountability requires that a broad range of organizational leaders be involved in the SGSG's processes. Not surprisingly, the majority of members on the group may represent staff rather than management. Role representation is critical, but distributing representation in order to favor management leadership is not. Ensuring breadth and diversity of representation is far more important than ensuring that most of the representatives come from management. For one thing, effective decision making depends on the diversity of the members. Therefore, the following should receive due consideration when the SGSG is formed:

- service pathway staff
- service pathway management leaders
- support systems leaders
- quality control staff
- departmental management leaders
- information systems staff
- medical staff leaders

- senior administrative staff
- trustees

The process of selecting team members depends on the dynamics of the organization. Clearly, the SGSG should include the best and the brightest but at the same time include those who play key roles in the organization. Selection of steering group members should be based on the following criteria. Each member should:

- hold a key position in the organization
- have good group skills
- demonstrate a commitment to redesign, the reengineering process, and the implementation of shared governance
- demonstrate a commitment to self-development
- have the ability to engage in dialogue with diverse individuals and to participate fully in the work of the steering group
- have the administrative or leadership support of those the person will represent
- have the ability and willingness to remain with the process through its completion
- have the time and the energy to commit to the level of intensity of activities associated with implementing shared governance

The character of the interface between members is a critical issue. Nothing is more disheartening than to have the wrong mix of players involved in as serious an undertaking as implementing a new structure. The more diverse the behavior, leadership styles, and gifts of the members of the steering group, the more effective the process of deliberating and decision making. Also, a clear commitment on the part of the members to the process they are undertaking is essential for the "sustainability" of that process. High turnover and short tenure of members can be very disruptive. It should be clear to all members what the time frame expectations are, why a strong commitment is necessary, and what the expectations are for each role.

THE INITIAL DEVELOPMENTAL PROCESS FOR THE SHARED GOVERNANCE STEERING GROUP

Once the steering group members have been selected, nominated, or elected, their frame of reference, knowledgebase, and other foundations for deliberation should be equalized as much as possible. Clearly there will be different levels of understanding and application of shared governance principles at the outset of the SGSG's work. There must be a mechanism in the organization that makes it possible for the knowledgebase and understanding of the members of the steering group to be developed and their learning cycle to be accelerated. Obviously, the organization wants to ensure that good and sound decisions are made. The activities related to redesign and to shared governance implementation must be correlated in the developmental framework of those who will lead the process. As participants are obtained for the reengineering process (including members of the SGSG), integration of their activities and the

> *In creating a learning organization, there is no better place to start than the steering group. Its development and skill building will be essential to the quality and thoroughness of the restructuring.*

activities associated with implementing shared governance will need to be a focus of SGSG deliberations. Education and development sessions and creation of a schedule for establishing a common frame of reference constitute an essential first step. This step can be accomplished in any number of ways, but the following topics need to be covered:

- the mission, purposes, and goals of the redesign process
- the principles of point-of-service organizational design
- the principles of decentralized management and accountability-based work systems
- the principles of shared governance and the use of the concept of a seamless organization as a foundation for restructuring organizations
- the characteristics of effective organizational change processes and their application to whole-systems shared governance

The developmental cycle is critical to obtaining the breadth of knowledge the members will need in order to undertake the activities of redesign. While development is by definition a work in progress, the implementation process will itself teach the members about the application of whole-systems shared governance to the organization. Therefore, there should be opportunities to take risks and to experiment with the application of new concepts. The spirit of experimentation will create a frame of reference that allows decisions to be implemented without the kind of confidence that is based on previous experience. Since new structures

> *There is no one model of structure that must be implemented. A system's culture drives the development of models. It is principle that is constant, not the process.*

are being created to respond to a new age and changing demands, it should be expected that some of the processes implemented will reflect different ways of thinking. Staff are applying elements that have never been applied before in a framework for decision making that is relatively untested. Each of these elements should be anticipated and incorporated into the process of implementation and the work of the steering group.

The membership of the SGSG should be reminded that there is a certain amount of serendipity and uncertainty in any change process. The dynamics of the environment, the shifting social context, the design of change, and other components of the change process (e.g., patient care redesign) all create new demands in the organization. Each of these has an influence on the character and content of the restructuring. The steering group members should take into account all of the factors that can influence the rate and timing of change (see Figure 3-4). The group's response must evidence a commitment to fluid and flexible processing that shifts and adjusts as the demand for it is altered. Flexibility in membership work and function keeps the members from creating rigid structures that are as unchangeable or impermeable as the structures they are attempting to remove and replace.

CONCEPTUAL DESIGN FOR SHARED GOVERNANCE
IMPLEMENTATION

Before the SGSG can fully begin the implementation, it must be aware of two principles of change: all sustainable change is comprehensive, and change that occurs in one place in a system affects every other place in the system. Therefore, it is important for the SGSG to be well informed about the redesign and other structural changes going on in the organization. Having a representative from whatever

> *Development of a work group is as essential as the work it does. Failure often results from what a group did not know rather than what it did not do.*

leadership group is undertaking the redesign or reengineering activities provides a solid foundation for a linkage between the SGSG and the group. Information and connection to this group will be critical to the ongoing work of the SGSG. Harmonizing the strategies and timing of the two efforts will increase the effectiveness of both.

It is a further obligation of the SGSG to be fully aware of organizational constructs, theory, and function. As the organization gets retooled, there will be broad implications for the entire system. Therefore, it is important that solid principles and good conceptual foundations be established. Members of the group should know about the complexities of systems and be able to apply organizational principles to their own system in order to ensure that the new structure is reared on solid foundations. Much has been written about shared governance, but perhaps

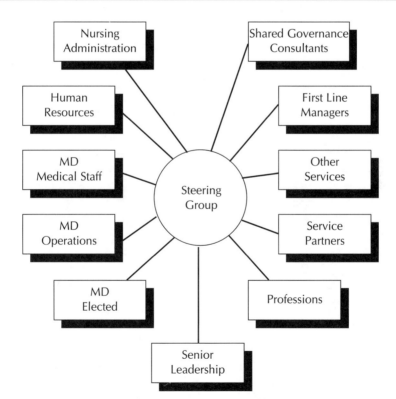

Figure 3-4 Shared Governance Steering Group Membership

the most significant models of implementation are those that have been used in highly complex nursing organizations.

NURSING SHARED GOVERNANCE

> *Nurses make up 60 percent of point-of-service providers. If they do not change, it does not matter who else does.*

In many hospitals and organizations, the nursing service has used principles of whole-systems shared governance as a foundation for implementing point-of-service empowerment processes (see Figure 3-5). As a result, many organizations assume that shared governance is strictly a nursing concept. Nothing could be further from the truth. While many of the service delivery models that exist in health care operate within the nursing service, the conceptual foundations come from a much broader theoretical and research frame of reference. Shared governance is most common among nursing services for two main

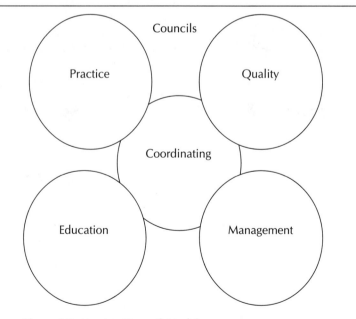

Figure 3-5 Nursing Council Model

reasons. First, the large aggregate of diverse members that make up a nursing service has a large impact on services. Second, most nursing services encompass a range of differentiated functions that need to be integrated in order to deliver patient care services efficiently. In addition, nursing services have implemented empowerment point-of-service processes for 10–15 years—processes that provide a strong foundation for shared leadership, shared decision making, and shared governance.

Shared governance is a systems concept, not a nursing model. It began with nursing because it could and because nurses are the largest group of providers closest to the point of service.

It has always been understood by those promulgating the concept of shared governance that it could not be limited to a single discipline in any system. In a health care system, the integration, coordination, and facilitation of disciplinary relationships among the various members of the health care team are critical to the effectiveness of service provision and the continuum of care. The need for a connection between the disciplines will likely become increasingly important, and thus, the principles of broad-based shared governance will continue to grow in value. Time and circumstances have created a situation in which shared governance can be expanded from use in single disciplines to the entire organization (see Figure 3-6).

In many organizations, the nursing shared governance may be the natural beginning point for the application of shared governance principles to the broader organization. As outlined in Chapter 2, different considerations arise when implementing shared governance in an entire organization instead of a single component (e.g., nursing services). Therefore, nursing-specific design and application of shared governance is essentially nontransferable to the whole system. The principles are unchanging but the approach is highly variable. Culture always provides the final framework for the implementation of any concept or process. Each health care culture has created its own framework for the implementation of nursing shared governance. It will also

Nursing shared governance does not disappear in whole-systems approaches. It does expand to accommodate all the partners that make a system work.

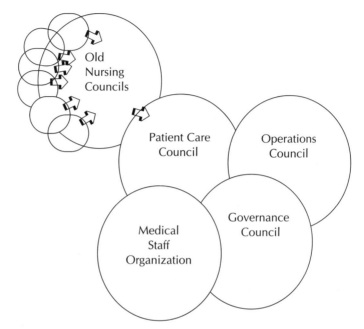

Figure 3-6 Moving from a Nursing Model toward a Whole-Systems Model

need to create its own framework for expanding shared governance to the whole system.

> **Nursing representation now expands to the system. If nurses are to have the impact on decision making they should, they must expand their frame of reference.**

In an organization in which nursing shared governance exists, the organization is not obligated to adapt to the nursing shared governance framework. Instead, the nursing shared governance component must fit itself within the broader framework of whole-systems shared governance. The benefit of having begun shared governance within the nursing service is that the largest group of point-of-service providers in the organization is already operating within the appropriate framework. That increases the chance of a successful organizationwide implementation of shared governance. In particular, it creates an opportunity to extend the necessary patterns of behavior, styles of leadership, and characteristics of point-of-service decision making to the remaining components of the organization, building on what is already present in the nursing service.

INTERDISCIPLINARY SHARED GOVERNANCE

Inviting others in the organizational system to become involved in shared governance does not guarantee that there will be an increased level of interest. In many instances, other disciplines and work groups in the organization may see shared governance simply as an externalization of the nursing service and another opportunity for nursing to influence or control its relationships with the rest of the system. This viewpoint is inadequate. It is reasonable to assume that if empowerment, shared leadership, and shared decision making are to occur in an organization, all of its members must ultimately participate. When clearly half or more of the point-of-service providers are nurses, it is also reasonable to assume that implementation of empowerment processes, shared leadership, and shared decision making should begin with that large group. Regardless of what other group might be willing to engage the change process, if the largest professional group in the organization has not moved a significant distance toward acquiring the behaviors associated with shared governance, it will not matter who else has. Simply in virtue of its volume, location, and diversity, the nursing service will require additional time, effort, and energy to acquire such behaviors, and allowing it to have a head start is not a bad idea. In many instances, it is for this reason alone that shared governance begins with the nursing service—although of course it should not end there.

> *Shared governance represents the partnership between all who provide service and support in a system. It requires their engagement in decisions and actions that support their work and relationships.*

Following the collection and dissemination of information on the theory, principles, and foundations of shared governance activities, the SGSG must begin to assess the activities it will undertake in order to facilitate the translation of theory and concept into practice. In doing this, the SGSG should follow a particular pattern of deliberation and decision making.

SHARED GOVERNANCE STEERING GROUP BASICS

The initial activities of the SGSG concern its own functions and activities. Setting up the rules of engagement and defining the issues associated with undertaking its work is the first step in the SGSG's design and construction of a shared governance structure. This step encompasses

> *Teams are the future of work.*

- creating a clear statement of purpose and direction as a foundation for its work
- outlining the obligations of membership, the commitment expected, the meeting schedule, the work to be done, and the shared obligation for that work
- delineating the decision-making processes and tools that are available and will be used for stimulating dialogue, seeking direction, defining work content, resolving conflicts, and seeking solutions to problems
- devising a timeline to guide the SGSG's work and the evaluation of the team's processes
- enumerating the mechanisms of linkage with the other reengineering processes going on in the organization
- defining the mechanism for communicating and intersecting with other leadership groups in the organization to ensure that each is informed and involved to the extent necessary
- defining the specific accountability of the SGSG in light of its obligation to implement shared governance throughout the organization
- outlining the evaluation activities that will be used to measure, evaluate, and validate the stages of implementation and their impact on the organization

> *Membership requires commitment, which in turn requires presence. You cannot commit to anything when you are not present.*

These first rules of engagement are an essential foundation for the work of the SGSG. Like all teams, it requires a clear understanding of its mandate, the tools that it will use to undertake its work, the expectations of those who are members, the time frame for accomplishing its objectives, and the outcomes required. Also, it must establish linkages with components to key parts of the organization—those that depend upon its work or that the SGSG depends on for completing its work successfully.

There are a number of stakeholders in the organization who are going to be very interested in the work of the SGSG. Whoever these stakeholders are (e.g., administrators, service pathway leaders, support services staff, board members, medical staff), a mechanism should exist for either incorporating or communicating with them so that they understand the developmental process and the activities related to it. In shared governance implementation, there are no hidden agendas, no secret meetings, and no closed-door processes. It is assumed in shared governance that investment, engagement, and ownership operate across the board. Initially, any member of the organization who has the time and interest has the option to either observe or be involved in decision making.

UNDERSTANDING THE LIMITS

The SGSG must also understand the expectations and limitations that exist. No group can successfully undertake its work free of the constraints imposed by limited resources, limited time, and competing demands. All areas of activity must be balanced in a meaningful way to provide appropriate support for the work of the SGSG and there are

> *Commitment always demands personal ownership. No responsibility, no rewards.*

several issues that must be addressed in order to ensure that the realities of the organization are fully taken into account.

Budgetary Availability

There should be a delineation of the costs associated with the work of the SGSG. The budgetary allocation for this work should be clarified in advance so

> *Don't ever attempt to produce what you can't pay for.*

that, when the SGSG undertakes its activities, it knows the financial parameters within which it must operate. No decision group that gathers key players together operates without having a cost impact on the organization, and the time, energy, commitment, and the results of the deliberations of the group all affect the viability of the organization. Thus, the financial impact of the

SGSG's work should be anticipated to the fullest extent possible before the group begins its activities and should be incorporated into its deliberations. Furthermore, the SGSG should make a commitment to help generate whole-systems budget enhancements, revenue reductions, cost reductions, and performance improvements that total more than the costs associated with its work.

Deadlines

No group can insulate itself from demands made by the organization to accomplish its ends. Deadlines are a requisite for motivating and guiding work in any system. They should be clear and outlined in advance of the undertaking of activities. The time frames for associated activities, such as budgetary activities, should be communicated to the leadership of the SGSG so that it can incorporate them into its planning.

Workload

Obviously, the work of the SGSG is affected by the availability of the team members. The workload of the members in their regular work setting must be moderate enough to allow them to fulfill the duties of the SGSG. If the workload requirements make it impossible for members to commit their energies to the SGSG, then the SGSG's performance will be seriously impaired. A discussion of the workload, time, availability, and obligations

> *Time is as much a resource as money. Neither should be wasted.*

of each of the members is essential during the formation of the SGSG. Workload adjustments can easily be justified, by the importance of the work of building a new structure.

Individual Differences

People in a work group are different. They bring a variety of skills and talents to the work group. Some are assertive and creative, innovative and energized, and able to verbalize their thoughts with great ease. Others are reflective and cautious and will need to be coaxed into making a contribution. Knowing the various characteristics of the members of the group, understanding their unique talents, and utilizing strategies that capture most of what each has to offer will be the job of the leadership. Use of techniques and tactics that allow every member of the group to contribute is essential, as is careful planning and a sensitive awareness of the ever-changing balance of participation.

Other Resources

The SGSG should not assume that its membership possesses all of the expertise and insight it needs. There will be times when other players will have to be involved and incorporated into the SGSG's decision making. If a non-member has required information, expertise, leadership abilities, or insight, that person will need to be brought in as an adjunct. In any work group there are essentially three kinds of members: core members, expert members, and ad hoc members. Core members are those that have been appointed, and they make up the continuing membership of the group. Expert members are individuals who are included in the deliberations of the group because they have a requisite set of insights and skills. Ad hoc members are individuals who are positioned either by location, power, or role to have useful information, insights, and relationships. At varying times expert and ad hoc members must be joined with the core members in order to ensure effective deliberation. Such fluidity in its membership allows the SGSG to focus on the proper issues and perform its work successfully.

> *Any work group should have available to it whatever resources it needs to do its work. No support, no outcome.*

Development and Training

As mentioned previously, development is important—continuous development. There will be points in the implementation process where the SGSG membership may need to stop in order to assess what it knows and what it needs to know to advance its work. A constant commitment to development, growth, and advancement is critical to the ongoing competence of the work group.

> *You cannot do what you do not know how to do. Learning is as important as the work that it enables.*

Authority and Decision Making

The group must be clear at the outset as to what decisions it is accountable for making, what authority it has for making those decisions, and the extent of its ability to implement the decisions made. Clear support from the leadership of the organization and enumeration of the authority and decision-making power of the group are essential to the group's ability to accomplish its work. Clarity of authority at the outset is essential to its accountability and its ability to implement its recommendations. It would be unfortunate if those who have been given the task of spreading empowerment throughout an organization did not themselves have the necessary power to accomplish this task. Clarification as to what it can do and cannot do will help form the framework and parameters for its deliberations and decision making.

> *Every work group must have access to whatever information it needs to make decisions. The major reason for inadequate decisions is lack of the right information at the right time.*

Information Access

In performing its work, the SGSG must have access to all the information it requires. Without access to the tools that it needs, including appropriate information, the SGSG will achieve only limited success, and the organization therefore must ensure that it always has what it needs.

Determination of Boundaries

As important as it is to know what the group can do, it is also important to know what lies beyond the scope of the group. Increasingly, in an integrated organizational system there are different loci of control and decision making. In the redesign process, groups responsible for varying components may have authority to make decisions within the appropriate context. Their authority and the boundaries that define it must be clear also to the SGSG. On the other hand, the boundaries of the functions and activities of the SGSG must be made known as early as possible so that when those boundaries are reached and the involvement of other components of the organizational system are necessary to continue the work of the SGSG, that will be clear to the members and incorporated into their deliberations.

THE PLANNING PROCESS

The above are important issues for any steering group involved in implementing shared governance. Again, clear accountability is the foundation of any team's efforts to accomplish its work successfully. If this and other basic components are in place, the SGSG can begin to undertake the design and implementation of a whole-systems shared governance

> *Every team must know what it can and cannot do. There is nothing more destructive than assigning a team its work and not giving it the authority necessary to do it.*

structure. Clearly, the first step is the delineation of a plan that sets out the SGSG's goals and objectives and the creation of a timeline that sets their time of accomplishment.

The planning process appropriate for this kind of a work group is not the incremental, long-range planning process so familiar to health care organizations in the past. The planning activities need to be directed toward delineating expectations, outcomes, and design components for a shared governance structure. The following three elements of the planning phase are critical to the initial work.

Expectations

The design and implementation of a shared governance structure depends on what processes and structure are anticipated. It is important that the shared governance principles be enumerated clearly so that they can be used as a database for implementation and later as a tool for evaluating the stages of implementation and the ultimate success of the design. The expectations, presented in a bulleted format, should be stated in such a way that they can be used to measure the functional components of the design and implementation. For example, the statement that there will be no more than two levels of management leadership and the statement that 90 percent of all decision making will occur at the service pathway level each indicate a principle and a device for measuring the effectiveness and appropriateness of any structure based on that principle.

Functional Components

The second task is to identify functional components of the new structure. For example, if the word *council* is used to refer to a deliberative body, the SGSG must define what this particular council does and what its decision-making authority is. As another example, it might need to define what a team is and what its authority, functions, activities, membership, and accountability are.

Roles and Positions

Once the principles and structural and functional components of the organization are clearly articulated, the next step is to delineate the new roles and positions. In the change to shared governance, a number of roles will have to be modified and others will have to be eliminated. For example, in the switch to a whole-systems design, vice-president and other senior management positions may become systems consulting positions, and the content, functions, obligations, and relationships associated with these positions will of course change as well. Each of the functional shifts should be identified in the planning process so that every member of the organization is clear about the implications of the move to shared governance for his or her position and role in the organization.

In addition to the three elements described above, the SGSG needs to develop a vision of how the organization will look. This vision should be "expressed" graphically and it should include the basic elements of the organization; the relationship of the functions and structures to each other; the interface between the individual structures; and the work, accountability, and decision-making authority of each of the components of the organization. A shared governance design cannot be described using a line and box chart. Since shared governance depends essentially on the interfaces between as well as the accountability and relationships of the various players and components of the organization, intersecting circles and cycles of relationship are often used to indicate authority, position, relationship, and accountability in a shared governance organizational chart.

> *The steering function requires sufficient time to do its work. However, the timelines for this work must be established at the outset, and they must be clear to everyone in the system.*

There are two types of models that are important in the design of a shared governance organization. The first consists of the linkages and intersecting lines of functional accountability, relationship, and position in the organization. The second consists of the management and leadership intersections along a continuum of decision making from the point of service to the system level. These two models, while closely related, display different categories of accountability. The first identifies the accountability of groups within the system, the second identifies the accountability of individuals within the groupings in the system. Constructing these models is one of the main tasks of the SGSG's planning phase.

Through use of these tools and the design processes, a better picture of the implementation process begins to emerge within the group. It is important to note that the beginning design is not permanent. It is simply a demarcation point, a place for the dialogue to begin. No structure is permanent. The parameters and design of a structure are forever shifting in response to the surrounding realities. This must be understood and accepted by everyone in the steering group. If the steering group does not recognize the need for fluidity, its efforts may result in the building of a permanent, rigid structure—the very thing the redesign process was intended to do away with.

> *The steering group must know that designing is merely the beginning of its work.*
> *Implementation of the design will change where it takes the system.*

THE WORK OF THE STEERING GROUP

Over the life of the SGSG, there will be many activities related to the implementation process for which it will have summary accountability. Anything related to the design and implementation of the shared governance structure falls within the auspices of this group. It therefore is critical to make sure that all of the phases of implementation, stages of development, and components of the structure fall within the purview and range of accountability of the SGSG.

> *Design is like art—necessary to human experience but subject to the tastes and judgments of others. You will never satisfy everyone.*

In doing its work, the SGSG has many diverse mechanisms and options available. Clearly, control of all of the elements of the shared governance implementation process should rest in the hands of the SGSG leadership. However, work groups, task forces, implementation groups, and various other tools can be used to delineate the steps in the implementation process. In many cases, implementation around the point of service or along the service pathway in the continuum of care will require the creation of culturally based work groups that fall within the auspices of the individual service pathways. Also, as teams get better defined and more thoroughly developed, leadership for team development will become a service pathway responsibility. While the SGSG may be accountable for application of the principles of shared governance, the framework for decision making, and the range of accountability and authority of teams and other decision-making bodies within the service pathways, the actual functions and activities related to the implementation of shared governance will unfold in the cultural context of each pathway.

> *The steering group must be free to do its work. Its accountability must be clear up front, and the support it needs must be articulated before it makes critical decisions. Countering decisions after they are made destroys the credibility of both the group and its work.*

The primary goal of the SGSG is to facilitate the implementation of shared governance and to ensure that it proceeds basically uniformly throughout the system. A secondary goal is to ensure that, where possible, the principles of shared governance are applied with enough flexibility to allow important unique characteristics of the individual service pathways to survive the restructuring.

In undertaking its work, the SGSG must address the following:

- the fit of the shared governance implementation schedule and the patient care and systems redesign schedule
- the design of a shared governance structure that integrates the whole organization
- the linkage of the medical staff organization and the point-of-service, empowered shared governance structure
- the design and creation of the patient care council and the design of its relationship to the service pathways and the teams of which they consist
- the design and creation of the operations council (the design should integrate management and resource decision making throughout the system and within each component of the system)

- the design and creation of the governance council (the council's main role is to integrate the shared governance structure so that it functions like a seamless decision-making network)
- the participation of the board of trustees in the conception, design, and implementation of whole-systems shared governance within and across the components of the organization
- the definition of the roles, functions, levels of management and leadership, and administrative relationships at the support and systems level of the organization
- the development and implementation of a learning and development model for the clinical and resource leadership
- the enumeration of learning organization characteristics and tools operating at different levels of the organization (e.g., team-based learning; support service roles; consultation roles; and revised administrative, governance, and medical staff relationships)
- the delineation and appointment of work groups, task forces, and other activity groups directed toward the implementation of components of the shared governance structure
- the delineation of accountability and authority at every decision-making point in the organization
- the evaluation of the effectiveness of the implementation of shared governance for the whole system through assessment of
  —the consistency of application of the shared governance concept
  —the effectiveness of decision making by individual providers, individual leaders, team service councils, and system councils
  —the impact of empowerment on the efficiency and effectiveness of decision making (taking into account decision timelines, appropriateness of decisions, and decision outcomes)
  —staff investment in system-level decisions and staff compliance and satisfaction with the empowerment resulting from point-of-service decision making
  —the effectiveness of the new roles for administrative officers and the impact those roles have on council decision making, service pathway decision making, and leadership development
  —the critical flow of decision making and communication throughout the organization (the focus is on effectiveness, efficiency, flow problems, and inadequacies in the communication system)

Each of the above items encompasses functions that will be essential to effective implementation of whole-systems shared governance. In subsequent chapters, each of the elements of the implementation for which the SGSG is responsible will be discussed in relation to the development of the main components of the shared governance organization. What should be clear already is that fundamental accountability for the success of the implementation of whole-systems shared governance rests with the SGSG.

THE CHANGE PROCESS

> *The steering group must be flexible and fluid. The conditions present at the beginning of its work will not likely be the same as those later in the process. The possibility of change of course must always be built into planning.*

It should be clear by now how time-bound and transitional each element of the implementation of shared governance is. External and internal variables will affect the rate of change, the intensity of change, and the time frame for change. Further, there are definite stages of change, and these must be understood by the SGSG and incorporated into its implementation plan. These stages include planning and preparation, design and movement, creativity and application, testing the value of the application, integrating the components of change, and evaluating the effectiveness of the change over the long term. The SGSG should be aware that these stages are highly variable. Certain pathways and teams will develop at a faster rate and in a different way than other pathways and teams, and this fact will need to be taken into account in devising the timeline and the evaluation process.

Often, adjustments in what was planned will have to be made to respond to unexpected internal developments. Chaos and complexity theory states that the serendipitous often has an influence on the formal and controlled part of change. Room for the serendipitous (and for anticipated problems) will need to be incorporated into the strategy and planning of the steering group. As it moves through the implementation process, challenges will inevitably arise, and it must be prepared to react efficiently. "Gridding out" or flowcharting the stages of shared governance implementation can provide a tool for measuring progress and handling the variability embedded in the implementation of a comprehensive restructuring.

The SGSG should always keep in mind that it is undertaking an activity that has few precedents. Redesigning an organization using shared governance principles is a relatively new type of under-taking. There are few tools and models that can be replicated by the organization as it begins to alter its structure to fit the emerging service and care delivery system. Undoubtedly, there will be many times the organization will need to redirect activities, alter plans, and adjust the implementation process.

Whole-systems shared governance has few precedents—it is a new application of systems principles. The designers are living the script as they write it. Adherence to the principles will help ensure the integrity of the process.

Flexibility and a good understanding of the elements of change within a whole-systems context will serve the SGSG well as it facilitates the implementation of shared governance. The task will require insight, patience, and determination. However, if the key elements of the change process, as outlined in this chapter, are incorporated into the functional components of design and implementation, the tools necessary for success will be available to the SGSG. It should be remembered by the SGSG leadership that the application of the principles of shared governance is critical to the sustainability of any shared governance design. Using the principles as a template and applying them consistently throughout the implementation process ensure that a meaningful relationship exists between the organization's services and the structures in place to support them.

SUGGESTED READING

Andrews, H., et al. 1994. *Organizational transformation in health care: A work in progress.* San Francisco: Jossey-Bass.

Bennis, W., and M. Mische. 1995. *The 21st century organization: Reinventing through reengineering.* San Diego, CA: Pfeiffer and Co.

Blendon, R., and M. Brodie. 1994. *Transforming the system: Building a new structure for a new century.* The Future of American Health Care Series, ed. R. Blendon, vol. 4. New York: Faulkner and Grey.

Byrne, J. 1993. The horizontal corporation. *Business Week*, 20 December, pp. 76–81.

Conrad, D. 1993. Coordinating patient care services in regional health systems: The challenge of clinical integration. *Hospitals and Health Services Administration* 38:491–508.

Edwards, G., et al. 1994. Unit-based shared governance can work. *Nursing Management* 25, no. 4:74–77.

Freeman, R. 1994. *Working under different rules.* New York: Russell Sage Foundation.

Graham, M., and M. Lebaron. 1994. *The horizontal revolution: Guiding the teaming takeover.* San Francisco: Jossey-Bass.

Porter-O'Grady, T. 1995. From principle to practice: Whole systems shared governance. *Journal of Shared Governance* 1, no. 3:21–26.

Porter-O'Grady, T., and S. Finnigan. 1984. *Shared governance for nursing.* Gaithersburg, MD: Aspen Publishers.

Wilson, C. 1991. *Building new nursing organizations: Visions and realities.* Gaithersburg, MD: Aspen Publishers.

Chapter 4

Building for Service: The Center of the Enterprise

Kami English, Curtis Takamoto, and Tim Porter-O'Grady

The first order of business is to build a group of people who, under the influence of the institution, grow taller and become healthier, stronger, more autonomous.

Robert K. Greenleaf
"Servant Leadership"

As indicated in previous chapters, shared governance is an accountability-based organizational design. This means that the involvement and invest-ment of individuals is sought after, not because of a commitment to democratic principles, but because each player in a system has a fundamental contribution to make to the work of the system and to the achievement of its goals. Therefore, it is in the interest of the system to define each person's potential contribution, incorporate the contribution into role expectations, and evaluate the person's performance in light of the outcomes toward which it is directed. An accountability-based sys-tem not only empowers each person in the system but sets a high level of expectation for each person's perfor-mance (see Exhibit 4-1).

> **Accountability is the foundation for good systems design. It is not participation that defines a good organization; it is, instead, sustainable results.**

Shared governance is intended to provide a framework for ensuring that an accountability-based approach can be sustained over an extended period of time. The effectiveness of a shared governance system is dependent upon the full and complete engagement of those who make it up. A system that creates barriers to

Exhibit 4-1 Key Principles of Shared Governance

1. Always build both decisions and structure on a point-of-service foundation.
2. Stakeholders are always involved in their own decisions.
3. Shared governance is an accountability-based approach, not a participative management model.
4. Team-based strategies are always basic to any shared governance structural design.
5. The locus of control in a system is placed wherever appropriate for the decision required.
6. There are no approval structures in shared governance.
7. Managers focus on context; staff focus on content.
8. Partnership, equity, accountability, and ownership are the principles that undergird shared governance.
9. Shared governance reflects the relatedness between people and systems, not their status within the system.

the engagement of workers or uses parental strategies to control and manage workers creates the basis for its own undoing. New organizational constructs, the emergence of the knowledge worker culture, and point-of-service–driven work arrangements have changed the relationship between the participants in the workplace and created a basis for the design of a shared governance structure.

PATIENT CARE: THE FOUNDATIONS OF HEALTH SERVICE

The ultimate aim of the health care system is to improve the health of the general public. While this purpose may have been obscured over the years by the focus on treatment of illness rather than the much broader goal of building healthy communities, there is a new emphasis on health care service driven by capitation, the demand for quality outcomes, and the growing focus on the continuum of services.

> *The primary aim of health care systems is to improve the health of the general public. Many health care professionals have forgotten their mission and have instead become self-serving.*

The design and structure of the health care system is being radically altered. There is now occurring a shift in focus from illness and intervention toward primary care and community health. This shift in focus creates an essential shift in the design, structuring, and integration of the point-of-service delivery of health care.

Newer notions of work and how it is organized have changed some of the constructs and contexts for the delivery of health care services. Organizing around patient pathways, critical paths, and product or service lines is an example of the changes. In all of them, integration, interdisciplinary relationships, care management, demand management, and the continuum of care serve as a foundation for the design and structuring of the future of health care.

Always, in any design and delivery approach, the focus is on appropriate use of resources. During the first stage of health care reform in the United States, cost has been the driving force, but ultimately it will not be sufficient as a factor motivating increased effectiveness. The issue of quality must become a focus for building a comprehensive approach to managing and delivering health care services. Again, in order to ensure the viability of an organization, all stakeholders must at some level be involved in activities that address cost, quality, and service. Within the shared governance context, most of those activities must occur at the point of service, requiring the involvement and investment of stakeholders whose work it is to deliver cost-effective services and to evaluate the quality of the services provided.

> *While cost may be the portal through which we enter a period of significant change, it is not sufficient alone to sustain either effective service or viable outcomes.*

It is no longer an option for those at the point of service to be freed of all responsibility for ensuring the value and effectiveness of the work they do. Increasingly, knowledge of the outcomes of work activities is used to delineate and assess the delivery of health care services individually and collectively. Through the use of tools such as clinical protocols, best practices, service algorithms, and care maps, the appropriateness and value of point-of-service activities are gradually becoming better understood. The information infrastructure of an organization can supply meaningful data on the efficacy of the services provided. The avail-

> *It doesn't pay to live in the past . . . There's no future in it!*

ability of this information, its locus of control at the point of service, and the necessity to know the outcomes of one's work converge to create the conditions that require ownership, investment, evaluation, and response to what the data show about clinical practice. In health care systems, as has been learned in the business community, decision making should be located at the point of service, and thus health care systems require information services and systems to support the activities and decision making of those at the point of service.

> *Achieving value is more than simply controlling costs and providing a service. It is the "tight" balance between what is done, what it costs, and the results obtained that forms the foundation for real value.*

One purpose of a shared governance structure is to create a configuration that not only allows but requires those at the point of service to fully participate in decision making, planning, and evaluation. In particular, a shared governance structure is designed to lack any other process, position, or location for making decisions that properly belong at the point of service and to provide a legitimate context supporting point-of-service decision making.

THE FUNDAMENTALS OF THE PATIENT CARE COUNCIL

The structure of the organization should provide just enough format to ensure that decisions that belong at the point of service are not made elsewhere. Therefore, it is important to determine what kind of decisions are made at what places in the organization (see Figure 4-1).

> *It can no longer be assumed that one's competence increases as one climbs the organizational ladder. Competence does not necessarily change, but access to information is enhanced.*

Clearly, critical decision making and supportive interfaces require a sharp delineation of the appropriate location for each kind of decision. Summary authority (i.e., the right to make increasingly broader based decisions as one moves up the hierarchy of control) is not a valid principle of decision making within shared governance,

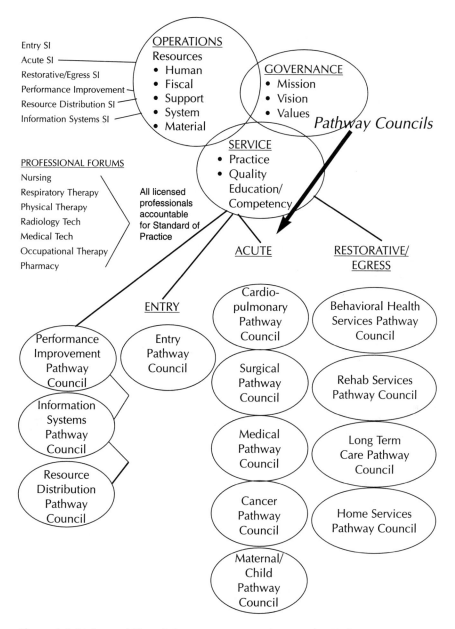

Figure 4-1 Linkage of Shared Governance Councils

which instead is based on the recognition that competence to make decisions does not necessarily increase as one climbs upward. In a truly effective organizational system, it would be known who the best person to make a decision would be—and that person would indeed make the decision.

As noted in Chapter 3, decisions related to team functions and clinical activities must be made at the point of service. The structure of the system should prevent those decisions from being made any other place, and it should provide the decision maker whatever supports and tools are necessary for evaluating the options and choosing the one most likely to lead to a positive outcome.

> *It does an organization no good to have the right competencies located in the wrong place.*

At the service pathway level, a different set of decisions—those related to the integration of relationships, critical paths, and best practices—are located. Here the focus is on linking the various teams along a particular clinical continuum. The service pathway devotes all of its resources and activities to the task of providing services to a specified group of patients.

> *A service pathway organizes work around the patient, not the provider. It depends on a good "fit" between the nature of the service provided and the demand of the consumer.*

The service pathway leadership is interested in the linkage and viability of the activities of each team. It does not have the obligation to define the activities and functions that belong to a team. It only looks at the interface between teams and the integration of their activities.

The service pathway council, which includes representatives from all pathway teams, deals with the broad issues of integration, intersection, continuity, effectiveness, efficiency, cost, relationship between services, and outcome. In fact, the service pathway council's role is to view the pathway as a whole in relationship to the population that it serves.

The notions of integrity and fit lie at the center of the work of the service pathway council. Its focus on integrity and fit keeps the council from making decisions about functions and activities that fall within the authority of the individual teams. It is only when a relationship between teams becomes problematic, when clinical protocols or pathways are incomplete, or when a team's activities are clearly inconsistent with the service pathway's purposes and work that the council pays close attention to specific activities. Further, since the service pathway council is made up of team leaders, focusing on it is the place in the system where their issues are worked on.

The service pathway council and the pathway teams make up the core of the governance structure in a health care organization. More than 90 percent of the decisions are made and implemented within the pathway, and it is here where the critical work of building effectiveness, efficiency, integration, and relationship as well as evaluating the outcomes and service components of patient care delivery is undertaken. It is rational, therefore, to structure the organization in such a way that information and evaluation tools are available within the service pathway.

> *All services are now organized around the patient, not the provider. It is the tightness of fit between the population needs and the services provided that creates the conditions for sustainability.*

> *The service pathway is focused on the specific culture of the services. The system is focused on the support of the services and their fit with the system's purposes and goals.*

THE PURPOSE OF THE PATIENT CARE COUNCIL

Any system must have a mechanism for maintaining its integrity. As mentioned previously, much of the structure of a shared governance organization is designed to support its point-of-service activities. The critical framework for those activities consists of the various service pathways that cater to the different populations served. Because each pathway is unique, there must be a mechanism to link the pathways and represent the purposes and principles of the organization as a whole. It is, after all, the organization that has an obligation to meet the full range of community health care needs.

While each of the service pathways looks at the functions and activities for a defined culture or patient population, the patient care council articulates the mission and objectives of the organization in light of the patient care processes devoted to providing appropriate and meaningful services to its community of consumers. The patient care council is also a place where the provider leadership can deal with issues of relationship, integrity, effectiveness, competence, and quality. Since the primary obligation of providers is to look after the interests of patients as both advocates and suppliers of care, it is important to ensure that conflicts between providers are addressed expeditiously. Resolving conflicts is one of the key functions of the patient care council.

> *The patient care council integrates the service pathways in a decision-making process that addresses their relationship across the system.*

> *In organizations, as in all structures, the system is simply not the sum of its parts. A system is exemplified by the seamless linkage of all the elements that define it.*

THE PATIENT CARE COUNCIL MEMBERSHIP

The patient care council is not a management council and is therefore not made up of management leaders. Most of the members are clinical leaders, selected from the various service pathways in a way that provides linkage between the pathways and the council (see Figure 4-2). Since the responsibility for clinical decision making rests with the clinical providers, it is logical that the responsibility for decisions concerning the delineation and delivery of health care services also rests directly with the providers. Within a shared governance context, they have the obligation to maintain control and have accountability for these kinds of decisions.

Other members who help integrate the system, such as support service personnel and administrative personnel (e.g., the information services staff in the finance office), should also be linked to the patient care council in a way that provides it with the essential information it needs to make effective decisions.

> *The patient care council is driven by clinical decision making. Therefore, it is made up of providers from the variety of pathways in the system.*

It is recommended that half the members of the patient care council represent the licensed disciplines and the other half represent the service pathway (Exhibit 4-2). This ensures that the two groups get an equal hearing.

Authority for decision making is invested in different bodies of the organization, and each decision-making group must have available to it the necessary competencies, support systems, and decision-making tools. Likewise, in the framework of shared governance, point-of-service decision-making supports must be available to ensure that appropriate decisions are made at the point of service (within teams and the service pathways).

> *The patient care council must not assume authority for decisions that belong elsewhere in the system. Decisions are accountability based, not authority driven. The notion of summary control is anathema to shared governance.*

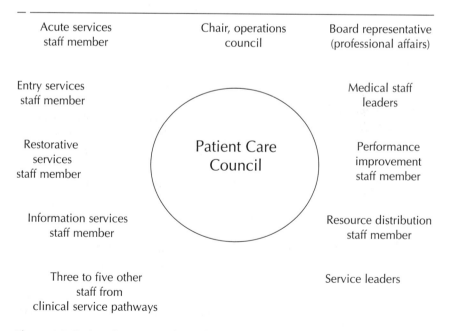

| Acute services staff member | Chair, operations council | Board representative (professional affairs) |

Entry services
staff member

Restorative
services
staff member

Information services
staff member

Three to five other
staff from
clinical service pathways

Patient Care
Council

Medical staff
leaders

Performance
improvement
staff member

Resource distribution
staff member

Service leaders

Figure 4-2 Patient Care Council Membership

Exhibit 4-2 Principles of Council Membership Selection

- Each pathway should be represented.
- All members should be practicing staff or point-of-service workers.
- Tenure of service should be defined in advance.
- Expectations of service should be outlined in advance.
- All time spent doing council work should be compensated for.
- All councils should have access to any resource needed for decision making.
- Required qualifications should be published in advance.
- Work schedules should accommodate council work.
- Council accountability for decisions should be clear to members.
- Requirements of member roles should be understood prior to service.

To enhance organizational integrity, the patient care council should include representatives from the board of trustees, the medical staff, the administration, and the operations council. The inclusion of these representatives creates an interface between key decision makers and increases the probability that appropriate

In shared governance, a seamless linkage between the decision-making components of the organization is a basic expectation.

information and support will be available to facilitate sound decision making within the patient care council. It also ensures that the patient care council has access to persons who are accountable for the effectiveness of decision making, the provision of services, and the quality of the outcomes. (See Exhibit 4-3 for a list of basic council member responsibilities.)

DEFINING THE WORK OF THE PATIENT CARE COUNCIL

The patient care council is accountable for ensuring

- the appropriate delivery of patient care services according to the standards and expectations set by the board of trustees and the patient care council
- the appropriate delineation, measurement, and evaluation of the outcomes of service delivery.
- the continuing competence and development of the professional and support staff

Exhibit 4-3 Council Member Responsibilities

Council members are expected to
- agree to fully participate in council decision making
- ensure availability in work schedules
- become informed regarding organizational issues
- accept key decision task assignments
- communicate effectively with the point of service
- represent the council in other forums
- support the decisions of the council in dealings with others

But although the council's accountability for service, quality, and competence is one focus of its activities, it also has an obligation to look at the whole organization and the relationship of the parts to the whole. Its tasks include defining, implementing, evaluating, and controlling the broad-based principles, priorities, plans, and programs the organization commits to for the achievement of its goals. By focusing on these four P's, the patient care council keeps its attention focused on the decisions over which it has authority and away from those decisions that belong to the service pathways.

While it is the obligation of the service pathways to deal with clinical standards, protocols, and practices, the patient care council provides the framework for those activities. The system councils (including the patient care council) operate at the system level (the level of principles, priorities, plans, and programs) with the goal of creating a foundation for the pathway councils and teams to operate at the service level (the level of standards, protocols, critical paths, team processes, quality measures, and outcome determinations). The division of labor builds checks and balances into the system and helps to ensure that decisions are made in the appropriate places (see Figure 4-3).

> *The patient care council focuses on those issues that give direction to clinical decision making. It does not make clinical decisions.*

SERVICE PATHWAY COUNCIL AND TEAM ACCOUNTABILITY

The presence of checks and balances creates in a horizontal, nonhierarchical organization an opportunity to ensure that decisions are implemented, outcomes are obtained, and confusion regarding locus of control and decision making is

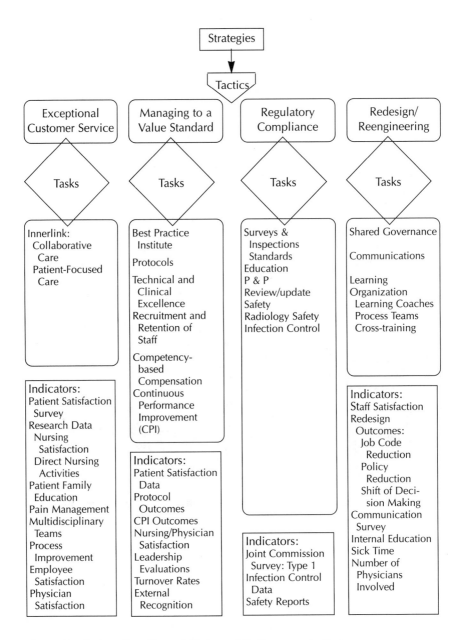

Figure 4-3 Patient Care Council Tasks and Performance Indicators

> *The councils are a locus of control, with the authority to make the decisions for which they are accountable. Their authority should not be located anywhere else in the system.*

reduced or eliminated. The delineation of accountability provides a vehicle for determining expectations and performance measures within the context of each category of decision making. It is critical, therefore, that the delineation occur early on in the restructuring process. Since shared governance is an accountability-based system, the delineation of accountability is essential to the effectiveness of the organization. Further, it must be remembered that a continuum of horizontally linked decision-making and service processes is being constructed to better configure patient services (see Figure 4-4).

The role of a team within a service pathway is to configure itself around the specific patient population it serves. In order to function effectively, it must have accountability and authority for all decisions concerning its relationship to other teams and the services it provides to patients.

As already indicated, all groups possessing accountability have a defined range of authority sufficient to meet their acountability. A team is no different. In shared governance, the team is the basic unit of service, not the individual. The accountability for desired outcomes belongs to the team. Indeed, sus-

> *Parallel decision-making processes constitute a major obstacle to empowerment. They indicate a lack of trust by the leadership and a lack of commitment to the empowerment process.*

tainable outcomes of a comprehensive nature along a pathway can never be achieved unilaterally. It is through the congruence of the activities of team members that outcomes get sustained. Therefore, individual accountability is defined specifically within the context of team accountability.

> *It is as important to know the results of a team's work as to know its processes. Work has no value if there is no desired outcome.*

Obviously, the construction of teams is a major organizational task.

Figure 4-4 Service Pathway Linkages: Building the Continuum

Since teams are the basic units of service in the organization, they demand the strategic, planning, and developmental resources necessary for success. In addition, considerable energy should be devoted to educating staff about team functions.

Typically, the core areas of team accountability in shared governance are as follows:

- identification and delineation of the functions, performance, and accountability of team members
- development, approval, and implementation of team-based clinical practices, activities, and functions along a clinical pathway
- discussion of all issues related to the development of team activities and review, approval, and application of team standards concerning the clinical delivery of patient care services
- determination and articulation of the roles and responsibilities of team members and their relationships
- assessment and resolution of conflicts, controversies, and interpersonal issues
- review, revision, and application of quality improvement activities
- determination of performance compliance, evaluation of individual and collective performance, assurance of team discipline, determination of recom-

mendations for disciplinary action, and assessment of individual and team competency and development needs
- determination of service pathway council and/or the patient care council membership eligibility and participation in service pathway-related decision making
- acceptance and implementation of council decisions within the context of the team's specific service requirements

Each area of accountability has many functional components. Clearly, as teams develop and refine their ability to perform, interact, and meet accountability demands, a broader framework for their activities will emerge. It should be clear in reviewing the above areas of accountability that increasingly teams have a high level of accountability for the functions and activities that constitute the content of their work.

Teams are free to attempt to meet their obligations in any number of ways. Obviously, along with this authority comes the consequences of its application. Both the service pathway council and the service leadership have a right to expect each team to perform the duties it has accepted in a manner consistent with the standards they have set. In addition, it should be clear that the consequences of performance (both rewards and disciplinary actions) are also part of the obligations of the team. The team, having accountability for specific functions, including the assignment of tasks to individuals, needs to identify the appropriate consequences for an individual's performance of his or her tasks. Since an individual's performance at the team level is critical to the system's effectiveness, clarity and applicability of accountability are also critical. By specifying performance requirements, evaluating performance, and rewarding good performance (and addressing poor performance), the team can help an individual member develop the skills necessary for acting as a representative on the service pathway council or the patient care council.

THE ACCOUNTABILITY OF THE SERVICE PATHWAY COUNCIL

Just as the team is accountable for the focus, functions, and activities related to the delivery of patient care services and the relationship between the team members, the service pathway council is accountable for the integration, facilitation, and coordination of the various team functions along a service pathway continuum of care. The role of the service pathway leadership is to bring together the components of the service pathway in a way that links the teams and the support structure, ensuring continuity along the continuum of care (see Figures 4-5 and 4-6).

> *Accountability creates its own set of checks and balances. That is precisely why it is not located in just one role or place in the organization.*

Since the service pathway council is made up of representatives of the teams in the pathway, it is a place where issues related to performance, the fit between team activities, coordination, and comprehensiveness can be dealt with in a realistic way and where guidance and direction can be obtained. Therefore, the specific areas of accountability of the service pathway council are as follows:

- integration of discipline-specific activities throughout the continuum of care
- design, initiation, and evaluation of critical processes, clinical paths, best practices, protocols, and other processes or devices that help define the integrated, interdisciplinary complex of care services

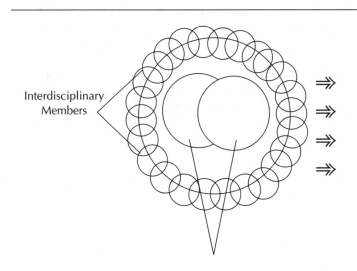

Interdisciplinary Members

Provider-Subscriber

Figure 4-5 Point-of-Service Team

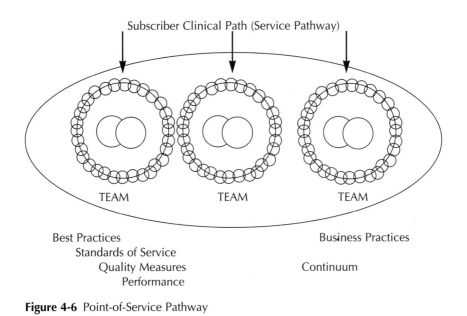

Figure 4-6 Point-of-Service Pathway

- establishment of standards, protocols, policies, and practices that facilitate team functions, decision making, problem solving, performance evaluation, and clinical services evaluation across teams and along the continuum of care
- establishment of service pathway policies regarding the design, implementation, and evaluation of performance standards for the various roles within the teams that make up the service pathway
- design and development processes for evaluating individual performance as well as team performance
- delineation and articulation of quality criteria for evaluating the protocols, practices, pathway activities, and team-based activities
- creation of a novice-to-expert development program for the various disciplines and the associated mechanisms for measuring progress and ensuring individual advancement
- design and implementation of an educational program specific to the service pathway as well as mechanisms for the educational advancement of teams and individuals
- collaboration with other pathways and with the patient care council directed toward integrating the service pathway within the system as a whole and link-

ing it with other components for the purpose of facilitating its clinical activities

- definition of generic team performance standards for the purpose of creating a framework for team functions, resolving conflicts between teams, evaluating the effectiveness of team functions and team interfaces, establishing performance criteria for team leaders, and comparing team performance data against service performance outcome data for the service pathway as a whole
- implementation of the service pathway principles, priorities, plans, and programs defined by the patient care council

The service pathway council's two main obligations are

1. to facilitate the decisions and work of the teams along the service pathway's continuum of care
2. to link the service pathway with the activities of the system as a whole

The service pathway council provides an interface between the system and services in a way that links the decisions of the system and the decisions of the services. Conflicts, challenges, and opportunities arising from the interface are the focus of the council's work. The council also has an obligation to refine the activities of the teams and help the teams to mature and become more effective.

THE WORK OF THE SERVICE PATHWAY COUNCIL AND THE PATHWAY TEAMS

The delineation and distribution of the activities associated with decision making and the establishment of a framework for designing, implementing, and assessing the activities of the service pathways and their teams are critical organizational tasks. Clearly they take time—and they also require the investment of all players in the organization. At the team level, it is expected that team-based obligations and team decision making are rotated among and assigned equitably to the members of the team. Clearly the skills and abilities of each member of the team determine what contribution the member can make to the performance of the clinical and relational activities of the team. The delivery of effective services will be impossible if there is not sufficient time for defining what effectiveness is, how it is obtained, and how it is to be evaluated.

This also holds true at the service pathway level. Here, however, more formalization occurs. Selection or election of team members who will represent the teams on the service pathway council may help rotate the responsibility for pathway council activities among the members. Regardless, it should be the expectation of all members that they will participate in the making of decisions that will influence the efficacy of the service pathway and its teams. Meeting times, agendas, tools, processes, mechanisms, activities, and evaluations are all part of the work of the service pathway council and of team decision making. Each of these will be affected by the culture of the particular service pathway. The various approaches may address the issues differently, but one underlying assumption of shared governance is that all members of a team have something to contribute to the team's activities and its fundamental work—and potentially to the work of the service pathway council as well.

> *In an accountability-based approach, there is no place for nonparticipation or nonownership of the process. If you are a member of the organization, you are expected to be invested in its processes. If not, why are you there?*

There must be a rotating leadership member who is selected or assigned, depending on the mechanism used by the service pathway, to provide linkage and to represent the service pathway council on the patient care council. Since the patient care council makes system-level decisions that have a direct impact on the service pathway, representation on the patient care council is important to the viability of the service pathway and its integration into the system. The representative also, in a sense, represents the patient care council in dealings with the service pathway and the teams that compose it. This type of dual representation is an inherent characteristic of shared governance decision making. Also, embedded in the disciplines associated with the establishment of standards, expectations, and decision-making practices are the checks and balances necessary to ensure that each decision is made in the appropriate place and that the individuals who have a stake in the outcome of the decision participate in the making of the decision as well as its implementation.

> *At the pathway level, it is expected that all staff will play some role in decision making, either through representation or through implementation. No one is exempt from the role of stakeholder.*

THE ACCOUNTABILITY OF THE PATIENT CARE COUNCIL

The patient care council does not have the authority to make decisions that are carried out at the service pathway or team level of the organization. Each service pathway and each team has its own unique range of accountability. It is the duty of the patient care council to make sure that no decision that properly belongs to a team or a service pathway is usurped by the patient care council. The development of staff accountability is the most significant work of the organization (see Figure 4-7).

> *System councils focus on integration, not operation. They must not usurp the role or authority that rests within each service pathway.*

The only need for a system council to deal directly with a service pathway arises when the service pathway's activities and functions are not congruent with the principles, priorities, plans, and programs of the system council or with the organization's mission and objectives as defined by the board. In such a case, the system council has the authority to delve into the service pathway council's activities, but only to the extent of facilitating the service pathway's revision of its activities and functions. It is the role of the system council not to make decisions for the service pathway, but to see to it that the service pathway and its teams are functioning at the level their accountability demands. It does not act as a surrogate for the service pathway or its teams or take on the task of making their decisions. It simply ensures that they are capable of fulfilling their obligations.

> *Good decisions require good data. All councils should have access to whatever information they need to make the right decision at the right time.*

The patient care council, as a system council, is oriented toward the whole. It is the duty of the patient care council to ensure that a comprehensive approach to the delivery and evaluation of patient-based care is undertaken across the service pathways. The patient care council provides the consistencies and commonalities necessary to ensure that there is appropriate system integrity.

The patient care council focuses on those areas that give guidance or provide a frame of reference or a set of principles that can be utilized by the leadership at

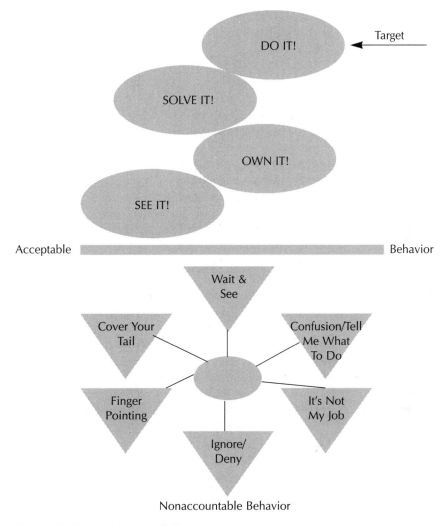

Figure 4-7 Steps to Accountability

the service pathway level and throughout the system. Therefore, the patient care council has accountability for the following:

- design, implementation, and evaluation of an integrated, coordinated patient care delivery system that operates cohesively and seamlessly

- design and application of standards for and normative approaches to clinical delineation, the planning and implementing of care services, and the designing and structuring of team activities
- development of a framework for and a systematic approach to the quality review of clinical practices across service pathways
- creation of an organizational framework for a learning system directed toward continuous staff development and advancement
- outline of an accountability delineation framework to help guide the consistent delineation of accountability within each service pathway
- outline of a performance criteria development framework to help guide the consistent development of performance criteria
- development and maintenance of an intra- and interdisciplinary set of mechanisms for dealing with standards, licensure, regulations, competence requirements, and service requirements within each discipline and across disciplines
- maintenance of a system of continuous team development and maturation within the various service pathways
- development of a comprehensive continuum-based system community clinical services plan that reflects the needs of the community of subscribers
- identification and delineation of a team-based disciplinary and corrective action program or model that is adaptable to the individual culture of each service pathway and possesses a uniform set of action criteria and a flexible implementation framework
- development of a mechanism for translating the board-mandated mission and objectives into the priorities, plans, programs, and specific service pathway objectives as a mechanism for their full implementation.

While the above tasks do not exhaust the patient care council's accountability, they are central to its role as a decision-making body oriented toward the whole. The patient care council has systemwide accountability for defining consistent, organizationally driven constructs that either provide a generic framework for clinical processes or a context for the management and application of teamwork within each service pathway. The council also provides tools that can be modified to fit each service pathway's culture. Here again the system perspective keeps the council's work broadly focused so that it does not impede service pathway accountability or create barriers to ownership of that accountability at the team and service pathway level.

THE TRANSITION FROM NURSING SHARED GOVERNANCE TO WHOLE-SYSTEMS SHARED GOVERNANCE

As indicated earlier, many health care organizations have already instituted nursing shared governance. As the next level of organizational maturity emerges—the linking together of the disciplines in a whole-systems approach— many of the nursing shared governance models are placed in a critical position. A transition to the next stage of development needs to be undertaken in order to ensure the viability of shared governance and the practical application of its principles across the entire system.

> *A good nursing shared governance model can serve as the underpinning for the whole-systems approach. One does not preclude the other.*

The move from nursing shared to systemwide shared governance can be challenging. While the same set of principles apply, the shared governance structure developed in the nursing department is not necessarily transferable to the system as a whole. This does not mean, however, that the nursing department must dismantle its shared governance structure. Indeed, the nursing model may be an appropriate shared governance model for dealing with discipline-specific issues and requirements as the organization becomes more interdisciplinary and multifocal.

Each discipline should have a shared governance mechanism for undertaking accreditation, legislative, licensure, regulatory, and standards development work. It should also have a shared leadership, shared decision-making model as a prerequisite for working within the

> *Each discipline will have to have a specific shared governance function that deals with the discipline-specific issues that only it can address.*

interdisciplinary structures of whole-systems shared governance. It is expected that as each discipline uses its shared decision-making model, it will take care of its discipline-specific issues itself and refrain from bringing those issues unresolved to the interdisciplinary forums (service pathway council, patient care council, operations council, governance council, and team-based decision making).

In building an integrated approach to whole-systems shared governance, the nursing model can be used as a guide for the development of the patient care council, the service pathway council, and team decision making. At the team level, the nursing-driven team functions can now expand to become an interdisciplinary frame of reference, so that other partners and players are included in decisions about patient care. This should also happen at the service pathway level in the organization. All disciplines that make up the key decision-making team have a right to representation and partnership at the service pathway council level, and all disciplines that play a key role in patient care planning and delivery should be involved at the patient pathway council level and on the teams (i.e., the medical staff and the therapeutic disciplines as well as nursing).

> *It is not the obligation of the organization to attend to the requirements of each discipline. It is the expectation of the organization that each discipline has a mechanism for attending to its own affairs.*

EXPANDING THE NURSING PRACTICE COUNCIL

In some organizations, nursing's practice council has been expanded to become the organization's patient care council. While challenging, this strategy does facilitate the linking of the nursing service's shared decision-making structures with the organization as a whole. However, in most organizations a new patient care council is formed at the outset, and all of the appropriate representatives from nursing's patient care council, education council, and quality council are included as initial members of the patient care council as a way of connecting the nursing shared governance structure and the integrated whole-systems shared governance structure. Here again, the discipline-specific shared-decision-making model remains intact and gets linked to the systemwide shared governance model through representation. These or any number of amenable approaches can be used to build integration.

Perhaps the most significant challenge in creating a whole-systems model will be some of the sentiment of proprietary ownership of shared governance that may come from the nursing service. It is hoped that this feeling or sense will dissipate quickly as effective integrative models for shared decision making and shared leadership emerge in a whole systems frame of reference. It should have been clear and continue to be clear to the nursing service that while initiating the model in nursing provided a firm foundation for nursing's involvement in shared decision making, it simply served as a pretext or template for the inevitable implementation of much broader whole-systems approaches. As mentioned in Chapter 1, it has been the author's experience that those organizations already with an existing nursing shared governance model find it much easier, faster, and more facilitating to move to whole-systems approaches than those organizations that have no shared decision-making models.

INTERFACING WITH THE MEDICAL STAFF

In traditional health care organizations, the organized medical staff has always been viewed as an entity separate from but correlated with the hospital organizational structure. In integrated health care systems and integrated service structures, a compartmentalized approach to the relationship between physicians and the organizational structure is no longer appropriate. Increasingly, methods of integration, participation, investment, and ownership in the clinical process and clinical decision making are emerging as preferable models. Shared governance is nonexclusive. All stakeholders are expected to be invested in the design and implementation of the shared governance model—including the medical staff. Physicians are members of teams and sit on service pathway councils and the patient care council (see Exhibit 4-4).

> *Connecting with the medical staff early in the process of structural change gets at their issues sooner. There will be plenty of work to do with the doctors; delaying the work will not make it any easier.*

Integrating the current organized medical staff structure and the emerging whole-systems shared governance structure is usually no easy task, because of the opposing points of view regarding leadership, organization, and role. However, activities can be undertaken to begin linking physicians to the decision-making process as the organized medical staff constructs shift toward becoming more partnership and ownership oriented. There are some suggestions for ensuring that occurs:

- Representatives from the medical executive committee should sit on the patient care council as it establishes the protocols and framework for the delineation of clinical practice for the system.

Exhibit 4-4 Key Principles of Physician Involvement in Shared Governance

- Physicians are always engaged at the point of service.
- Physician membership on service-oriented bodies is not optional.
- It is more important to link physicians at the point of service than anywhere else in the system.
- The physician is a partner in deliberation, not a control point. Interface is necessary, hierarchy is not.
- Physician practice is evaluated within the continuum of service, not separate from it.

- Service chiefs, associates, chief residents, or other physicians should sit at the service pathway council in order to participate in making decisions related to standards, clinical protocols, the interface between disciplines, the evaluation of team-based activities, and the delineation of continuum-based performance expectations.
- Teams should be designed around specific patient populations in a way that includes attending physicians, residents, and interns as full partners. Since the teams are clinically driven and implement and refine clinical protocols, care maps, best practices, and clinical pathways, the presence of physicians on the teams should be unquestioned. Difficulties related to the appropriate role of the physicians must be resolved in a way that takes into account the nature of the teams, the role of the physicians, the character of the teams' work, and the teams' approach to collective decision making.
- As the medical staff get increasingly tied to point-of-service decision making and operate within the patient care council and services structure, modification of current medical staff decision making and problem solving will have to be undertaken by the system and the medical staff leadership.
- Increasingly, the locus of control and authority for implementing clinical process and resolving clinical difficulties is at the point of service, and thus there is a decreasing role for physician problem solving at what were once considered the higher echelons of the organizational system.

Since point-of-service accountability brings critical decisions regarding clinical practice and relationships to the point of service, the role of the physician in decision making is increasingly moving there as well. The design and implementation of physician-based decision making and problem solving at the point of service is crucial for the inclusion of physicians in whole-systems decision making (see Exhibit 4-5).

Involving physicians more fully in the shared governance structure increases their ownership of protocol development, quality determination, performance evaluation, and outcomes determination. Moving decision making to the point of service facilitates their inclusion and investment in all clinically driven decision processes and the evaluation of the outcomes of these processes.

PATIENT CARE INTEGRATION

In shared governance, facilitating the development of the continuum of care is a fundamental activity of patient care professionals. The patient care council and its relationship to the service pathway council and teams provide the framework for increased practitioner involvement in delineating the continuum of care (see Figure 4-8) and ensuring the attainment of outcomes and the evaluation of variance. Since the point of service is the fundamental place of decision making in the organization, it is critical that patient care design facilitate decision making at that point of service (see Figure 4-9).

> *The centerpiece of all activity within the health care system is health services delivery. Nothing should impede the delivery of services.*

There is a great deal of development that must occur at the point of service before interdependent and independent decision making can occur there. Historically, it was the role of providers at the point of service to undertake actions that had been defined and planned at other places in the organization. In shared governance those places are eliminated, which means that the providers can no longer expect others to offer guidance and information and make decisions on their

Exhibit 4-5 The Role of Physicians on the Patient Care Council

- Medical staff problem solving as it relates to the continuum of care
- Critical pathing the standards of care across the continuum of care
- Integrating the physician's role and the roles of other clinical providers
- Modifying the delivery system to strengthen the links between the providers of care
- Establishing a strategy for harmonizing the service priorities and the priorities of the system

Figure 4-8 Patient-Service Path

behalf. Increasingly, the goal is to ensure that providers have the support, tools, and structure necessary for clinical decision making.

Supporting clinical management at the divisional, departmental, and unit levels used to be the primary role of the system. As health care has become more decentralized and moves more fluidly along a continuum of service, the support-

Figure 4-9 Pathway Structure: Conceptual Basis

ing structures and services must move accordingly. Building the information infrastructure in a way that supports its use by providers in the making of judgments about cost, effectiveness, process, and outcome becomes an important developmental task for the system (see Figure 4-10), as is the task of creating direct relationships between financial, information, marketing, and systems, and human resources and leadership at the point of service.

Providing a supportive decision-making structure, facilitating the appropriate locus of control and accountability, and ensuring the creation of tools to support the achievement of defined outcomes constitute the central work of the systems councils. The patient care council simply serves as the primary interface between clinical providers, the system, and the community. The patient care council and the service pathway councils, along with the service pathway teams, form the composite of relationships necessary to ensure the effective integration of decision makers and the provision of services along the continuum of care. Such integration is not only an empowering process for the participants and members in the organizational system but reflects the growing dependence on point-of-service

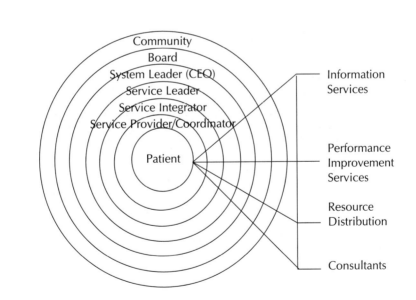

Figure 4-10 Point-of-Service Design

> *As the patient care council carries out its work, it inexorably fulfills the purpose of linking and integrating patient care with the other operations and the governance activities of the system.*

accountability and the expectation that each member of the system is included in the activities of decision making, is committed to building a sound process, and recognizes an obligation to achieve excellent clinical outcomes. Each member, playing his or her role, exercising the accountability that is the extension of the rights of that role, helps ensure the effectiveness of the system and the quality of the services it provides to the community and to each patient it serves.

SUGGESTED READING

Bell, C. 1994. *Customers as partners*. San Francisco: Berrett-Koehler.

Bowers, M., J. Swan, and W. Koehler. 1995. What attributes determine quality and satisfaction with health care delivery. *Health Care Management Review* 19, no. 4:49–55.

Davenport, T. 1994. Saving its soul: human centered information management. *Harvard Business Review* 72, no. 2:119–131.

Dunham, N., D. Kindig, and R. Schultz. 1995. The value of the physician executive role to organizational effectiveness and performance. *Health Care Management Quarterly* 19, no. 4:56–62.

Elliott, C. 1994. Leadership without bosses: Shared leadership in the creation of a health network. *Health Care Management Forum* 7, no. 1:38–43.

Evans, K., et al. 1995. Whole systems shared governance: A model for the integrated health system. *Journal of Nursing Administration* 25, no. 5:18–27.

Handy, C. 1995. Trust and the virtual organization. *Harvard Business Review* 73, no. 3:40–50.

Porter-O'Grady, T. 1992. *Implementing shared governance*. Baltimore: Mosby.

Porter-O'Grady, T., and S. Finnigan. 1984. *Shared governance for nursing*. Gaithersburg, MD: Aspen Publishers.

Porter-O'Grady, T., and C. Krueger-Wilson, 1995. *The leadership revolution in health care: Altering systems, changing behaviors*. Gaithersburg, MD: Aspen Publishers.

Relman, A. 1988. Assessment and accountability: The third revolution in medical care. *New England Journal of Medicine* 319:1220–1222.

Zander, K. 1995. *Managing outcomes through collaborative care: Care mapping and case management*. Chicago: American Hospital Publishing.

Zuckerman, H., A. Kaluzny, and T. Ricketts III. 1995. Alliances in healthcare: What we know, what we think we know, and what we should know. *Health Care Management Review* 20, no. 1:54–64.

Chapter 5

The Operations Council: Managing the Horizontal Organization

Jeff LeFors and Tim Porter-O'Grady

Judge a tree by its fruit,
not by its leaves.

Euripides

Perhaps the most significant change in the design of whole-systems organization relates to the management structure. In old models of organization, the management structure was more vertically defined, reflecting Newtonian concepts of compartmentalization and distinctions between categories of work and the functional organization of work activities. Each of these models represents a way of thinking of work and workers that is no longer viable in integrated whole-systems organizations. Indeed, the whole way of integrating and lengthening the components of the organization is altered in a whole-systems approach. This creates a need to change the role of management, redefine the function of manager, and establish new relationships between all players in the organization.

In a point-of-service organization, it is critical to view the role of management in a different context. In the old organization, management had summary authority for the direction and decisions of the organization. Managers delegated those decisions down the chain of command and implemented them as expected at the point of service. In a whole-systems organization, the recognition of the partnership between those who do the work and those who link

> *The world of work is being radically altered and changing relationships and interactions forever.*

and integrate the system changes the format of the relationship between the players, and in fact partnership is driven by the realization that the future sustainability of the organization is dependent upon the linkage and integration of the activities of all of its members. Of course, many of the decisions that affect the viability of the system are made at its point of service, and it is critical that those decisions be effective and that the stakeholders implement those decisions in a way that creates ownership of and commitment to the purposes and outcomes of the work of the organization.

ENSURING EFFECTIVE DECISION MAKING

The only way to ensure good decision making at every point in the system is to foster the committed involvement of all players in decision making and implementation throughout the organization. This requires a shift in mindset and in action. First, everyone must be brought around to accept the following principles, which articulate the specific management and workplace changes within the new paradigm:

> *In the old organization the manager predominated and had summary control over decision making.*

- Managing knowledge workers is different from managing assembly line workers. Knowledge workers own the inputs of their work and therefore have a direct and dramatic influence on its outputs or outcomes.
- The organization is essentially a gathering of adults, and adult-to-adult interchange requires a different communication and relationship dynamic than the parent–child, superior–subordinate, and master–servant interactions common in the past.
- The results of service and production depend almost entirely on the efficiencies and effectiveness of the interactions and intersections at the place services are provided and products are produced. It is increasingly apparent that sustainable quality is caused by the effectiveness of decisions and functions at the point of service more than by any other single factor.
- The role of the manager increasingly encompasses functions associated with linkage, integration, fit, and information.
- The manager is servant to the system and those who do its work. The primary role of the manager is to integrate the system activities design to fulfill its mis-

sion and achieve its objectives. A subsidiary goal is to build a foundation of empowerment throughout the organization, ensuring that appropriate decisions are made by the right people in the right place at the right time.

- An organization should have the number of managers that organizational integrity and functioning require—but no more. One of the key roles of the manager is to develop the leadership skills of others in order to improve their decision making and increase the level of their interdependence.

EMPOWERMENT

Empowerment is widespread in an organization when the following is true:

- Workers possess accountability for their own destiny.
- Workers exercise the right to define their own purposes and develop their own vision.
- Staff emotionally invest in their work environment.
- Workers recognize that they have an obligation to partner with those historically located above them, not to simply wait for direction from leaders.

CHANGING CONCEPTS OF MANAGEMENT

Many of the old notions of management developed during the Industrial Age. Managers were led to believe that an organization was essentially an entity independent of those who composed it. Management represented the board and the senior level of the organization and made certain that the desires and wishes articulated by those at the top were carried out by the workers. It was assumed that there was an ownership relationship generated from the board through senior-level management to line management that ensured that the work performed at the point of productivity or service was consistent with the desires of the owners.

> *Empowerment is recognizing the power already present in a role and allowing it to be expressed.*

The board and senior-level managers were looked at as the stakeholders in the organization. They essentially represented those who invested in the organization—in some cases, the stockholders; in other cases, the public; and in still others, private entities. In the old model it was assumed that it was the exclusive obligation of those who represented the owners to make decisions about the mission, purposes, and the direction of the organization and to ensure that the activities of workers were consistent with these decisions. The line management role was to essentially operate as a link between the board and those at the point of productivity or service (see Exhibit 5-1).

This notion of the relationship between owners and workers goes back a long way. It represents a particular set of economic realities and builds organizational behavior on those realities. In the traditional corporate mindset, owners were assumed to be those who invested financial resources and thus placed their financial resources at risk, in return, of course, for a portion of the profits generated by the organization's productivity. Financial investment was viewed as the significant critical measure of the value of the organization, and those who invested and managed the financial resources were viewed as producing or creating future financial advantage for the organization and for those who invested in it. On the other hand, those who simply did the work of the organization and were paid for it were primarily seen as users of its resources. The main obligation of managers was to improve productivity and maintain the organization's financial viability, and they thus were required to keep costs and inflationary factors (including the size of the employee pool) to a minimum.

The traditional corporate mindset, while modified, is still the underlining construct of the economic enterprise that is health care in America. This mindset, itself based on the belief that those who own the means of productivity also own the rewards of that productivity, is threaded through all the work activities in almost every organization in a traditional free enterprise system.

TECHNOLOGY-DRIVEN SYSTEMS AND WORK

In the late twentieth century, changes have occurred that have altered work relationships dramatically. As technology and knowledge have exploded, they

Exhibit 5-1 Mentor or Coach Behaviors

- Stimulating enthusiasm
- Maintaining high expectations
- Giving credit for performance
- Being approachable
- Listening to new ideas
- Encouraging risk taking
- Helping people learn from their mistakes
- Showing sensitivity to feelings of others
- Believing people can be more effective

have changed the economic conditions and the nature of work. The variables affecting the production of profits, the sustainability of systems, and the future growth of businesses have been radically altered.

Organizations are increasingly dependent on technology. Their dependence on technology has changed the locus of control and affected how they operate. Those individuals who have the knowledge to create technology, utilize it, and manage it become the stakeholders in the process of technical application. Indeed, organizations are becoming more dependent on individuals who have technological knowledge and less dependent on individuals who represent the organizations. This is especially so in health care.

The interdependence of multiple technologies creates a different relationship between providers than existed previously. Health care today is essentially knowledge work and requires a high level of education and a firm foundation in one's specialty. Much of the learning and expansion of skills occurs outside of the work setting. Knowledge, now one of the major prerequisites of work, is no longer under the control of the organizations that must have it. Knowledge is now portable, fluid, and increasingly owned by those who have it. Its portability alters the locus of control for work and the character of work relationships, and it also affects the various organizational roles.

THE KNOWLEDGE WORKER

Managers today, at the end of the twentieth century, coordinate the resources and facilitate the work of knowledge workers. The knowledge worker in today's world owns the means of doing work and must increasingly be invested in the processes related to work. This creates a challenging situation for the manager.

First, the manager can no longer direct work that is dependent on the knowledge of those who do it. Second, the knowledge worker has as much investment in the exercise of his or her knowledge and the unfolding of work as the manager has investment in the system. There must be a convergence between the two in order that the appropriate integration and desired outcomes are achieved.

The problems arise as a result of the shift between the industrial model and the new framework needed to support the knowledge worker. The old expectations regarding workers and work are now in conflict with the new reality. Because of the tradition of "parenting" by management, workers have become essentially dependent in mindset and behavior.

Because managers have a history of directing and controlling and the workers have a history of doing as told, contradictions now emerge between the behavior of the players and the expectations of the workplace. It is these contradictions that create the foundations for significant change processing and for shifting both role and structure in the organization to support a different understanding of relationships in the emerging sociotechnical age.

As we mentioned in Chapter 4, the patient care council and the service framework are designed specifically to ensure that 90 percent of the decisions that depend on the knowledge worker at the point of service are made there (and that generally decisions are made where they belong). Although in the past most decisions were made in the management structure, managers must be precluded from making decisions that do not belong to them.

This creates a huge challenge for the organization. One new expectation is that managers will focus on different areas of accountability than before. The role of manager is directly related to the management of the system. Therefore, the manager represents the system and all of the efforts that the system undertakes to fulfill its mission, manage its resources, and ensure that those at the point of service are supported in a way that is consistent with its purposes.

DISTINCTION OF ACCOUNTABILITY

One of the chief characteristics of shared governance is the clear distinction that is necessary between areas of accountability and between associated roles. Indeed, as indicated in Chapter 2, clarity of accountability is an important foundation of shared governance. This is certainly true for the role of manager, which must be a clearly defined range of accountability that does not overlap the accountability that belongs to others or diminish their accountability. Accountability should not be delegated or supervised. It is applied and evaluated within the context of the role of those who possess it, although all who depend upon the accountability are involved in its evaluation.

Everybody whom the accountability impacts has a right to address its appropriateness. Therefore, hierarchical notions of supervision and unilateral control and delegation no longer apply. Indeed, the relationships in the organization must become increasingly horizontal.

Horizontal relationships require adult-to-adult interchanges, equality in the roles around the point of service, and mutuality of accountability. It is the obligation of each player to be aware of the impact of the activities done to meet his or her accountability and also to be aware of the impact of others' accountability-related activities.

MANAGEMENT ACCOUNTABILITY

The need to limit the role of manager to its proper range of accountability requires an investigation into what the proper range of accountability might be. Further, it is important to be able to understand the difference between the accountability around "context" and accountability that represents the "content" of work.

The providers at the point at service have the predominant accountability for the content of work and for achieving meaningful outcomes. That accountability can be characterized as content accountability. On the other hand, the manager, who is not accountable for undertaking the activities associated with producing clinical outcomes at the point of service, is accountable for ensuring that the support given to the providers is appropriate and effective. In other words, the role of management is basically to create a supporting context for the performance of work. Contextual accountability relates specifically to the stewardship of the organizational resources directed toward supporting those who do the work. It is fundamentally reflective of the organization's linkage and support functions—the functions that allow those at the point of service to undertake the clinical work.

> *There should be as few levels of management as possible in the organization. The greater the number of managers, the less efficient the system becomes. There is an inverse relationship between the number of managers and the effectiveness of a system.*

Contextual accountability is essentially resource based. All the functional roles of the manager are resource driven, and the fundamental accountability of the manager usually relates to the delineation, distribution, and utilization of resources in support of the mission and objectives of the organization and its point-of-service activities.

Using Mintzberg's framework, we can identify the following areas of resource accountability: human, fiscal, material, support, and systems resources. Together these areas form the central core of the management role. Accountability for the right use of resources belongs both to individual managers and to management as a whole.

Each area of the resource accountability has specific functional requirements. Each is also defined in terms of outcomes so that the focus of managers is not so much on process as on achievement of goals (Exhibit 5-2). Obviously there must be a mechanism or process for articulating what is expected of each manager.

THE TWO LEVELS OF MANAGEMENT

In the approach to management presented in this book, there are essentially only two types of managers—those that integrate the system and those that integrate the service. The nature of the accountability of the types is fundamentally the same, but the breadth of accountability and the obligations associated with the types differ.

For example, those who act as system integrators have an obligation to maintain a linkage with the external community (e.g., the board of trustees, other health agencies, health partners, etc.). On the other hand, each leader of a service pathway has an obligation to maintain linkages with other pathways as well as linkages between the various components of the service pathway. While each pathway is functionally complete (in the sense that it has its own accountability and focus), all the pathways are interdependent. For example, no system integrator (senior manager) could undertake the implementation of change in community health priorities without first consulting the service pathway leaders (unit managers) whose services would be impacted by the change. Conversely, no service pathway leader would undertake a strategic change in the service content of the pathway without consulting system integrators about the possible effects on the organization's mission, objectives, integrity, and linkages. The range of accountability of each type of manager differs, but both types depend on each other in their attempts to support the integrity of the system and the functional efficiency of the service pathways.

While the accountability of each of the roles can be clearly defined, this is not true for the interface between the roles—or the impact that a manager's actions can have on the organization and the individual players. One of the drawbacks of an accountability-based organization is the ability of any one player to make decisions independent of other people and to have a dramatic and possibly negative impact on the integrity and effectiveness of the organization. The fact that each leadership role is a locus of control entails that destructive conflicts will arise if there is no mechanism for ensuring that the decisions made are consistent with the organization's tactics, strategy, and direction. It is for the purpose of addressing this problem that the operations council is created.

Exhibit 5-2 Management Accountability

Human Resources

- There is a unit staffing plan that takes into account staffing guidelines, productivity measures, and the hospital plan of care.
- There is a staffing system that meets identified customer and service needs through the utilization of available resources.
- There is a mechanism for selecting personnel who meet the identified needs of the unit.
- There is a mechanism for removing personnel who do not meet the identified needs of the unit.
- There is compliance with all applicable policies, regulations, and laws.

Fiscal Resources

- There is a unit business plan based on products and services provided that is in alignment with the overall goals of the organization.
- There is a system for effective management of the business plan based on monitoring and modification of operations.
- There is a process in place for communicating the business plan to all involved parties.

Material Resources

- There is an ongoing mechanism for assessing material and capital needs.
- There is an effective plan for meeting material and capital needs utilizing available resources that is consistent with the goals of the organization.
- There is an ongoing system for effectively managing material and supplies usage on the unit.

Support Resources

- There is a work environment that effectively achieves the goals of the organization.
- There is a process in place that empowers employees through the relocation of decision making.
- There is a mechanism in place to measure quality and to ensure that quality relates to goals.
- There is a system in place that facilitates staff development, including a performance appraisal process.
- There is an approach to problem solving that utilizes facilitation skills and tools to achieve unit objectives.

continues

Exhibit 5-2 continued

> • There is a plan that assesses and meets the ongoing developmental needs of
> the manager.
>
> **System Resources**
>
> • There is an approach to work systems that is multifocal, multidisciplinary,
> and patient based.
> • There is an approach to operational systems that ensures effective interde-
> partmental linkages.
> • There is an approach to technological systems that ensures support for work
> and operational systems.
> • There is a mechanism in place for integrating and evaluating systems within
> and across units to support partnerships.

THE FOUNDATION OF THE OPERATIONS COUNCIL

It is in the operations council that the management team meets together to create a broad-based framework for ensuring the integrity of the system and the
effectiveness of resource decisions throughout the system. The same objectives
pursued by the patient care council—integration, seamlessness, effectiveness,
broad-based accountability—give direction to the activities of the operations
council. The main difference is that the operations council acts as an organ of the
system and focuses on the delineation and integration of resources from the perspective of the whole. While its structure is similar to the nursing structure, it has
a much broader set of obligations (see Table 5-1).

In fact, its obligations will broaden as departmental structures diminish and the
organization begins to configure itself around services, components, and pathways. The organization now is built on its functional services and the methods
and mechanisms through which those services are provided. The linkages in
shared governance are predominantly horizontal (see Figure 5-1), and thus the
council's focus is on addressing linkage, integration, and intersection of decision
making in a way that enhances the effectiveness of the system. Because of the
pathway format, there is increasing need to emphasize the role of the councils in
ensuring appropriate linkage and facilitation of decisions likely to affect the system as a whole or alter any component of the system.

Table 5-1 Comparison of Nursing Management Council and Operations Council

Nursing Management Council	Operations Council
Limited to nursing	Multidisciplinary (includes support areas)
Single facility	Corporate accountability across individual facilities
Narrow scope	Broad, whole-systems scope

SUPPORT FOR THE MANAGEMENT ROLE

Before we can clearly delineate the role of the operations council, other changes in the management structure must be enumerated. Since the point-of-service leaders assume the critical leadership role in the system, other roles in the

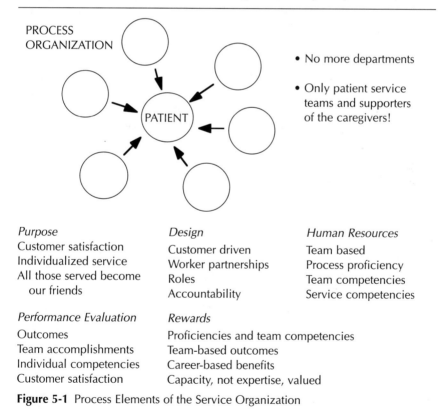

PROCESS ORGANIZATION

PATIENT

- No more departments

- Only patient service teams and supporters of the caregivers!

Purpose
Customer satisfaction
Individualized service
All those served become
  our friends

Design
Customer driven
Worker partnerships
Roles
Accountability

Human Resources
Team based
Process proficiency
Team competencies
Service competencies

Performance Evaluation
Outcomes
Team accomplishments
Individual competencies
Customer satisfaction

Rewards
Proficiencies and team competencies
Team-based outcomes
Career-based benefits
Capacity, not expertise, valued

Figure 5-1 Process Elements of the Service Organization

system once thought of as line roles (with specific summary responsibility for the functions and decisions at the point of service) now change in both character and content. Some senior management roles even disappear.

In the old approach, there were often senior-level administrators for finance, human resources, planning, marketing, and development as well as various other operational vice-presidents, and all of the organization's functions, activities, departments, and structures were essentially distributed among the various vice-presidential roles. In the shared governance approach, the distribution now occurs within a service pathways framework. First, there are the services provided directly to patients, and these are configured within a specific service pathway; second, there are services oriented toward the whole system or intended to support the individuals in direct contact with the patients (Table 5-2).

As for the old administrative senior-level positions, the majority no longer remain line positions in shared governance. Instead, they become consulting positions whose purpose is to assist, providing service to the system and the service pathway leaders and others in the system. Since summary line responsibility cannot act as a frame of reference for the organization's design in shared governance, the identification of certain individuals as senior managers ceases to have value.

Real value in the organization now depends on the relationship of all roles and functions in the system to the service pathway and the point of service. In keeping with Deming's challenge, shared governance requires that each person either be providing a service or serving someone who is. One consequence is that senior management plays more of a support role in the system (see Chapter 6).

Table 5-2 Comparison of Service Integrator and Service Coordinator Roles

Service Leader	Service Coordinator
Management-level position	Staff-level position
Accountable for resource management	Accountable for coordinating daily activity in a functional area
Accountable for budget development	Accountable for operating within budgeted guidelines
Overview perspective of operations	Involved at the point of service with daily operations
Organized around pathways	Organized around points of service

PURPOSE OF THE OPERATIONS COUNCIL

The operations council is the gathering place for the management leaders accountable for the resources of the organization. Both levels of management (system and service) are represented on the operations council. It is this council where the leaders meet to delineate issues affecting the system and the services. Also present are the systems consulting partners (formerly senior administrators), whose role is to provide information and support to the council during deliberations. The primary focus of the council's work comprises linkage, integration, effectiveness, and the tactics intended to achieve the objectives set by the governance council.

The operations council also deals with capital planning, operational budget, and strategic initiative issues that mainly concern one pathway but may affect the integrity of the system. The council is in fact the place where the managers of the organization make decisions that affect the integrity and efficacy of the organization as a whole.

The council deliberates issues related to its fundamental accountability for the management of resources throughout the system. Elements of the council's accountability might include the following:

- delineation and distribution of resources, including budgetary, operational, capital, and contingent financial resources
- delineation of issues associated with the provision of the material resources necessary to meet the service needs of the system and the individual service pathways
- delineation and provision of support and clerical services
- delineation and evaluation of the resource distribution system to ensure equitable, appropriate, service-based distribution
- design and implementation of an appropriate management and resource information network to ensure that the appropriate informational components are available to monitor the effectiveness of resource distribution and use
- delineation of human resource requirements and a legal framework to meet applicable federal, state, and organizational standards regarding the management of human resources
- provision of an operational and leadership connection between the various service pathways as a means of problem identification and solution seeking in an effort to reduce policy, priority, service, and mission conflicts
- integration of the decisions and activities of the various service pathways to ensure congruence in decision making and service provision

- identification of organizational and service pathway problems and conflicts and establishment of a mechanism for deliberation about and resolution of these problems and conflicts
- establishment and maintenance of communication routes between councils, between pathways, and between councils and pathways to facilitate the delineation and sharing of information
- creation of a mechanism for developing the management leadership of the organization both individually and in groups to ensure the ability of leaders to meet the different role expectations associated with shared governance
- appropriate operations council representation on other councils and on task forces, work groups, and other functional groups needing the insight of operations council members and their integration and leadership skills

These tasks are indicative of the accountability of the operations council, but each individual organization will add other obligations. The main point to keep in mind is that the organization's environment, framework, and support structures and the information foundations necessary to support the work at the point of service and to link it with mission and objectives of the organization lie at the center of the operations council's role.

As with the patient care and governance councils, any group, committee, task force, or functional group focusing on any specific task or requirement of the operations council must be appointed by the operations council. In addition, all of these appointed groups are accountable to the operations council. The council is the appropriate locus of control for the work that relates to its accountability. It also has the right to delineate how that work is to be done. If the work is assigned, accountability for its completion remains with the council and cannot be delegated away.

The incapacity to delegate accountability away from its legitimate locus of control is a critical element of shared governance. The formation of committees and other kinds of work groups can tend to fractionalize the organization and diminish its effectiveness. The councils must maintain control over the work of the organization in a disciplined way and make certain that accountability for its outcomes never shifts from the councils and that any functional activities associated with this accountability are carefully managed by the councils.

THE ROLE OF THE OPERATIONS COUNCIL

The role of the operations council is to bring managers and their patient pathway perspectives (nondepartmental and point-of-service driven) together to facilitate the decision making related to resource management. In the old hierarchical structure, a project or proposed system change may have been initiated by a manager, and its success was directly related to the manager's ability to persuade or cajole necessary top-level stakeholders into supporting the initiative and providing the necessary staff. Staff at the point of service may not have been involved at all in developing the plan or have any ownership of the project. Indeed, they may not even be aware a change in their functional area was being developed.

The move toward shared governance always causes some leaders to complain that it represents "decision making by committee" and that group decision making is inefficient and expensive. Such complaints are based on a misunderstanding of system constructs and how to design decision work. In the past, in a number of work groups, the decision-making process was undisciplined, group techniques were almost never used, and process skills were almost never present. It is rarely true that engaging stakeholders in decisions that will have an impact on their lives is a poor strategy. However, it is true that, unless a well-structured decision-making process and a disciplined deliberation methodology are in place, both time and money can be lost in the engagement of others in decision making.

Furthermore, when such processes are not consistently undertaken and efficiently designed, the decisions made tend to be incremental and short term. Also, since the decisions require continual repetition, the staff become more passive and dependent on leaders for making the decisions. It is not that groups are incapable of good decision making but that they need appropriate accountability and the necessary tools and skills.

THE OPERATIONS COUNCIL MEMBERSHIP

The membership of the operations council should reflect the resource leadership configuration of the organization (see Table 5-3). It is critical that the operations council be composed of decision makers and representatives from all service pathways so that all perspectives have a hearing. The consequences of not having the complete representation include the making of decisions that neglect the needs of a stakeholder group or have little credibility in the rest of the organization.

In many settings, the council membership is determined initially by the shared governance steering group (SGSG) during management restructuring deliberations. The SGSG often organizes the council membership around the newly developed pathway structure by including representatives from all pathways on the council. And not only are clinical service areas from all over the organization included, but support areas are often included, which brings a valuable support

Table 5-3 Operations Council Membership

Member	Expectations
Service integrator	To bring a systems overview perspective to the council's deliberations
	To help ensure that the focus of the council is appropriate
Service leader	To bring the individual pathway perspective to the council's deliberations
	To participate in deliberations as an objective steward of corporate resources
Physicians	To bring the physicians' clinical perspective of the M.D. to the council's deliberations
	To act as a communication link to other members of the medical staff
Chief financial officer	To bring financial expertise to the work of the council
	To assist council members in developing their financial understanding and analytical ability

perspective to decision making. In this approach, such areas as information systems and finance are actually involved in making clinically related decisions and the implementation issues surrounding them. Having a full range of perspectives results in everyone having a better understanding of each other's perspectives and in better overall decision-making and implementation processes.

Individuals who represent significant stakeholder groups should be considered for membership. These include the chief financial officer (CFO), a consulting partner, someone from medical affairs, several service integrators (one, two, or three senior administrators), and a member of the board of directors. As the medical staff structure gets more fully incorporated into the shared governance structure, the president of the medical staff is also added to the operations council membership.

> *The operations council provides a forum for resource-based decisions around which all the stakeholders are configured.*

These individuals bring specialized and invaluable experience and viewpoints to the process. The CFO can help raise the council members' level of understanding of the financial workings of the organization. The consulting partner, the medical affairs member, and the president (or other officer) of the medical staff bring a physician perspective to decision making. The service integrators are in a position to provide a broad systems overview and needed context. The board member brings knowledge of the workings of the board as well as a community perspective.

All members of the operations council face a steep learning curve. Not only must they understand the management structure of the organization, but they must also have a thorough understanding of shared governance principles. Most members will find themselves gaining a new perspective on the financial operations of the corporation and will need education on basic business tasks, such as budget development, capital planning, and financial statement review, as well as basic accounting practices. They will also need education on the current stage of certain business processes, such as strategic planning and site planning. It is critical that the council identify as many educational needs early in the development process so adequate resources can be found to fully educate members. At the end of their term on the council, members will have gained a level of understanding of the business of health care comparable to what used to be attained by a chief operating officer or divisional vice-president.

Initially (and sometimes thereafter) the chair of the operations council, like the chairs of the service and governance councils, is selected from the SGSG. This ensures continuity with the original work performed in laying out the new structure and defining the new roles of managers. The council's first order of business, besides determining its accountability, is to decide on the functional aspects of its operation, including the selection process for members, term limits, meeting times and locations, and other details. The role of the chair is to lead the meetings in a man-

> *The operations council requires that each member maintains a view of the whole system, not simply a view of the part he or she represents.*

ner that focuses the participants on the core issues, disciplines the dialogue on the issues, and facilitates decision making by consensus. The chair is also empowered to make critical decisions on behalf of the council (as is the case for all council chairs), including the commitment of corporate resources when time does not allow for a council meeting. When a critical decision is made by the chair, he or she has an obligation to report the decision back to the council at the earliest opportunity.

The role of the manager in shared governance shifts in content and expression. It now involves supporting, mentoring, and coaching staff at the point of service so that they will better understand the truly empowered nature of their positions. With the move to a flatter organization and the relocation of decision making comes the need for a decision-making body to deal with operational and resource issues that cross the boundaries between areas of the organization. It is this need that the corporate operations council is intended to meet.

> *The chair has power to act delegated by the council. It is characteristic of the governance notion as applied to a system.*

The tearing down of the old hierarchical power base and the move to a council structure based on data and outcomes is a paradigm shift for everyone involved. A great deal of education and development of council members is required if the council is to achieve full functionality. Former managers and administrators who now find themselves without a hierarchical power base will need to adapt to the new structure and to the new management role.

MAKING THE OPERATIONS COUNCIL WORK

In the operations council, projects related to the organization's priorities are scrutinized by a management panel and by the organization's financial experts. Since the council includes representatives from all pathways, all perspectives are shared at the table during the process. The council focuses on data "fit" within the context of a strategic plan or priority list, so politicking for a particular project or idea is excluded from the decision-making process. The council also serves as a focal point for systems, processes, and projects that span multiple pathways. While it is primarily a decision-making body, the council is accountable for ensuring that certain tasks are completed and certain outcomes achieved. Thus, it is required to delegate responsibilities to facilitate the completion of tasks.

> *The role of manager must be broadened in a way that makes it impossible for the manager to continue to do the work that has always been expected.*

One of the major challenges facing a newly formed operations council is to find the right context for decisions. In the old hierarchical structure, the context may have been as simple as one administrator's feeling that a particular idea was a good one and should be acted upon. As decision making becomes more of a council-driven, data-based process, an overriding context must be found that facilitates the comparison of projects and the arrival at satisfactory decisions.

THE OPERATIONS COUNCIL PROCESS

A good example of a major operations council issue would be the capital purchase of a new treatment technology. In the old structure, a physician (or department manager) might research a new technology and decide unilaterally that it would make life easier or achieve better outcomes within the organization's scope of care and service. The physician would then try to "sell" an administrator on the need for the technology by pointing to a currently important issue (e.g., cost containment, poor patient satisfaction, etc.). The administrator might then try to sell the idea to senior management stakeholders depending on the size of the purchase, and ultimately the CFO would have to buy into the idea. This process is typically very time consuming, since an individual meeting has to

> *In the operations council approach, it is not possible for an individual to control decisions or project a personal agenda.*

be held with each stakeholder. Different questions might be asked at each meeting, requiring additional research and investigation. Each person might have unique issues in mind as he or she evaluates the purchase, and the feelings and viewpoints of the stakeholders may not be congruent with the overall goals of the organization. At the end of the process, the involved parties, tired of being hounded by the champions of the new technology, may cave in and agree with the purchase. By this time, supplier discounts may have been missed because of the length of time required to get approval, or the scope of the pro-

> *There are no other approval mechanisms outside the council structure. There is a single locus of control for all decisions.*

ject may have grown or shrunk and be completely different than the original proposal (see Table 5-4).

CLARITY OF ISSUES

The operations council provides an opportunity to expedite the planning and decision process and keep the discussion focused on the key issues. For example, a capital purchase may be identified by a service coordinator or a provider team and communicated to the service integrator associated with the pathway. The service integrator is accountable for ensuring that all the necessary homework is completed for a purchase, including a detailed financial analysis for presentation to the operations council. At the council meeting, members hear the presentation (see Exhibit 5-3) and discuss the fit of the purchase with organizational strategies and capital resources. Since the discussion takes place with all the stakeholders in the room, a decision can be made immediately. Politicking and hidden agendas become nonissues, since the justification for the purchase is based on data and the purchase's fit with the priorities of the system. Once the decision is made, there is no further approval process required. A service leader presents his or her proposal only once.

The challenge for the council is to clarify the context for decision making. There is generally no shortage of good ideas coming forward for approval. Trying to understand what resources are available or clarifying strategies to a point where they are helpful in the decision process can be the biggest challenge for the council. In the old hierarchy, vague strategies or a fuzzy logic and/or indicators of available capital could be used to move personal agendas forward. In data-driven discussions, the source of information must be clear and to the point. This may require a review of existing strategic plans including implementation details and

Table 5-4 Old and New Decision Processes

Old Process	Operations Council
No shared understanding of standard	Projects are evaluated based on an understanding of fit
No context for consistency	Operations council approves all major processes and items
Narrow point of review and approval	Projects are evaluated by a diverse group of stakeholders
Ability to project a personal agenda	Decisions are made by consensus
Ability to force a request or demand through the system	All decisions reflect the organization's priorities and goals

Exhibit 5-3 Presentation Guidelines

---

1. Project steps
- Problem statement
- "As is" statement
- Brainstorming
- Option design and selection
- Implementation plan
- Follow-up and benefits statement

2. Checklist
- Does project meet strategic requirements?
- Is project budgeted?
- Does project exceed budgeted dollars?
- Is project consistent with capital plan?
- Is this a subproject of previously approved project?
- Are stakeholders identified and included in project process?
- Did physicians have input and express agreement?

3. Option selection
- List of benefits
- Cost analysis
- Type of decision requested
- Nonbudgeted projects (add justification or reasoning)

---

generation of new financial reports that give a good picture of capital availability to the organization.

CLARIFYING OPERATIONS COUNCIL ACCOUNTABILITY

One of the critical first steps to undertake in developing any council is to firmly establish in writing the accountability of the council (see Exhibit 5-4). This provides a focus for council members and serves as a tool for communicating the purpose of the council to stakeholders. This work requires creativity and perseverance until all members feel comfortable with the wording of the accountability statement and fully understand its meaning. It is important that each organization take the time to develop its own accountability statement to take into account its unique characteristics. The accountability statement, which should clearly

Exhibit 5-4 Operations Council Accountability Statement

Material Resources

To provide the linkage, communication, and action between service and governance as it relates to material resources within the corporation and the community as evidenced by

- capital priorities that are consistent with the corporate mission and strategies
- a corporate capital plan based on products and services provided that is in alignment with the health goals and mission of the organization
- establishment of parameters for monitoring and evaluating material resources
- a process for communicating the capital plan, material resources parameters, and other actions of the council

Human Resources

- There are corporate policies and strategies regarding recruitment, retention, and utilization of human resources that reflect the philosophy, mission, and values of the organization and are consistent with applicable laws.
- There is a communication and action linkage between the service and governance councils regarding human resources.

Support Resources

There is a framework in place that

- facilitates the transition to shared governance
- provides educational resources for the development of staff and management
- supports the relocation of decision making and redefining of management accountability
- facilitates the removal of organizational obstacles to point-of-service decision making at all places they exist in the organization

Fiscal Resources

There is collaboration between leaders and representatives from the appropriate disciplines and services to develop an annual operating budget and a long-term capital plan, including a strategy to monitor the implementation of the plan. The budget review process includes consideration of the appropriateness of the organization's plan for providing care to meet patient needs.

continues

Exhibit 5-4 continued

There is a communication and action linkage between service and governance regarding fiscal resources within the organization and the community, as evidenced by

- program evaluation consistent with the organizational mission
- consistent linkage and integration of strategies, service pathways, and prioritized budgetary resources
- facilitation of the fiscal activities of the service pathways, including
  - the monitoring of appropriate budget indicators
  - the monitoring of appropriate business plans
  - the sharing of resources across service pathways
  - the removal of obstacles to fiscal integrity
  - a corporate business plan based on products and services provided that is in alignment with the health goals and mission of the organization
  - a process for communicating the business plan and other actions of the council

Systems Resources

There is evidence that each service pathway, discipline, or service group has established and individualized its functional accountability within the context of a whole-systems shared governance framework.

There are integrated information systems that serve as a foundation for the linkage of all services across the continuum, as evidenced by

- an approach to work systems that is multifocal, multidisciplinary, and patient based
- a method of determining and interpreting systems models, policies, and strategies to create a shared governance systems framework
- an approach to new technological systems that ensures support for work and operations, with attention to work flow and how work flow will change
- a mechanism for integrating and evaluating systems within and across work areas to support partnerships
- a mechanism to deal with systems problems at the level where they occur

Appropriate application of systems resources will be evidenced by

- the linking of systems within the work area and across the service pathways and the defining of their purpose

continues

Exhibit 5-4 continued

- the utilization of a project management or continuous quality improvement (CQI) process for systems development, maintenance, and improvement
- the assurance of work area system alignment with the organizational mission, goals, and values
- the implementation of systems in the work area within the context of a whole-systems shared governance framework
- the implementation of a clinical information system to meet the needs of patient-focused care

As the operations council, we define

- linkage as the flow of communication between related points
- multifocal as the viewing of an issue or a system from more than one perspective
- partnership as the organizational relationship between stakeholders who have shared accountability
- systems as tasks, activities, and information flows that are interconnected (every change in a system has potential repercussions in every other system)
- whole-systems shared governance as the organizational system that supports the work of the organization through the application of the principles of partnership, equity, accountability, and ownership

define the charge of the council in a theoretical fashion, must delineate the council's specific areas of control, authority, and decision making. Noted should be the absence of control of or accountability for work, quality, competence, and the outcomes of the relationships between team members at the point of service.

THE OPERATING BUDGET PROCESS

As previously mentioned, many activities formerly performed in different areas of the old hierarchy become included in the accountability of the operations council in a shared governance structure. For example, development of capital and operating budgets is overseen by the operations council

> *Stewardship is a key role of the leader. Control of the resources facilitates growth when done well and ensures decline when done poorly.*

rather than by the CFO or finance department. The council monitors the budget process at certain checkpoints to ensure that financial targets are being met and budget assumptions and implementation plans are coordinated across pathways. Much of the coordination of the process remains with the technical experts, who facilitate the completion of large fiscal projects. However, the locus of control rests with the operations council.

Once the budget is developed, the operations council monitors the financial performance of the organization and makes the decisions necessary to ensure that targets are met. Variance reports generated by the finance office are reviewed monthly by the council. Action plans submitted by service leaders are reviewed to ensure the correction of any performance shortfalls.

The accountability for financial performance provides discipline when targets are not met. The operations council serves as a support for service leaders, reviews all variance reports with a systems perspective, and looks for trends or patterns across pathways. The council can direct resources to be rerouted from one pathway to another or can balance budget shortfalls with budget overages in other areas. Note that the role of the council is not to control or manipulate point-of-service leaders but to support them in meeting their particular accountability for financial performance. Thus, council members must have a clear understanding of the personal accountability of individual service leaders. If a service leader demonstrates a pattern of nonperformance, the operations council recommends actions to be taken by the appropriate council or organizational leader.

THE CAPITAL BUDGET PROCESS

As previously mentioned, the operations council spends a good portion of time reviewing capital purchases. While routine capital budgeted items fall within the high signature limits of individual point-of-service leaders, items that are unbudgeted or require expenditures over the relevant signature levels must be reviewed by the council prior to purchase. The purpose of this review, which represents another clear departure from the way a hierarchical organization functions, is to determine the priority of the item being requested. The council members must therefore be aware of the amount of capital resources available and the strategic

All workers are stakeholders in the sharing of the resources of an organization. Each must play a part if the resources are to be equitably distributed.

priorities of the organization. In many cases, the discussion centers on the consequences of trading one capital expenditure for another.

This type of capital analysis may require new reports to be generated by the finance consultants. Monthly reports of capital purchases need to be reviewed to understand how much of the available capital has been spent to date, how much was budgeted initially, how much capacity remains in the system, and what major expenses loom on the horizon that may change the financial picture.

CAPITAL PROJECT PRESENTATIONS

Another aspect of the council review process involves development of all leaders, clinical and management, in the art of project presentation. Guidelines need to be developed by the council that indicate what kinds of questions may be asked during a presentation and thus provide a framework for the presentation. Leaders with previous management experience in a hierarchical organization may have been conditioned to "sell" capital items. A selling type of presentation has no place in the operations council. Discussion of the merits of a project should be based on data and financial analysis rather than intangible benefits that cannot be measured.

Prior to each project presentation, the chair must carefully preview the presentation to ensure that the necessary facts are included and all questions are anticipated by the presenter, with adequate answers at the ready. As experience is gained, the discussion of projects in the council becomes more and more disciplined. Use of continuous quality improvement (CQI) techniques, such as process flowcharts and a formal project management process, help further regulate the dialogue so that frustration is minimized for both the council and the presenter.

> *In all proposals for consideration by the operations council, the goal is not to convince others of the value of the proposal. Instead, proposals simply validate through data analysis the central viability and outcome they are supposed to address.*

THE PRIMACY OF FINANCIAL ACCOUNTABILITY

While the accountability of the council covers all five categories of resource management, the majority of council time will likely be taken up dealing with the financial matters. Development of the operating and capital budgets, variance monitoring, and capital purchase review are basic functions that will dominate the work of the council. These are common business functions, but performing these tasks in a shared governance structure means the routine steps may require modification. The challenge for the council is to understand where accountability lies for completion of tasks, set expectations for performance, and take appropriate action when targets are not met.

SETTING TARGETS

Important components of operations leadership include understanding the importance of target setting and placing the accountability for outcomes in its proper place. It is common knowledge that in the current health care environment, most health care organizations are experiencing decreasing revenues and increasing costs. As a consequence, an organization's financial picture influences nearly every decision made. It is not possible to focus on any

> *If you do not know where you are going, anything will get you there.*

patient care issue without considering the financial implications, nor is it possible to focus on financial performance without considering its impact on quality. The balance of cost and quality defines value. If this balance is used as the overall template for the organization—setting financial targets to achieve maximum value—the result will be a good fit between cost and quality. In other words, all financial activities should be disciplined by the mission and purposes of the organization.

OPERATIONS COUNCIL COMMITMENT

Membership on the operations council demands a significant commitment of time and energy. There is generally enough business in a large organization to require biweekly meetings of the council. In the early stages of council formation and development, a great deal of time is spent discussing the accountability of the council and other details of its implementation and operation. As the council begins to take on the real business of the organization, every presentation or process becomes a learning experience for the council members.

Discovering which questions are important in getting to the bottom of an issue takes time and experience (and can be facilitated by CQI techniques). Likewise, presenters must learn how to formulate presentations based on data—a process that may take time for those who have had years of experience playing political games rather than responding to fact-based arguments. The council must constantly remind itself that its role is to provide support for managers and act as the steward of the resources of the system, not function as a high court handing down summary judgments (see Exhibit 5-5).

CONSENSUS-BASED DECISION MAKING

Council members need a thorough understanding of the consensus-based decision making. Most of us have experience with groups that make decisions using a voting process. While this process results in majority support for decisions, it is not the best process for an accountability-based model.

> *Consensus is not simply agreement. Instead, it involves the group's acknowledging what is right and then doing it.*

In reaching a decision by consensus, every participant in the decision process must understand and agree on the points that make up the decision. This does not mean that every point will meet with everyone's complete approval. The end result of a consensus process is a decision that everyone understands as the right one and can support, since all the relevant data have been analyzed. Some participants may not be totally satisfied, but all can support the decision based on logic, data, and fit.

There is no voting in consensus decision making; instead, there is a determination of where the group is with its understanding of the pertinent issues. Included is a strategy to broaden understanding and knowledge and to provide sufficient data to form a solid foundation for whatever decision is reached. Seeking a consensus in this way prevents members from holding on to a minority view and sabotaging the decision. It also prevents issues from being constantly revisited. In explaining his or her attitude toward a consensus decision, a participant might state, "I do not fully agree with the outcome of the decision-making process, but I understand the reasons why this decision was chosen and can support it."

When an organization moves toward a shared governance council model in which workers are truly empowered, managers are forced to cope with their perceived loss of power. The loss of power is difficult for anyone but can be especially traumatic for individuals positioned at higher levels. Directors, administrators, vice-presidents, and even presidents must all come to terms with the fact that

Exhibit 5-5 Rules for Building a Consensus

A consensus requires that everyone involved in the decision must agree on the individual points discussed before they become part of the decision. Not every point will meet with everyone's complete approval. Unanimity is not the goal, although it may be reached unintentionally. It is not necessary that everyone be satisfied, but everyone's ideas should be thoroughly reviewed. The goal is for individuals to understand the relevant data and, if need be, accept the logic of differing points of view.

The following rules are helpful in reaching a consensus:

- Avoid arguing over individual ranking or position. Present a position as lucidly as possible, but seriously consider what the other group members are presenting.
- Avoid "win–lose" stalemates. Discard the notion that someone must win and thus someone else must lose. When an impasse occurs, look for the next most acceptable alternative for both parties.
- Avoid trying to change minds only in order to avoid conflict and achieve harmony. Withstand the pressure to yield to views that have no basis in logic or the supporting data.
- Avoid majority voting, averaging, bargaining, or coin flipping. These techniques do not lead to a consensus. Treat differences of opinion as indicative of an incomplete sharing of information, and so keep probing.
- Keep the attitude that the holding of different views by group members is both natural and healthy. Diversity is a normal state; continuous agreement is not.
- View initial agreement as suspect. Explore the reasons underlying apparent agreement on a decision and make sure that all members understand the implications of the decision and willingly support it.

either their role no longer serves a purpose in the new organization or has changed into a support role. The shared governance organization does not place any value on the symbolism or trappings of hierarchy. Large offices, individual secretaries, and special privileges are all looked at carefully during the transition. While they certainly do not necessarily all disappear, they may be distributed differently to reflect a new emphasis on the point of service and the achievement of goals.

This attitude toward the trappings of power is inconsistent with the rewards managers (including senior-level managers) have grown to associate with power and authority and "climbing the ladder." Many who have spent their work lives climbing to the top of the organization may feel like the rug has been pulled out from under them. A sense of concern and confusion may also permeate the staff as the power base of individuals they have worked for is stripped away. During this transition, the chief executive officer (CEO) plays an essential role in holding things together while pushing the parameters of the organizational hierarchy. With feelings of loss experienced by everyone on the leadership team, the CEO's ability to motivate the other leaders during this shift is critical.

> *There is nothing that causes more fear and pain than a shift in the power base of a leader. All the work done to obtain power and keep it is lost in the "noise" resulting from a change in the locus of control.*

SHARED VISION

One common consequence of the move toward shared governance is the discovery that the organizational vision is not broadly shared. In a hierarchical structure, senior management may have a common understanding of the organization's mission and major strategies, but their penetration to the lower levels of management may be suspect. When a project or tactic is discussed in a council meeting, it must be debated within the context of the mission, vision, and strategic plan of the organization. All council members must have a common understanding of these before a well-founded conclusion can be reached. In most health care organizations, a great deal of time is spent in efforts aimed at adding clarity and specificity to the strategic plan, by providing supporting documents and relevant information, for example, in the attempt to build a solid foundation for determining tactics.

The operations council must be given substantial authority, and decisions should require no further approval than that obtained at the council. In an empowered shared governance organization, the chair of the operations council (always a point-of-service manager) has the same signature limit as the CEO (see Exhibit 5-6). Decisions of the operations council are final unless they involve a capital expenditure above a dollar amount that requires board of directors approval. The transition to this type of approval process requires an education process not only for the council chair but for all stakeholders who have resource stewardship or fiscal accountability. Everyone who is impacted must be educated, including the board and the accounts payable and materials management staff, as they may be involved in the purchase process.

Exhibit 5-6 Council Chair Duties and Powers

- Calling meetings
- Controlling the agenda
- Moving the council to a consensus on decisions
- Removing nonparticipating members
- Making group assignments
- Making critical decisions on behalf of the council as needed
- Calling emergency meetings if needed
- Acting as mentor of the chair-elect
- Executing signature authority for the council

In a shared governance organization, the operations council assumes areas of accountability that formerly belonged to the chief operations officer or the CFO. Rather than simply being a new place to perform old tasks, however, the operations council plays an important role in supporting the entire shared governance structure. Besides reviewing capital purchases and projects, the operations council is accountable for all resources at the corporate level. When the administrative process does not give way to the council's role, the council's involvement simply evaporates in the face of the administrative position where the "real" power to decide resides. This "escape option" must be eliminated if true accountability is to exist and get expressed by the council.

While service leaders are accountable for managing human, fiscal, material, system, and support resources within their service pathways, issues that involve multiple pathways or have a substantial impact on the organization are handled by the operations council. For example, while daily staffing is managed at the point of service by service coordinators, service leaders are accountable for acquiring an adequate staff with the necessary qualifications to meet the needs of the pathway for which they are responsible. The operations council, with its systems perspective, is accountable for the compensation system used to pay all staff members within the organization. This illustrates the difference in focus at different levels of accountability. The operations council is mainly accountable for translating the strategies of the system into actions and outcomes (see Figure 5-2).

> *There cannot be two places where a decision is made. Preference is always given to decisions made closest to the point of service.*

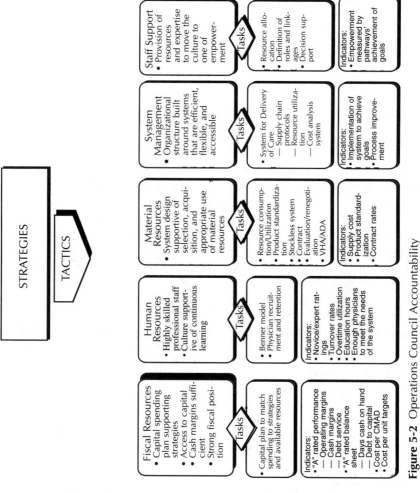

Figure 5-2 Operations Council Accountability

SYSTEMS ACCOUNTABILITY AND SUPPORT ACCOUNTABILITY

Although human, fiscal, and material resource accountability is fairly self-explanatory, systems accountability and support accountability require further elaboration. While the term *systems* may suggest that the focus is on the organization's computer system and information system, the operations council's definition encompasses all systems that form the organization. In fact, there is a connection between its understanding of the concept and "systems thinking" (see Chapter 3). As noted already, the interrelationships between all business processes must be understood in addition to the subsystems and the individual tasks.

This concept is often difficult for many in the organization to embrace. It is one primary reason that the learning organization approach plays a central role in the development of all personnel. It should be expected that everyone who is part of the organization will have role transitions to confront and they will need the insight gained from engaging in an effort to understand and work within a whole-systems shared governance framework. The operations council has an obligation to ensure that everyone has the opportunity to learn and adapt. If the council does not facilitate the achievement of a higher level of systems understanding, the organization will fail to undergo essential change.

> *All work, all relationships, must be seen from the perspective of the whole, not of each part. A system is not simply the sum of its parts.*

Its accountability for support entails that the council must provide a framework for supporting behaviors that resonate with shared governance throughout the organization. The leadership must commit to removing obstacles to full implementation of the values that will undergird the restructured organization. The operations council is the locus of the debate about how the new structure should work, how roles may need to change, and what systems may need to be altered. Therefore, its members must exhibit a high degree of creativity and develop a thorough understanding of the basic principles of shared governance.

LINKAGE TO THE OTHER COUNCILS

Linkage between the councils is critical to the integrity of a shared governance system. As should be clear to the reader, communication and interaction in the building of collateral relationships is a requisite of shared governance. Consequently, considerable attention must be paid to the linkage and communication processes that support accountability and effectiveness within the councils.

Council representation is one important means of linking councils to each other. Just as the operations council leadership should be represented on the patient care council, so should the patient care council leadership be represented on the operations council (and both should be represented on the governance council). This type of cross-representation helps ensure that decisions made in any one part of the organization do not impede the decisions made in another part. It also begins to address the issue of equity and integrity in a horizontal or equity-based organizational system. Shared governance demands that no one part of the system either make decisions that belong in another part or jeopardize the integrity of decisions made elsewhere. The only way to guarantee that this does not happen is to create linkages throughout the system.

Each of the council leaders represented on the operations council has the full right of participation in the decisions of that council. Indeed, it is expected that the patient care council's chair will articulate the impact of budgetary considerations and tactical planning on the decisions made in the patient care council. Further, the patient care council's chair communicates the framework for decisions generated in the operations council in conjunction with the operations council leadership representatives on the patient care council. The same strategy is used in the operations council—the chair and the patient care council leadership representatives communicate decisions made in the patient care council.

CAUTIONS ABOUT CONTROL

One of the most challenging shifts in the locus of control in a shared governance organization relates to the authority of the manager and the framework for decision making. In the old model, ego awards, personal fulfillment, and role expectations centered around the authority of managers to make summary decisions regarding the services that they led, and the old expectations and behaviors are hard to extinguish. Yet they need to be eliminated if the new management role expectations are to be met.

One major focus of the operations council is to develop new leadership skills and to establish a behavioral framework for the new management role. Coaching, development, education, mentoring, and other tactics for changing behavior become essential. The operations council should look carefully at the new role, the shift in expectations, the shift in evaluation of performance, and the new behavioral models of leadership as part of its accountability for supporting the transition to shared governance.

It should be understood that not every manager will be able to make the move to a new kind of leadership. Managers who obtained personal rewards and satisfaction in the exercise of the old role may find the new role to be unfulfilling. The operations council should recognize this reality and make it possible for individuals to move out of unsatisfying roles and into roles that fit their needs and likes. While the transition to shared governance can be a challenging and traumatic time for the organization, it is also a time when the organization can configure its support structure so as to provide a solid foundation for the creation of effective and meaningful roles.

SUPPORT FROM THE CEO

The position of CEO is still a critical leadership position in the new organization. While operational concerns are transferred to the operations council and the lean point-of-service management structure, the CEO remains a visible figure focused on the community interface and serves as a focal point in guiding the organization into the new paradigm. During the transition, while the staff are learning their new empowered roles, they may continue to look for leadership from their traditional leaders, who are themselves learning new roles—or possibly leaving the organization. The CEO is in a position to send a powerful message to the staff and provide strong support for the new values. For this reason, it is critical that the CEO be brought along during the entire process. Without the support of the CEO, the predicted chaos of the transition may be amplified.

The CEO, although a leadership figure in a visible position, is also vulnerable to attack from all sides during the transition. Physicians, board members, and staff will all turn to the CEO at some point for support and reassurance. For this reason, the CEO must have a firm grasp of the theory and application of shared governance, fully understand who is accountable for problem solving, and be willing to take great criticism from nearly everyone while providing an anchor for the organization. The CEO must demonstrate a sensitivity to the traumatic changes the organization is going through and be willing to direct people to the right place in the new structure to get problems and concerns dealt with. Even the slightest wavering in the CEO's commitment will be amplified and used as evidence that the new structure is not working.

OTHER ADMINISTRATOR CHANGES

While the role of the CEO remains basically intact in the new structure, the roles of other senior managers become more consultative in nature. The need for many senior management roles simply disappears in the new structure as staff members assume accountability for decision making, and the remaining senior managers are required to provide special expertise throughout the organization and develop a teaching–learning relationship with the point-of-service managers (see also Chapter 8). These consulting managers (called consulting partners in this text) also play a very important role at the council level.

Since the operations council assumes accountability for many of the critical financial decisions, the expertise of the former CFO is essential for operations council deliberations, and thus this particular consulting partner is in regular attendance at the council meetings. As the need arises for different types of expertise, other consulting partners can be accessed by the council. Indeed, the consulting partners are expected to be present at the operations council meetings so that the council can obtain any information it needs to make good decisions. Also, the other councils and unit or point-of-service groups and teams have the right to access these consultants for deliberations and problem solving whenever it becomes apparent they need expert assistance.

OTHER MANAGER TRANSITIONS

For some members of the senior management group, the loss of perceived power entailed by surrendering ownership of "their" employees and budget cost centers presents substantial difficulties. The ones who adapt more easily will be those who come to understand they are being offered an opportunity to become more deeply involved with interesting projects and to have a broader impact on the organization by improving the skill level of new managers. It is here where the learning character of the new organization becomes critical to the role change of the leadership. Strong support and a learning framework provide the bridge between old and new role behaviors and performance expectations.

> *In shared governance, the old vice-president or senior management roles disappear. Instead the role of systems consultant emerges, available to all who need support for decision making.*

CONCLUSION

Even with a fully empowered work staff and flat management structure, not all decisions can be made at the point of service. For very large projects that cross multiple clinical services and pathways and exceed the scope of the point-of-service leader, a forum must be established to review the projects and act as a steward for the major categories of resources.

The operations council brings together managerial stakeholders with a variety of perspectives and acts as a decision-making body for far-reaching systems issues. Decisions are made faster and are of higher quality because the issues are examined in the open by leaders with a wide range of perspectives and expertise. By fulfilling its role, the operations council contributes substantially to the implementation of shared governance and ensures the long-term viability of the organization.

SUGGESTED READING

Ackoff, R. 1994. *The democratic corporation*. New York: Oxford University Press.

Beckham, D. 1994. The vision thing. *Healthcare Forum Journal* 37, no. 2:60–70.

Block, P. 1991. *The empowered manager*. San Francisco: Jossey-Bass.

Block, P. 1993. *Stewardship: Choosing service over self-interest*. San Francisco: Berrett-Koehler.

Dumaine, B. 1993. The new non-manager managers. *Fortune* 127, no. 4:80–84.

Edwards, G., et al. 1994. Unit-based shared governance can work. *Nursing Management* 25, no. 4:74–77.

The end of delegation? Information technology and the CEO. 1995. *Harvard Business Review* 73, no. 5:161–173.

Garvin, D. 1993. Building a learning organization. *Harvard Business Review* 71, no.3:78–91.

Griffith, J. 1995. The infrastructure of integrated delivery systems. *Healthcare Executive* 10, no. 3:12–17.

Hale, G. 1995. *The leader's edge*. New York: Irwin Professional Publishing.

Lawler, E., III. 1994. *Motivation in work organizations*. San Francisco: Jossey-Bass.

Limerick, D. and B. Cunningham. 1993. *Managing the new organization*. San Francisco: Jossey-Bass.

Chapter 6

Building Seamlessness: Governance at the Crossroads

Tim Porter-O'Grady and Bruce Perry

New directions are always suspect and usually opposed without
any other reason but because they are not already common.

John Locke

LINKING THE SYSTEM

So far, this book has covered the service and operational components of the
clinical health system as it reconfigures itself for an integrated continuum of care
approach to health services. Now is the time to address the governance and linkage components of the organization.

Shared governance is fundamentally a point-of-service framework that tends to
link the greater community with specific patients and the internal community.[1]
The assumption is that, while the organization serves the community as a part of
its mission, each provider can serve only one patient at a time. Consequently, providing excellent service to an individual patient is a way of serving the community as a whole.

Linking the external and internal
communities previously has been a
function of the board of trustees,[2]
whose main goal, of course, is to help
achieve the mission and objectives of
the organization within the context of
the community. However, in the emerging integrated environment, linking
activities can no longer be looked at in

> **The system focuses on the entire community. The point of service focuses on the community one member at a time.**

the same way, nor is the traditional view of governance appropriate for an integrated health system.[3]

NEW NOTIONS OF LEADERSHIP

In the new paradigm, a new set of rules applies to all the functions of the organization, including those related to governance. The clear distinctions between the roles of one level of an organization and another (vertical design) are no longer sufficient to delineate new kinds of relationships. In the movement from vertically integrated structures to horizontally integrated systems, a large-scale change occurs in the relationship between the functional elements of each part of the organization.[4] The clear distinction between such elements no longer has meaning and value, for the following reasons:

- Ownership is no longer a model for control in horizontal systems. Shared risks now become the foundation for relationships.
- Functional integrity at the point of service requires a clear understanding of the system's mission and objectives.
- The fit between decisions that relate to the system as a whole and those that impact on work at the point of service must be clearly understood. It can no longer be assumed that a governance decision need not have the same content or context as a point-of-service decision.
- In order to ensure the continuing engagement of empowered individuals, some reference to and linkage with governance in functional decisions must be maintained as an ongoing part of the organization's work.
- Effective decisions are made as close as possible to the place where they will be carried out. Therefore, anything that impedes the ability of those at the point of service to understand the implications of governance decisions can no longer be tolerated. Decisions that impact a group of individuals should not be made without somehow including those individuals in the decision-making process.

LINKING GOVERNANCE AND FUNCTION

In an accountability-based framework, the linking of all components of the organization is essential for the judicious exercise of accountability (see Figure 6-1). Decisions regarding the organization's mission and objectives (decisions typically made by the board) are usually carried out by those at the point of service. In an empowered organization, those at the point of service are expected to

> *Assuming governance decisions can be made without including those they will impact is no longer tenable in the new systems paradigm.*

play some role in making such decisions and in determining how they will be implemented.[5]

Linkage of decisions between one component of the organization and another depends on understanding the implications of the decisions throughout the system, especially the places they will be implemented. Decisions made at some point always affect decisions made elsewhere, and consequently it is appropriate to delineate decisions in an accountability-driven system based on their appropriate locus of control and then to intersect the decisions in a way that engages the individuals who will carry them out. Also, work related to decisions depends on the decisions having legitimacy where they are made.[6] For example, making a decision about a way in which care will be delivered should be made in the places where accountability for providing the care exists.

> *Once the locus of control for a decision is affixed, the major task is determining how to engage those whom the decision will impact directly.*

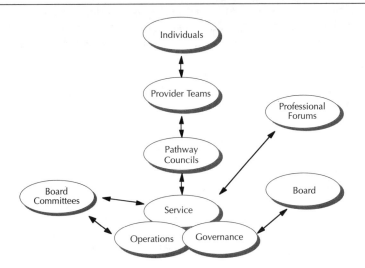

Figure 6-1 Whole-Systems Shared Governance: Integrating the System

The delivery model and clinical framework should not be the province of the administrative leadership—and in shared governance they are not.[7] Therefore, empowering an administrative group or board group to choose the model for the delivery of care is inappropriate. It is equivalent to precluding certain decisions from being made in certain parts of the organization regardless of who might be there and what perceptions of their authority might exist.

In shared governance organizations, it is critical to view decision making as a partnership activity. Each partner in a partnership has a specified role to play—a role that contributes to achieving the goals of the partnership.[8] What is essential is for each partner to be clear about the functions and extent of decision making that falls within the ambit of his or her role (see Figure 6-2).

In an organizational system, such as a health care organization, the partnership framework works in the same way. When a partnership has been forged between the various components, it becomes imperative to delineate what roles and functions are appropriate for which partners. The concept of partnership is inconsistent with the concept of hierarchy, but decision making among partners still requires the delineation of decision-making obligations.

> *In shared governance, the status of one's position is no longer a viable determinant of value. It is instead the consonance between the decision and the accountability for its implementation that defines role value.*

This is also true at the council level. A partnership between the councils is created to ensure that specific decisions are made, work is accomplished, and desired outcomes are achieved.[9] Each role and function, range of accountability, and outcome expectation is delineated by the stakeholders. Because there is a recognition of stakeholder obligations, there can be a negotiation between the stakeholders to clarify their obligations. Once the obligations have been clarified, it is expected that they will be met. The checks and balances in the system are designed to ensure that accountability is exercised and desired outcomes are achieved.

TRANSLATING BOARD ACCOUNTABILITY

One of the biggest challenges presented by point-of-service models is to ensure that the goals envisioned by the board are translated into functions and activities at the point of service and implemented in some sustainable format.[10] It is clear

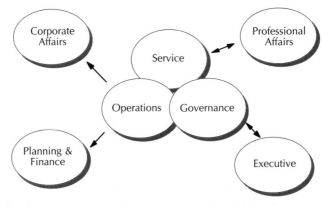

Figure 6-2 Whole-Systems Shared Governance: Structural Interface

that, in a point-of-service model, sustainable outcomes can be achieved only by those who have a strong sense of ownership and have fully participated in the activities related to their functions and work. Consequently, decisions must not limit the ability of those at the point of service to own and influence the processes and outcomes of their work. This principle is critical for understanding of the shared governance process and point-of-service models. Increasingly it is apparent that whole-systems ownership and the investment of all of the stakeholders in the work of the system and the achievement of out-

> *If outcomes are to be sustained, those at the point of service must exhibit as strong a sense of ownership and investment in the system as those at the "point of governance."*

comes is necessary to make that achievement sustainable and gain everyone's commitment to continuous improvement.[11]

There must also be a clear understanding of the accountability and expectations that relate to the functions of the various components of the organization and the people who work there. The board, for example, is expected to act as a liaison between the organization and the community that it serves. In that capacity, the board defines the relationship of the organization to the community.[12] One priority of the board is to identify functions and activities that support that relationship (as well as the organization's viability).

> *The board is obligated to ensure an appropriate interface exists between the system and the community it serves. It is primarily a steward of relationships rather than resources.*

Unfortunately, the fulfillment of its stewardship responsibilities at the community level does not necessarily mean that the board's wishes and desires get translated into daily work. Indeed, there is often a disconnect between the perceptions of those who are doing the daily work and those who are prescribing the overall direction and goals of the organization—a disconnect that tends to create "systems noise." It is often only through the authority and energy of the administrative leadership that any portion of the board's vision ever gets translated into functions and activities at the point of service, and this is one reason hospitals and health care systems can wind up looking extremely faddish, frequently shifting between a whole range of initiatives and innovations that rarely are substantiated by any long-term process or by sustainable outcomes.[13]

> *In shared governance, the board is as accountable to its internal community as it is to its external community.*

TRANSLATING DIRECTION

In order to provide a meaningful linkage between the components of a shared governance organization, some process must occur that motivates the stakeholders to invest, either directly or indirectly, in the organization's operating system.

> *In shared governance, there is a linkage between the decisions of any of the operating bodies of the system, no matter whether vertically or horizontally related.*

Part of this process involves creating an interface between the stakeholders that engages them and facilitates their investment in the work and the outcomes envisioned by the board. Therefore, the board should be linked directly at key decision points in the shared governance system (see Exhibit 6-1).

In a shared governance framework, it is essential that there be linkages between all types of decision making

Exhibit 6-1 Governance Council Accountability

The governance council

- translates the board's mission and objectives into strategies
- sets policy and priorities
- ties corporate goals to the organizational strategy
- ensures system integration
- resolves conflicts between councils

along the vertical and horizontal continuum and that the players be enlisted in a meaningful and direct way in establishing direction, setting up objectives, and unfolding work. It is also essential that there be full participation by accountable individuals in decisions that affect their accountability. Through the representative process, the stakeholders at every level of the organization must be invested in a way that ensures both their understanding of the mission and objectives of the organization and their implementation of decisions that are made. The following principles apply:

- The mission and objectives will mean nothing if the language of shared governance is all that is generated throughout the organization.
- The mission and objectives must be translated into functions and activities.
- The daily activities and insights of those at the point of service must be consistent with the purpose and structure of the organization.
- The organization's mission must be translated into strategies, which must be further refined into tactics and processes. Consequently, the mechanism for decision making must get designated stakeholders to invest in each type of decision making—strategic, tactical, and functional.
- Equity demands that players throughout the organization be equally involved in establishing the strategies and tactics chosen to fulfill the organization's mission.

Further, there must be a place within the organization where all of the activities, from direction setting to care provision, converge—indeed, where linkage occurs. Principles that should guide this include the following:

- Strategy formation must occur in one place, yet involve all the necessary stakeholders.

- The fit between the strategies of the organization and their direction must be defined as clearly as possible.
- The strategies and their relationship to the tactics must be identified in a clear, succinct way.
- Individual and team performance must reflect the tactics chosen to carry out each strategy.
- Performance measurement and outcomes determination must be linked to expectations in every type of decision making, including the direction setting, strategy development, formation of tactics, and development of the personal objectives of individual workers. This range of activities is central to the work of the governance council.

In shared governance, structures are locations for the convergence of decision making. Linkages between the various components of the system require an identifiable structural format. It is critical to the integrity of the system that there be a place where the leaders representing the stakeholders come together. In a whole-systems shared governance structure, that place of convergence is the governance council.

The governance council replaces all executive-level groups, presidents, councils, cabinets, or other groups that reflected the hierarchical relationships that existed previously. Much of the value of those roles is diminished or eliminated with the change to shared governance. Consequently, having a body at the executive level whose role it is to make direction-setting decisions no longer makes sense. In a shared governance framework, the governance council assumes the accountability for tying the components and configurations of the organization together as well as the strategies and tactics that the organization undertakes to fulfill its mission.[14] Like all councils, the governance council is a decision-making body. Its decisions, however, are specifically related to

> *In shared governance, the governance council replaces all executive level groups as the core point of integration in the system.*

- translating the direction, mission, and objectives set by the board of trustees into specified strategies that give form to the work of the organization
- linking decision-making loci to ensure that each component of the organization is meeting its obligation to achieve its assigned goals

- dealing with linkage, intersection, and integration issues to ensure the fluid and effective functioning of all of the components of the organization
- addressing problems with linkage and integration as well as the implementation of tactics related to the strategies for which it is accountable
- evaluating the extent to which the strategies and tactics identified, agreed upon, and implemented by the councils and pathways are contributing to the achievement of the organization's objectives and the fulfillment of its mission
- reviewing the interface between capital initiatives and strategic plans to ensure that resources are directed to the priorities it has established for the organization

The governance council is a place where the key designated leaders meet to focus on issues of direction and integration. It serves as a forum for delineating and assessing both the integrity and the effectiveness of the organization's work.

GOVERNANCE COUNCIL MEMBERSHIP

The governance council includes as members the key decision makers and stakeholders in the organization. Since it is responsible for integrating the organization and ensuring that the work being done is fulfilling the mission and objectives set by the board of trustees, leaders who are accountable for achieving objectives properly belong on the council. Therefore, at a minimum the members of the governance council include

- the chair of the board of trustees (or a designee)
- the chair of the service (patient care) council
- the chair of the operations council
- the chief of the medical staff
- the CEO (and designated senior leaders)
- all senior leaders and consultants (ex officio)

The leadership of the governance council represents the leadership of all the major components of the system, not just the administrators and the board.

This list covers the primary members (see also Figure 6-3). It is important to note that senior leaders and consultants are present as ex officio members because of their involvement in

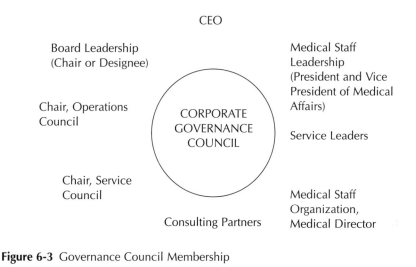

CEO

Board Leadership
(Chair or Designee)

Chair, Operations
Council

CORPORATE
GOVERNANCE
COUNCIL

Chair, Service
Council

Consulting Partners

Medical Staff
Leadership
(President and Vice
President of Medical
Affairs)

Service Leaders

Medical Staff
Organization,
Medical Director

Figure 6-3 Governance Council Membership

whole-systems applications across components. The leaders are mainly responsible for making critical decisions regarding the integration of the organization and the fulfillment of its mission, and the consultants provide information and support to the leaders.

THE ROLE OF THE CEO

The CEO is the agent of the organization and an officer of the system. As the designated link to the board, the CEO must ensure that the work of the governance council fits the mission and objectives set by the board. As noted, the governance council is primarily responsible for translating the mission and objectives into the work activities performed in all parts of the organization. It is thus secondarily responsible for developing and promulgating strategies to fulfill the mission. To meet its responsibilities, it uses its links with the patient care council, the operations council, and the service pathway leadership.

A further obligation of the governance council is to ensure that all leaders pursue the strategic priorities in a disciplined manner. Since the governance council constructs the priorities, it has an interest in seeing to it that everyone is focused on them and that no one gets sidetracked into spending undue energy on unimportant projects.

ROLE OF THE CONSULTING PARTNERS

As the old leadership team disappears from the organization, a new set of relationships emerges. In the hierarchical approach to senior-level structuring, there was a specific range of authority and accountability associated with each role. The chief financial officer had accountability for all financial issues. The human resources senior officer dealt with all human resource issues. Authority and accountability for anything involving those issues fell under the auspices of the senior officers (presidents, vice-presidents, administrators, etc.).

> *The greatest barrier to innovation is conventional wisdom.*

In a point-of-service system, as much authority and accountability for issues of control and revenue generation, for example, lie at the point of service as with the financial leadership. Utilization and regulation of human resources is also largely a point-of-service responsibility. The role of senior leaders is primarily to provide support to the point of service and the decision makers located there. Indeed, in some models the leaders who were designated vice-president delineations are now called consulting partners. For example, the chief financial officer may now be the consulting partner for finance. This consulting partner's role is to ensure that the various accountable decision-making groups and individuals at the point of service have the information, tools, resources, and guidance they need to make good finance-related decisions.

> *Hierarchy has no inherent validity. It is merely the accommodation to our failing to do the real work of relationship building in organizational and work systems.*

This same role shift occurs for human resources, information, marketing, planning, and other officers. The consulting partners have an obligation to be accessible to anyone making decisions about the utilization of resources or other key matters.

Consulting partners operate like any consultants. They seek to market their services to those who need them (at the pathway level and in the councils) and validate their performance effectiveness by their degree of availability, their impact on decision making, and the number of consulting relationships they establish in a given period of time. Consequently, they

> **The old vice-presidents now become consulting partners, providing resources and support to decision makers closer to the point of service.**

- are available at all levels of the organization upon demand for their services
- are prepared to provide educational and support services to advance the skill base of the point-of-service decision makers
- accept task assignments for research and planning related to major strategic initiatives
- provide advice and assistance to pathway leaders for decision making related to the management of their particular service pathways
- continue to refine the systems, services, and structures required for supporting point-of-service decision makers in all the places where decisions must be made

Needless to say, the shift to consulting partner for the system requires tremendous changes in behavior and function. Not all senior leaders can make this transition. A sense of loss and diminishment is sometimes associated with the movement of authority to the point of service and the change from being key decision maker to being key decision maker consultant. The organization must be prepared to meet the challenges presented by the dramatic change in role.

> **A shift in the role from senior officer in the system to consulting partner requires a major shift in role and behavior. Not all people can make this shift successfully.**

Much of the importance of the role of consulting partner derives from the value of the advice the consultants give key decision makers at the council or pathway level. Since councils and pathways in whole-systems shared governance are the only two loci of resource-related decisions, providing the information and advice is critical to the quality of the decisions made there. Indeed, the pathway leaders and council members require the same level of insight and knowledge as was once required of senior-level administrators. Moving decisions closer to the point of service does not reduce the need for good insights and comprehensive information. In fact, it is becoming apparent that high-quality decision making needs to occur more frequently at the point of service than at any other point in the organization.[15]

The consulting partners also have an obligation to the governance council. Since the governance council's role is to ensure the integration of the whole system, the governance council leadership needs the insights and the skills of the consulting partners to recognize the implications of strategic decisions and the linkages required to make the strategic initiatives successful.

The consulting partners usually have defined roles delegated to them by the governance council leadership to facilitate the translation of strategies into tactics at the pathway and point-of-service levels. The governance council does not develop tactics. It simply develops strategies. It does, however, have the expectation that tactics will be developed in the operations and service councils as well as in the service pathways. The main duty of the consulting partners is to help translate the strategies into tactics.

The consulting partner role is becoming increasingly important to the organizational integrity. Indeed, it can be argued that this role has broader implications than did the old vice-presidential roles that were defined compartmentally or by divisional allocations in the hospital structure. In the new approach, the consulting partners have a broad impact on the integrity of the organization, the effectiveness of decision making, and the delineation of expectations.

> *There is no value or future in believing something cannot be done. The future is always in making things happen.*

GOVERNANCE COUNCIL ACCOUNTABILITY

Like all other councils, the governance council has defined areas of accountability that determine its parameters and give it direction.

The areas of accountability of the governance council are necessarily broad since its role is to ensure the translation of the organization's mission and objectives into strategies, tactics, and ultimately functions and activities. In particular, the council is accountable for ensuring the existence of the following:

- a mechanism for reviewing evidence that the organization is achieving its goals
- a process for establishing priorities for the organizational strategies and initiatives

- a mechanism for ensuring that strategic initiatives support the achievement of the mission and objectives of the organization
- a framework for translating the organizational mission and objectives into strategies and tactics
- a mechanism for ensuring that all councils fulfill their obligations in a manner consistent with the mission and objectives of the organization
- a structure to ensure that all councils meet their accountability for making necessary decisions
- a system that provides necessary information to decision makers throughout the organization
- evidence that all work performed by the councils and pathways is consistent with the strategies selected by the governance council
- a clear linkage between the organization and the external community so that the needs of the community are met by the services of the organization
- an information infrastructure to support decision making throughout the organization
- a mechanism to ensure that all decision processes support each other and that the decisions made at the point of service and the team, pathway, and council levels are integrated in a way that contributes to the fulfillment of the organization's mission

BREADTH OF ACCOUNTABILITY

The governance council has general accountability for the effectiveness of the system as a whole. Consequently, it is especially concerned with the linkages between internal structures as well as the organization's linkage to the greater community. It has an obligation to make certain that the perspectives of the community and the organization's mission are what drive its own deliberations.

Ensuring seamless connections between the decision-making components of the organization is a critical goal of the governance council. Seamlessness is important to the integrity of decision making in point-of-service systems. Therefore, the governance council is always assessing the

> *The governance council ensures that there is a seamless linkage between all the points of decision making throughout the system and that they all work to fulfill the mission of the system.*

"fit" of the components with the other. The integrity of decision making at one place in the organization becomes a serious concern if it affects the viability of decision making in another place.

The whole-systems perspective of the governance council leadership is key for the ability of the whole council to perform its role. The council uses various information strategies and the reports to determine whether the decisions made throughout the organization are consistent with the strategies it has selected.

> *The governance council leadership is concerned with the "fit" of the components of the system and their congruence with the system's mission.*

Evaluating individual performance is not nearly as important as evaluating the integration of components committed to fulfilling their obligation to provide patient care services. However, the provision of patient care services may have a positive or negative impact on other components of the organization. Each component must operate within concerted service parameters yet facilitate the work of the other components if the continuum of services is to be viable over the long term. One part of the system (e.g., one pathway) operating in a way that creates an impediment for another part vital to its integrity is involved in an unsustainable activity. If the pathways do not intersect appropriately or if the work of one pathway is in conflict with that of another, some mechanism must be used to find a solution. It is the duty of the governance council to ensure that there are mechanisms for

- measuring the dissonance between the pathways
- identifying the source and nature of the problem(s) causing the dissonance
- linking each of the players involved so a meaningful dialogue may occur
- identifying and clarifying appropriate methods for problem resolution
- selecting a method and measuring its impact
- evaluating performance

The governance council also has an obligation to ensure that there are assessment mechanisms to measure the achievement of objectives. Note that, rather than it being the identifier of problems, the governance council makes certain that there are strategies, mechanisms, and systems in place to assist those at the point of service in identifying incompatibility or performance interruptions and in resolving issues and concerns.

THE QUESTION OF SYSTEMS

Clearly, organizational effectiveness over the long term depends less on the ability of the governance council to resolve specific problems and more on its ability to identify imbedded processes than can be used to correct problems or address issues.[16] The governance council has a predominant role in ensuring that such processes exist in the organization.

> *The governance council must be sure that the information infrastructure provides the range and depth of information necessary to clearly determine the seamless flow of data across the system supporting all outcome measurement.*

Key to the success of any systems approach is the quality of the information infrastructure. The internal information system (see Chapter 8) and the external information system (see Chapter 9) are critical tools for measuring the effectiveness of the organization. An information system is like a river that flows through the organizational system. Any player along the way should be able to "dip into the river" and obtain any information needed to guide decision making, correct deficiencies, and resolve problems. The insights, tools, and evaluative mechanisms necessary to determine effectiveness should be available at any given time to any player. It is the governance council's duty to see to it that the information system is in place, does operate, and meets the needs it was designed to meet. In the future, the information infrastructure of a health care organization will function as the framework for planning, implementing, and evaluating at every level. Since the governance council's focus is linkage and integration, the information system is a

> *Attachment to the current structure always impedes the ability to conceive new structures. In general, conceptual capture by the passing age makes it difficult to see the emerging elements of the new age.*

key vehicle for determining if integration has occurred and how effectively goals are being achieved.

THE GOVERNANCE COUNCIL AND THE CASCADE

Since there is no hierarchy in a shared governance system, the integration of decision making, the facilitation of partnership, and the interface between the components of the system are essential factors. In addition, a functioning system that assists the leadership in determining the proper direction for the organization and in moving the organization in that direction is critical to the organization's viability.[17]

The implementation of strategy is becoming increasingly dependent on the quality of the information infrastructure. Without it, data interface is virtually impossible in an integrated system.

The success of a strategic approach is highly dependent on the quality, breadth, and integrity of the information system. Since control can no longer be achieved by ownership of all processes, a shared risk framework requires not only good information but a good informational structure supporting the activities of the organization and their linkage.

A strategic cascade provides just such a structure. In this system, the board determines the organization's mission, objectives, and direction based on the demand for services within the community. As it links with the community, the organization defines its relationship to those it serves (see Figure 6-4). In fact, in a subscriber-based marketplace, the community is equivalent to the subscribers, both current and potential.

The governance council's role is to identify key strategies for fulfilling the mission established by the board. While the strategies that define the organization's direction may be few, they are broadly encompassing and create the framework for subsequent activities by the councils, the pathways, and the service teams (see Figure 6-5).

The board sets the direction for the system, the governance council translates that direction into specific strategies, and leadership of the system formulates tactics for their implementation.

Figure 6-4 A Strategic Cascade

As noted already, the board's work is to set the direction. The governance council's role is to translate the direction into strategies, mandates, capital plans, and other functional elements, and the strategies determine the organizational priorities toward which the energies and work of the system are devoted.[18]

Following the development of strategies, the governance council and the pathway leaders are required to develop specific tactics to carry out the strategies. These tactics identify sharply defined activities and functions that are intended ultimately to lead to the achievement of the objectives of the organization.

Because stakeholders are involved in every component of the system, staff at the team level, staff and management

> *Leaders from the point of service, the councils, the medical staff, and board converge at the governance council to integrate all efforts around the mission and objectives of the system.*

at the pathway level, staff representatives on the service council, management representatives on the operations council, and staff and management leaders as well as organizational leaders and consultants at the governance level all converge

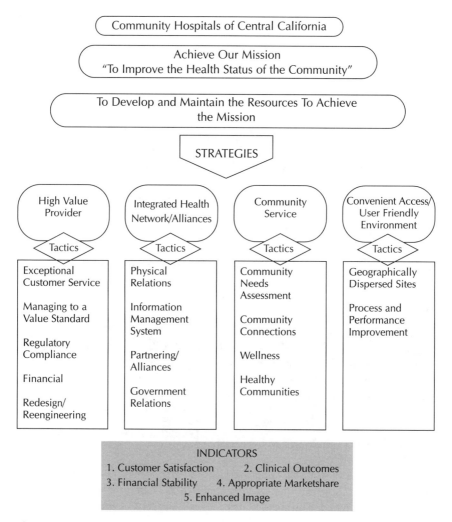

Figure 6-5 Translating Mission into Strategy

to provide a framework for the delineation and implementation of the tactics. Since the tactics are identified in an outcome format, the outcomes toward which the tactics are directed are identified in advance. Consequently, as the outcomes are defined, the organization simply backs into those behaviors, actions, or functions that will facilitate their achievement.

In the past, there was a heavy emphasis on process and action, but today the emphasis is on outcome. Recognition of the need to fit actions to outcomes is now part of the mindset of all leaders. Doing more work and using more resources is not equivalent to providing effective services, and much of the systems noise is caused by the conflict between the old functional expectations and the new focus on fit between resources and essential work.

> *The strategic cascade provides the necessary tools to link strategy, tactics, and outcomes within a seamless connection between elements of the system and the mission to which the system is directed.*

The cascade from strategies to tactics to performance creates an organized and systematic mechanism to link all of the pieces of the organization together and create a seamless connection between process and outcome as well as a linkage to structure. It provides the governance council with a way to continually address the issues of integration and continuum and to identify those places where there are problems or issues or a break in the connection between components. Further, it also creates efficiencies in the system, narrows the place where decisions are made, clarifies accountability, and raises the level of performance expectations. Again, it does not increase the number of points of decision making. Only two points should exist in the organization: the point where decisions are made about service to patients and the point where decisions are made about service to providers. The structure, in other words, should support the

> *The governance council should bring a level of clarity to the intersection of the components of shared governance that will allow any person to enter it and easily know how it works and what people do within it.*

providers in their work and the providers should support the patients in managing their lives and illness experiences along the continuum of service.

Hooking the cascade into the information infrastructure provides an ongoing interface between the daily activities, the clinical paths, the organizational goals and objectives, and the measurement of outcomes. Outcome measurement can occur all along the continuum, so that at every place decisions are made, information that relates to the decisions or any associated decisions is available to whomever needs it. The governance council has the duty to push the organization to further refine information and the information structure to make it possible for more people to have more information about their performance and their relationship with other parts of the organization.

CHALLENGES TO EFFECTIVENESS

There are many problems associated with getting the governance council to work effectively. Many of them arise because of the major shift in the organizational structure that is occurring simultaneously.

> *The most difficult challenge presented by the shift toward shared governance is changing parent–child behavioral dynamics into an adult-to-adult partnership at every level of the system.*

Clearly, the total impact of the changes in roles, expectations, accountability, and functions creates a tremendous challenge for each player in the organization.[19] The move toward consulting rather than managing, for example, causes the leaders to experience extreme stress. Altering their behavior, changing their expectations, defining new roles, building new measures of evaluation, and determining new processes associated with the roles—all of this together can be overwhelming to those undergoing the switch.

The effectiveness of the governance council depends on the performance of the service and operations councils, the effectiveness of the pathways, the integration of the pathways, and the functioning of individuals at the point of service. Developments such as the increased involvement of the medical staff in point-of-service decision making and the closer linking of the medical staff organization and the entire system create substantial noise during the transformation process. In order for

> *No incremental system change can be sustained if it ultimately does not engage the whole system. No one can change one part of a system without ultimately affecting every part of the system.*

effectiveness to be maintained, those at the point of service need development as much as the erstwhile senior-level managers.

SHIFTING THE FOCUS OF WORK

The transfer of work formerly done by senior-level managers into the councils and the pathways is slow and traumatic. Assignments that once belonged to specific vice-presidents now must move to the councils and to other players in the organization. The decision makers that are critical to the effectiveness of the pathways are now the pathway leaders (service leaders). As they develop and grow, they assume more of the responsibility appropriate to their roles. At the same time, responsibility is drawn away from the former vice-presidents, who are now shifting into corporate consulting roles. They experience a sense of lost power and need special support. One good tactic is to maintain an ongoing dialogue so everybody feels that they can have their say.

> *It cannot be expected that shifts in the context and content of work will be received by people with great joy and enthusiasm. The system must respond to loss as effectively as it deals with change.*

INTERFACE WITH THE MEDICAL STAFF

As the medical staff continue to refine their role as a partner in the process, their interface with the system will become increasingly critical. It is important that the medical staff play roles at the governance, service, operations, and point-of-decision-making levels (see Exhibit 6-2). Unfortunately, the movement of physicians from customer to partner also creates much noise in the system.

Physicians are accustomed to having summary authority and being the locus of control for clinical decision making.

> *Physicians play a more intimate role in the decisions of the system, but as partners, not customers. There is a greater focus on outcomes and relationships with other partners, requiring more integrating physician behavior.*

Exhibit 6-2 The Governance Council–Physician Relationship

The governance council
- translates the board's mission and objectives into strategy
- interfaces with the physicians
- ties its strategy regarding physicians to the organizational objectives
- ensures physician integration
- resolves conflicts with physicians

In a team-based format, responsibilities are more broadly defined, and a clear delineation of the accountability of each player is undertaken at the outset of each relationship.

In short, the physician's role undergoes a major change. The physicians must accept a loss of clinical control, develop a partnership orientation, and build relationships at the point of service with other providers. The challenges that these tasks present and the changes in the structure of the medical staff organization have an effect on the physicians' relationship to the shared governance structure.

ENHANCING EFFECTIVENESS IN SHARED GOVERNANCE

As the functional components of the organization move to higher levels of activity and achieve increasing success, the demand for the appropriate functioning of the governance council grows. Change is often slow. It becomes more evident every day during the shift to shared governance that the point-of-service functioning of the teams and pathways is an essential foundation of the viability of the evolving health care organization. As implementation of the whole-systems approach accelerates and begins to achieve desirable outcomes, the performance of the participants starts to stabilize.

> *Shared governance is a journey, not an event. It is not achieved overnight, and there is no conclusion—no point when it is fully in place. It only provides a foundation for further growth.*

The need for quality information, the development of a broad-based information infrastructure, the linkage of tactics to strategy, the need for increasing control over finances at the point of service, and the growing accountability of staff for effective utilization of resources all intensify the demand throughout the organization for support, for integration, and for clarity. It is to these ends that the governance council's work is directed.

CHECKS AND BALANCES

Because of the checks and balances that are inherent in an accountability-based approach, no one council can permanently or negatively affect the integrity of the organizational system. Clearly specified loci of control, point-of-service decision making, accountability-based expectations, a framework for clarifying the roles and functions of each council, and defined roles for managers—these are the types of checks and balances that ensure congruence, integrity, and effectiveness.

The governance council's focus on seamlessness of fit, the integrity of the relationship between the internal and external community, and the building of a supporting information infrastructure to help the system operate more effectively strengthens systemwide decision making. Of course, there will still be problems that arise in clarifying roles and getting the players at the governance council level to agree to act within the context of their emerging roles and in concert with other leadership roles. The demand for role congruence increases in every part of the system and maintains the energy necessary to address issues that have not yet been resolved.

As the cascade becomes linked to the information infrastructure as well as the work process and as the accountability of the councils becomes clarified, effectiveness, measurability, and outcome determination become easier to achieve. The immediacy of decision making, the ability of those at the point of service to make high-level decisions, the timeliness of decision implementation, and the ability of the system to correct errors quickly all represent a level of effectiveness probably never before experienced by the organization. Since the governance council's primary role is to ensure the effectiveness of the system, it is rewarding to the leadership to see desired outcomes being achieved throughout the system at an unanticipated rate.

CONCLUSION

The governance council's most critical role is to link the components of the system together to form a seamless whole. The goal of seamlessness demands that every component of the system serves the organization's objectives. As those objectives become more diverse, the various components must again focus on the outcomes identified at the point of service and evaluate them in light of the expectations of the board. Doing that as partners creates a definitive arena of accountability that ensures that the desired outcomes are achieved without violating the authority, autonomy, and control of any of the components. Every component, whether a council, pathway, or team, has clearly delineated accountability that at some level contributes to the fulfillment of the organization's mission in a very specific way.

Through integrating components, the governance council creates a mechanism for maintaining a focus on the organization's principles and mission. Further, all activities are tied to the direction of the organization as it responds to its obligation to serve the community.

> *To create, to endure, and to create again–that is the requisite course of innovation. Creativity, like change, is a relentless taskmaster, always requiring more growth, more insight, more work.*

At the governance council level, seamlessness becomes the driving force for effectiveness. The council's ability to support other components, its ability to act independently, its willingness to relate interdependently, and its respectfulness toward decisions made at the point of service create a framework for achieving the organization's objectives and sustaining the integrity of the shared governance process and the effectiveness of the organizational activities.

REFERENCES

1. T. Porter-O'Grady, *Implementing Shared Governance* (Baltimore: Mosby, 1992).
2. M. Brown, "The Purpose of Hospital Governance Is Purpose," *Health Care Management Review* 19, no. 2 (1994):89–93.
3. P. Block, *Stewardship: Choosing Service over Self-Interest* (San Francisco: Berrett-Koehler, 1993).
4. G. Beneveniste, *The Twenty-First Century Organization* (San Francisco: Jossey-Bass, 1994).
5. M. Graham and M. Lebaron, *The Horizontal Revolution: Guiding the Teaming Takeover* (San Francisco: Jossey-Bass, 1994).
6. G. Maurer, "True Empowerment: From Shared Governance to Self-managed Work Teams," *Journal of Shared Governance* 1, no.1 (1995):25–30.
7. K. McDonagh, *Nursing Shared Governance* (Atlanta: KJ McDonagh Associates, 1991).
8. H. Coeling and J. Wilcox, "Steps to Collaboration," *Nursing Administration Quarterly* 18, no. 4 (1994):44–55.
9. J. Jenkins, "Professional Governance: The Missing Link," *Nursing Management* 22, no. 8 (1991):26–30.
10. J. Lorsch, "Empowering the Board," *Harvard Business Review* 72, no. 6 (1995):107–118.

11. J. Nirenberg, *The Living Organization: Transforming Teams into Workplace Communities* (Homewood, IL: Irwin Professional Publishing, 1993).

12. R. Johnson, "The Purpose of Hospital Governance." *Health Care Management Review* 19, no. 2 (1994):81–88.

13. T. Kochan and P. Osterman, *The Mutual Gains Enterprise* (Boston: Harvard Business School Press, 1994).

14. K. Evans et al., "Whole Systems Shared Governance: A Model for the Integrated Health System," *Journal of Nursing Administration* 25, no. 5 (1995):18–27.

15. P. Russell and R. Evans, *The Creative Manager* (San Francisco: Jossey-Bass, 1992).

16. R. Blendon and M. Brodie, *Transforming the System: Building a New Structure for a New Century*, The Future of American Health Care Series, vol. 4 (New York: Faulkner & Grey, 1994).

17. N. Imparato and O. Harari, *Jumping the Curve: Innovation and Strategic Choice in an Age of Transition* (San Francisco: Jossey-Bass, 1995).

18. S. Wall and W. Shannon, *The New Strategists: Creating Leaders at All Levels* (New York: The Free Press, 1995).

19. W. Bennis and M. Mische, *The 21st Century Organization: Reinventing through Reengineering* (San Diego, CA: Pfeiffer & Co., 1995).

Chapter 7

Integrating Physicians and Building Provider Partnerships: A Community Hospital System Approach

Phil Hinton and Marsha Parker

The real voyage of discovery is not in seeking new lands, but in having new eyes.

Marcel Proust

THE FORMAL MEDICAL STAFF

The medical staff in most hospital settings is an independent, self-governing organization that reports to the board of trustees, not the hospital administration. In most hospitals, a single medical staff organization serves the system, and the top-level physician committee is the medical executive committee, which has responsibility for quality of medical care within the hospital, medical staff credentialing, delineation of clinical privileges, and the disciplining of medical staff members. The medical executive committee usually consists of the president, the vice-president (president-elect), the chairperson of each department (e.g., medicine, surgery, family practice, Ob-Gyn/peds, and clinical specialties), the chairperson of the credentials committee, the chairperson of the quality management committee, the chairperson of each medical staff council, and representatives from hospital management and the board (see Figure 7-1).

> *Physicians are no longer customers in the health system. They are, instead, partners, creating a whole new set of relationships.*

While a number of simplifications have been made as a result of the evolution to a single integrated medical staff, the remnants of the individual

192

Figure 7-1 Sample Medical Staff Organizational Structure

medical staff councils at each of a system's acute facilities is a reminder that there is a long way to go. Those councils often no longer align with the rest of the structure and increasingly are an obstacle to decisions being made at the point of service. They have less real authority, but everyone wants to include an informational step to the council before any final decisions are implemented. This often results in delays and turmoil that are not contributory to better decisions.

The current medical staff structure in most facilities is being redesigned to more closely align with the system's changing governance structure. Ideally, in a shared governance approach, there will be medical directors associated with each service pathway, and the aggregate group of pathway directors will constitute the new medical executive committee. In this shared governance structure, then, the linkage between the medical staff committee work and the point of service will be dramatically strengthened.

The redesign effort includes changing all medical director contracts to a performance-based format that accommodates medical director participation in the point-of-service multidisciplinary groups. This simplified, more aligned structure provides physicians more direct influence over practice in their most frequented areas. With the participation of physicians on the shared governance corporate councils, there begins real collaboration among the disciplines to govern and operate the whole system from the vantage of their own points of service. Unfortunately, there are some barriers to deal with along the way.

A PHYSICIAN'S VIEW OF BARRIERS TO SHARED GOVERNANCE

The bylaws of the medical staff at most health facilities are designed to protect the rights of the individual medical staff physicians rather than the rights of the patients (regardless of how they read). These bylaws are also intended to give the organized medical staff the maximum authority possible in how the hospital functions. The issue at the heart of the bylaws is control. Indeed, conflicts occasionally arise between the hospital and members of the medical staff, some of whom would like to believe that they should have "veto power" over changes in hospital staffing and organizational structure and decisions regarding hospital reorganizations or closures, mergers with other hospitals, and similar matters.

These same members threaten the hospital administration using time-honored tactics, including threatening to "vote with their feet" and move to other area hospitals if they are not afforded veto power over these decisions. Many members of the medical staff believe that their power rests in demands and threats—which may be true in the vertical, hierarchical power structures they are familiar with. Whole-systems shared governance approaches, however, hinge on team building, collaboration, partnership, interdependence, and accountability—a *horizontal* sharing of power.[1]

INFORMAL STRUCTURES AS BARRIERS

In addition to the formal medical staff structure, there exists another parallel system of informal physician political power related to personality strength, number of hospital admissions, abrasive behavior, racial alignment, religious affiliation, specialty association, heavy competition, referral relationships, and common economic benefits. Each physician feels that he or she is independent, is competent to make decisions of all kinds (regarding medical care, budgeting, planning, and personnel), and has a right to practice unilaterally and often without any constraint from the hospital or other physicians. Trying to organize physicians has often been likened to "herding cats."

In short, many physicians have felt that the hospital is simply their "workshop," a place that exists for their convenience and monetary gain. This historic cultural mindset is a major barrier to collaboration and partnership. Physicians have been acculturated to share power with no one, not even their own peers. In fact, the old medical staff structure is designed as an adversarial system, to "protect" individual physicians from the hospital and to "protect" individual physicians from the organized medical staff itself. As has been evidenced in a number of national cases, the rules as written often made it nearly impossible to discipline physicians for incompetence or intolerable behavior.[2]

> *The independent and unilateral practice of medicine in America is now dead. The physician of the future will exemplify a partner approach to practice in a much stronger team orientation.*

In medical school and residency, there are clear boundaries to behavior, set by deans and residency directors. Breaking the rules of proper behavior at that level of training can result in suspension from the program, so trainees usually behave well. But when the physician is truly "independent," having gained board certification and admission to the hospital medical staff, there are no such firm rules of behavior. The basic lessons learned in kindergarten, such as being nice, sharing, saying "please" and "thank you," are frequently forgotten, and adolescent behaviors are reverted to when any conflict occurs, even a simple dispute over the requirement that a history and physical examination be in a patient's record before a surgical procedure is undertaken.

CHANGES IN INCENTIVES

Before Medicare payments changed the landscape, physicians were paid on a fee-for-service basis, so their income went up as the number of hospital admissions and procedures performed went up. Similarly, the hospital was paid on a fee-for-service basis. Even with the advent of Medicare and hospital reimbursement by diagnosis-related group (DRG) and similar arrangements, the hospital had an incentive to admit as many patients as possible and offer an intense level of care in the shortest possible time. This helped to decrease hospital costs and maximize income.

> *There are no more resources. Anyone looking for more of anything in the current economic environment is engaged in a hopeless task.*

Physicians' incentives were somewhat different. Under the aegis of the new focus on quality of care, physicians gained maximum income by ordering multiple diagnostic tests and performing multiple procedures. Their physician colleagues benefited by multiple referrals during the hospital stay, and the longer the patient stayed in the hospital, the more money the physicians made.

With the implementation of managed care, both physicians and hospitals are paid by capitation, with a fixed fee for total care. This changes all the rules. With a fully capitated system, the incentive for both the physicians and hospital is to manage care. Most contracts provide for shared risks, so that excessive costs by either the hospital or the physicians come out of the pockets of both, and decreased costs by either the hospital or physicians advantages both (see Table 7-1).

In this transitional time, with some patients in managed care and others in fee-for-service arrangements, many physicians do not understand that hospital stays, diagnostic tests, and procedures are costs to the system, not income generators. Many still see the system with old eyes. Some still envision the hospital as the "enemy," trying to decrease physician income by encouraging early hospital discharge (decreasing length of stay [LOS]) and trying to maximize its own income by charging excessive amounts for services rendered and by cutting the number of caregivers to decrease salary expenses.

> *When the price for service is negotiated in advance of service, everything changes in the health system.*

PHYSICIAN DISCONNECTION FROM A SYSTEMS PERSPECTIVE

It should be clear that the medical staff functions in a way that keeps it disconnected from the core of the system. This disconnection, which results in delayed decision making and continuous conflict, weakens the care linkages to the point of service. One senior manager at a hospital created this personal breakthrough statement for working with the medical staff: "At this hospital the collaborative relationships among physicians partners and hospital staff will be so smooth they will result in a complaint-free medical staff." The first reaction to that statement was uproarious laughter from hospital staff and physicians alike. Was the idea expressed really in the realm of the ridiculous? Apparently it was thought to be.

One of the learning outcomes from shared governance and whole-systems theory is that there should be no blame—every member of the system is accountable for the problems generated by the system. Yet in many hospital organizations,

Table 7-1 Alignment of Incentives

	Hospital Admissions*	LOS†	Procedures‡	Patient Health§
Fee for Service				
Hospitals	+	+	+	−
Physicians	+	+	+	−
Medicare DRGs				
Hospitals	+	−	−	−
Physicians	+	+	+	−
Capitation				
Hospitals	−	−	−	+
Physicians	−	−	−	+

*Higher number of hospital admissions.
† Longer length of stay.
‡ Higher number of diagnostic and treatment procedures.
§ Better health for patients.

the historical relationship between physicians and administrators has been one of mutual blame. The physicians have often blamed the administrators for only caring about "dollars" for making cost-cutting decisions that endanger the quality of care, about falling behind on spending for high-tech equipment, and so on. The administrators sometimes blamed physicians for not being enlightened about basic business necessities, about endangering the viability of the organization, about only wanting to further their own agenda to the detriment of their colleagues, and so on (see Figure 7-2).

> **The notion of integrating the medical staff is so unusual that many in the health care system see it as impossible, thus limiting the vision necessary to it ever happening.**

Each side in this scenario expended a great deal of energy trying to find the pressure point that could gain it an advantage. At times, should either side get too much control, something radical would be done to rebalance the scale. For example, the senior management team might be fired or the hospital system might set up physician organizations for the purpose of breaking old referral patterns and shifting power among the physicians. Neither of these solutions led to a healthy relationship between the hospital and the physicians.

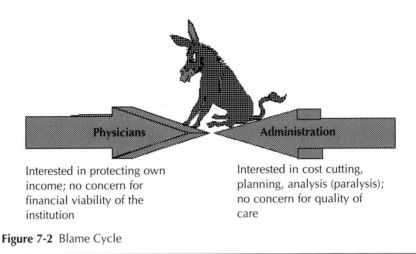

Interested in protecting own income; no concern for financial viability of the institution

Interested in cost cutting, planning, analysis (paralysis); no concern for quality of care

Figure 7-2 Blame Cycle

Clearly, the hospital administrators and physicians have seen themselves as countervailing forces in a system, needing each other but lacking a mechanism for integrating the relationship. Each faction has operated as though their business affairs were completely independent of each other, as by law they have been. Each has tended to the belief that when push came to shove, new physician–hospital relationships could be set up—a belief that increased the risk of never developing committed and more sustainable relationships.

Physician "bonding" activities undertaken by hospitals are often based on the assumption that this kind of relationship is natural and attempt to create loyalty by offering more "goodies" to their physician customers. There is a great deal of effort spent on trying to understand the needs of physicians and appeasing them. There is often some short-term gain from such programs, but the reality of the provider–customer relationship between physicians and hospitals is that demands by one or the other continually become the focus of contention.

> *In the past, physicians and hospitals bonded by offering more "goodies" to each other. Today there are precious few rewards that can be obtained without real partnership.*

Adding to the dilemma are the difficulties that occur when a large organizational system interacts with small group systems or individual systems. Administrators agonize over the anecdotal complaints of physicians that seem so narrowly focused and so broadly communicated that they are frequently impossible to respond to. The example of the angry physician who, having had a frustrating day, storms into the administrative offices and accuses the administration of "lousy quality of care" because of staffing changes in a patient care unit is not an uncommon one. In a classic scenario, the physician loudly recounts a situation in which one staff member proved "incompetent" at observing symptoms and was bathing a patient when a crisis occurred. In another scenario, a physician demands the manager of the area be fired because "patients are being harmed." The appropriate response is to agree there is a problem and to seek a resolution. However, it can happen that the manager, when researching the problem, finds that the problem occurred some time ago, has been corrected, and has nothing to do with why the physician is so angry. Yet the manager might well fail to provide feedback to the physician because there is no easy way to go back and tell the physician that there does not appear to be a replicability. Of course, the physician, receiving no satisfactory feedback, is reaffirmed in his or her belief that administration does not really want to work together on solving problems. It becomes a treadmill of failure, and the underlying causes remain unaddressed (see Figure 7-3).

> *Each physician sees the world from his or her own perspective, not realizing that there is a broader frame of reference that is driving all change in the health care system.*

Old structures and systems reinforce the problem of separateness. The medical staff structure is not only designed to be separate from the delivery structure, it is slow and cumbersome in its decision making, so that any attempt at meaningful learning or collaboration is drained of energy. Old administrative structures can be rigid, and a morass of decision layers can effectively stymie any change efforts. The administration and the medical staff are each independent systems built on the assumption that they are distinct. This is a recipe for conflict. In this arrangement, there is little reason for the members of each of the structures to feel part of the larger whole and accountable for making the system work. When a medical staff committee votes to give itself approval powers over operational changes and when the administration assumes the right to control independent medical care decisions, conflict is engendered.

The dynamic at work here could be viewed from an entirely different perspective that offers up new solutions. If the relationship between the providers is assumed to be central and partner interaction is necessary to manage a patient

Medical Staff

Hierarchy
Coercion
I am the customer
Discussion
Blame

Hospital Staff

Shared governance
Consensus
The *patient* is the customer
Dialogue
Accountability

Figure 7-3 Paradigm Collision

population to a set of standards, the organization takes on a different character. When the living systems are seen by the people who make them up as so interrelated as to be inseparable, the anxiety, fear, and mistrust are offset by the mutual business of taking care of patients. Moving each patient to health becomes easier when the system is healthy.

A lack of understanding of what is to be gained by taking this perspective is the biggest obstacle to obtaining the benefits. The question then becomes, "How can we all begin to feel part of the system, an integral and necessary part of the whole?" This is the fundamental question of shared governance. The first step is to create some sort of vision or shared dream of what the end result could be.

> *Shared governance requires a vision of the interrelated aspects of all the elements of a system, not just the impact of any one component upon the whole.*

VISIONING WHOLE-SYSTEMS SHARED GOVERNANCE

The very first step in developing the vision is to try to get a grasp of what the system is all about. Too many old assumptions keep getting in the way. To demolish the obstacles to understanding the relationships between living systems requires radical intervention. One good method is to engage in a "blank sheet exercise" in which groups sit down to a blank white board or flipchart and begin to discuss what it would take to manage a large, diverse patient population effectively and work toward an understanding of what would be needed beyond what currently exists. The first sessions foster the energy necessary to explore new solutions, and a shared view begins to emerge among the participants. These sessions can have shortcomings, however. If there are not enough physicians in the room when the exercise is done, the view is much too restrictive. In early discussions, the "whole system" is identified as the hospital system, the committed physician organization, and any contracted providers and suppliers. There is no consideration of the connections to other "whole systems" that significantly impact interrelatedness.

> *The stakeholders in a system must be present at the making of decisions that affect what they do. In this case, you must be present to win.*

What will change the perspective is the possibility of merger or partnering with other facilities. Suddenly the patient population numbers radically shift, and a new service mix is introduced. The obstacles to managing the patient population demand that the larger picture be considered. The overall impact serves to intensify the need for the key players to see themselves as part of the whole system rather than separate users of the system.

THE VISION

Once the view of the "whole system" and the shared governance framework emerge, the key players in the system begin to feel the need to restate the concept of their system in terms of an integrated health network (IHN). This approach is not limited to a subset of the local patient population but is designed to take care of a large, diverse patient population along the entire continuum of care. Because the network model is based on whole-systems principles, the most important part of the system is the relationships between the elements of the network and the relationships with the other living systems that contribute to the functioning of the network (see Figure 7-4).

> *The single greatest impediment to a new medical staff partnership is the old medical staff organization. One cannot hold onto yesterday while constructing tomorrow.*

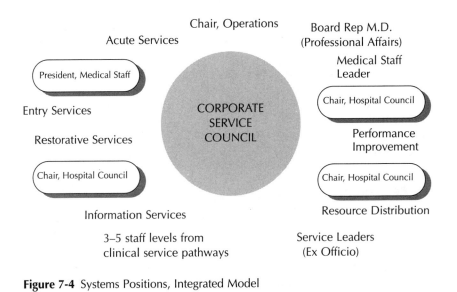

Chair, Operations

Acute Services

President, Medical Staff

Entry Services

Restorative Services

Chair, Hospital Council

Information Services

Board Rep M.D.
(Professional Affairs)

Medical Staff
Leader

Chair, Hospital Council

Performance
Improvement

Chair, Hospital Council

Resource Distribution

CORPORATE
SERVICE
COUNCIL

3–5 staff levels from
clinical service pathways

Service Leaders
(Ex Officio)

Figure 7-4 Systems Positions, Integrated Model

Interestingly, the physicians are going through significant turmoil in trying to get themselves organized at the same time. One of the major hurdles is their own political structure. Several groups exist in most health systems, such as practice groups, physician associations, an existing medical staff organization, and so forth. There are a number of players who still have not yet committed to one of those groups and are watching the activity from a distance. Others have been deliberately excluded. While many physicians realize the necessity of becoming organized to deal with the managed care pressures, they turn to political power and ownership control as a means of addressing the issues. As a consequence, the same dynamic that has kept physicians and administrators at odds for so long is also at work within the physicians' own ranks. Many fall back on old behaviors of mistrust and blame the hospital for their own leaders' inability to get the physicians organized.

Usually the physicians choose a "senior statesman" peer to help the various groups work through their issues and get organized into an "interdependent physician association" or a similar type of coalition made up of physicians committed to making the "system" succeed. When this strategy works and a significant breakthrough is achieved, the painful cost of the turmoil causes some physicians to leave the system. This radical change process reenergizes some of the hospital administrators to assist in integrating activities across the entire system, creating the IHN.

So work on the vision results in some form of IHN identified as the services, systems, and relationships that support the provision of health services and the management of the health of a population up to a set of value standards. The value standard formula is

$$\text{Value standard} = \frac{\text{quality (outcomes)}}{\text{cost (resources)}} \times \text{time (Service)}$$

In managed care, the definition of the "population served" now encompasses not just the managed care members but the whole community. It is the link with the community as a part of the network that helps illustrate how to better integrate the physician group.

STRUCTURING TO SUPPORT THE VISION

Driving much of the new vision is the urgent need to move to a managed care type of organization and to stay strategically flexible in the rapidly changing environment. The strategy is to implement a continuum model of care.

The continuum can be identified here as a master pathway where subscribers (people) are managed so they reach best health status and different detour pathways used when a subscriber is having an acute episode. The goal of the health system is to manage care in a way that moves members (subscribers) back to the master pathway as soon as possible. The master pathway is managed mostly by primary care physicians, and the detour pathways are managed mostly by specialists. The detour pathways within an integrated care model are arranged into at least seven major pathways, three of which are continuum of care pathways (entry, acute, and restorative) and three support pathways (information management, performance improvement, and resource distribution). The seventh pathway is a standards pathway that might be called the "best practice institute," and it is there, in large part, that a link exists for connecting physicians, the community, and the rest of the delivery system. Using a structure of best practices, physicians can sit with other providers and community members to perform a truly interdisciplinary assessment of community and subset population health needs. They then can develop standards designed to meet those needs and measure outcomes.

Conceptually, members enter the master path when they:

- sign up for a plan served by the IHN
- go to any IHN system entry point
- apply for agency assistance as indigents

The physician office and clinic are the most common entry points for most people. Interestingly, they offer the least information when the member arrives. In the new whole-systems vision, the physician-managed point of service (usually a physician's office) would be the place with the most information related to management of the life of the individual member. The structuring of the information system around this vision and the "whole systems" needs is one of the critical success factors in a whole-systems shared governance model.

> *Physicians must be tied into the information system early in order to change their practice so it is supportive of a systems approach.*

Information system restructuring began with the evolution of the information systems departments into an information management pathway and the placement of all the old information-collecting, -processing, -analyzing, and -reporting jobs into process teams accountable for outcomes. Those outcomes relate back to the continuum tactics (the work of the patient care and operations councils). The next step is to integrate the information management efforts of the medical staff organization with the hospital system efforts to create an IHN.

During the struggles to find the right kind of organizational structure, an informal survey of key physicians can be useful. The single question is, "If you had a magic wand and could make anything at all happen, what questions about managed care would you have answered?" The following questions are commonly cited:

- Where do I learn how to manage care in a capitated environment?
- How can I find out how I am performing compared with my peers?
- Where can I find the information and the method for managing a capitation budget so I know if I am making money doing this?
- How can I have input in setting the standards against which I am measured?

Answering these four questions provides a good foundation for the design of the organizational structure and the supporting systems. The design task is a huge undertaking and requires the board of directors to focus on the need for automated support for the whole integrated health network. The clinical information system, the network infrastructure, the shared governance decision support system, the office management systems, and electronic inpatient and outpatient medical record systems have to be selected and linked based on the answers to the above questions.

In designing the information process, the physician member of the information management steering committee (the chair, if possible) must have the expertise to understand the greater system design needs and the importance of including physicians in the information system redesign process as early as possible. However, just because some physicians and hospital staff come up with a great vision does not mean it is acceptable. Aside from vision and structure, there are other elements of successful physician integration to develop:

- visible inclusionary activities
- communication of the whole systems view
- results of "best practice"
- finding and fixing underlying causes of conflict
- participation in shared governance decision making

SEEING THE FUTURE

It is wise for hospital leadership to see the future clearly and make changes to prepare for managed care. This is easier for the hospital because it has an incentive, as it had with the old system, to manage costs for maximum benefit. Bringing the physicians along is more problematic. Even when presented with clear explanations of the changes, many physicians retain their fee-for-service mindset and sometimes refuse to let go of the idea that the hospital is their enemy (or at least their workshop, to do with as they like).

In the midst of this kind of turmoil, the hospital's leadership must look at the future anew. The CEO and the board must make a critical decision that in many ways will threaten the relationship between the physicians and the organization further—to proceed with a complete corporate reengineering, the institution of whole-systems shared governance, a radical flattening of corporate layers, and a redesign of processes to achieve breakthrough improvements in cost and quality. The hospital getting ready for the future must embrace change. Instituting shared governance entails a sweeping change of the corporate structure.

THE IMPLEMENTING EXPERIENCE

Making a change of this nature requires both commitment and caution. The first steps taken to implement a different way of making decisions will create organizational "noise" and will be difficult for the physicians to accept.

The medical staff and the hospital experience a paradigm collision in implementing shared governance. Before shared governance, it is hierarchy versus hierarchy, raw political muscle versus backroom politics in a balance of power not unlike that brought about by a state of mutual assured destruction. With the new hospital structure, the medical staff bureaucracy can run headlong into shared governance councils. Coercion confronts decisions made by interdisciplinary caregivers (like nurses and environmental workers). Physicians attempt to retain their customer orientation (I am the doctor, I am the customer). There is little evidence of a partnership mindset. There is still a desire to control (use of power to get what is wanted by avoiding facts that might be detrimental to a unilateral argument). In the beginning, no dialogue is undertaken (no putting assumptions on the table, no inquiring if there are other ideas that might show assumptions to be incorrect), and much blame is present. There is little evidence of personal accountability (adult-to-adult interaction). Predictably, the medical staff's formal and informal structures are increasingly ineffective in communicating need or resolving problems in the emerging shared governance structure (see Figure 7-5).

> *Polarization cannot survive in a partner-driven organization. No unilateral agenda processes can long thrive in such a system.*

INVITING THE MEDICAL STAFF

The initial response of the hospital shared governance councils is to invite the formal medical staff organization into the "points of power," teach the staff to dialogue, allow their participation in decision making, and demand accountability. This is a major change from the usual structure, in which the physicians' responsibility is merely to identify problems, complain about them, and expect someone else to solve them. The best strategy is obvious: align incentives for the medical staff so that the success of the hospital is their success, and vice versa.

> *In health care, there is no us or them; there is only we.*

As the shared governance structure gets started (the experimental prototype for the whole system), the medical staff council soon realizes that decisions are being made by the governance councils rather than individual hospital administrators.

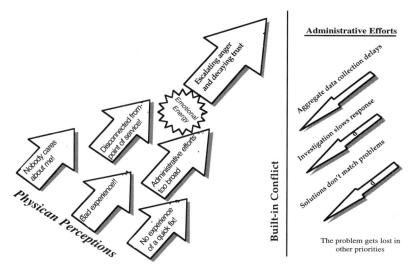

Figure 7-5 Perceptual Conflict

Sometimes in the beginning, the organization, in driving the creation of shared governance, adds members to councils from nursing, the administration, and other hospital disciplines and gives them a defined role in council proceedings. Wise implementors of the governance council usually add physician members.

INTEGRATING PHYSICIANS INTO THE WHOLE SYSTEM

When whole-systems shared governance is structured within the health system redesign, the new single medical staff organization often deals with many of the same problems on a larger scale. Physician members of the medical staff should be invited to participate in the governance council, operations council, and patient care council. Meetings must be scheduled so that the physicians can attend without disrupting their office hours. Even if this is done,

> *Commitment to the decision-making process in shared governance is necessary to ensure the long-term efficacy of team activity.*

however, physician attendance at the outset is frequently poor. Reluctance to attend sometimes derives from the structure of the shared governance meetings.

When the physicians realize that decisions are made after extensive dialogue and the uncovering of assumptions, and that other caregivers have an equal voice, they are less interested in participating. Their idea of participation is that, if an issue is of interest to them, they will participate and have their solution adopted. Rarely have they been part of a diverse decision-making process in which they are not the only stakeholders who have an important role.

As an example of what can happen, consider this possible scenario. The entry pathway council is where decisions are made about the process of care in the emergency room. A key medical staff member, such as the physician in charge of quality in the ER, might be invited to participate in the new council's deliberations. He is well liked by the nurses, other caregivers, and the medical staff in general. He is viewed as fair, experienced, and open to change. But when his "solutions" to the ER problems are challenged, sometimes even by the least powerful people on the team (e.g., environmental workers, ward clerks, or administrative partners), his feelings become hurt and he might complain that his broader medical knowledge is not affording him the influence over the decision-making process that he thought he deserved. He may characterize the shared decision-making process as "status collaboratis"—a condition similar to status epilepticus, where random chaotic flailing motions result in no forward motion. But suppose he is committed and persistent enough to stay in the process and does not quit the pathway council. As the council moves toward consensus on how to improve the processes in the ER, the physician might begin to understand the importance of looking at the process from the standpoint of the other stakeholders.

> **Physicians are members of the team. As members, they participate in the dialogue; they do not control it.**

The final decisions that emerge from the team process are clearly superior to the physician's initial proposed solutions, and he eventually ceases to enumerate at medical staff meetings the ways in which shared governance structure does not work. Indeed, he becomes a champion of the shared governance approach and defends the decisions of the council against the objections of his fellow physicians—and he might even seek their cooperation. He soon becomes accountable. Problems uncovered are owned and solved, not stated and complained about.

As the medical staff realize that their normal power base is eroding away, their first reactionary move might be to demand veto power over all decisions of the shared governance councils. When this move is (predictably) rebuffed, their next request might be to be afforded input into administrative decisions that will affect physicians and their work. This is a step toward acting in concert with the councils, because it fits with the shared governance principle that decisions should be made by those affected by the decision (stakeholders).

It is best to arrange a meeting between the medical staff leadership (members of the medical executive committee) and representatives of the shared governance and pathway councils at the beginning of the implementation effort. Each medical staff leadership position should be examined in light of its function and intended sphere of authority and responsibility and should be assigned a place in the shared governance structure. It should be recognized that a primary goal of shared governance is to bring 90 percent of all decision making to the point of service and that physicians retain power by being located at the provider team level, on the care units where the patients are served.

PHYSICIAN ROLES IN THE CORPORATE SHARED GOVERNANCE COUNCILS

Physicians must be present at critical decision making at the point of service where they have a major stake in its outcome.

The membership of the patient care council, since the council deals with the way the work gets done, should include someone who represents the president of the medical staff. The decision to have broad-based medical staff representation is justified by the wide range of responsibilities of the medical staff members. The top leadership of the medical staff has primary accountability for the quality of medical care delivered by the medical staff members. Other medical staff leaders may have responsibility for "site-specific issues" (mainly quality issues) of interest to the medical staff, and they should also be members of the patient care council or present at its meetings.

In return for sitting on the councils, the medical staff members are expected to communicate the council's decisions to the rest of the medical staff and defend those decisions. They are expected to provide input regarding the needs of the medical staff, not to try to subvert the decision-making process for their own ends. They are expected to respect the other members of the councils and treat them as equal representatives with viewpoints that must be considered before changes are made. Getting the medical staff to become invested in shared governance is a continuous, unending process that will require patience and persistence and an effective strategy (Exhibit 7-1).

Exhibit 7-1 Strategies To Win Over Physicians

- Role-model desired behaviors.
- Overeducate on concept.
- Keep overinformed.
- Ask advice frequently.
- Ask for help.
- Give credit freely.

THE MEDICAL STAFF, GOVERNANCE, AND OPERATIONS

The operations council must also have a representative from the medical staff leadership. This is necessary because the medical staff share in the deliberations regarding capital requests and their priority. The consulting partner for medical affairs (see Chapter 6) is also a full participating member. The leadership of the operations council must realize that the hospital-based physicians are critical to decision making about infrastructure, such as the information system, facility construction, and clinical equipment.

Representation reflects ownership of decisions and influence over key outcomes that define the viability of the system.

The governance council, which devises strategies for the system and translates the board's direction into a practical plan for implementation, should have a key member of the medical staff as a member. It is preferable that the chief or president of the medical staff be that member, since so much of the work of the organized medical staff must harmonize with the work of others in the system. Since setting policy, translating the mission into strategies, is the primary job of this council, this medical staff member is the most appropriate for the job.

MEDICAL STAFF INTEGRATION INTO THE PATHWAYS

Following are suggested assignments of the medical staff leaders to the decision groups developed within each pathway. The chair of the department of medicine sits on the medical pathway council, the chair of the department of surgery sits on the surgical pathway council, the chair of the Ob-Gyn/peds service sits on the maternal/child pathway council, and the chair of the department of family practice is assigned to primary care and sits on the home services pathway council.

The paid medical directors (e.g., the directors of cardiology, radiology, laboratory, rehab, and psych) are assigned to appropriate pathway councils and provider teams: the medical director of cardiology is assigned to the cardiopulmonary pathway council, the director of rehabilitation to the restorative pathway council, and so on. Many of the provider teams will want to participate in the orientation of the physician member to integrative and partner-based decision making.

THE MEDICAL STAFF AND DECISION MAKING

A fundamental shared governance principle is that those who are affected by a decision should have a voice in making that decision. The major part of the medical staff input, therefore, is at the service level, because the medical staff is primarily interested in how the work gets done, the quality of that work, the competency of the caregivers, and the education and health of patients. This means that the primary place to integrate physicians is in provider teams, pathway councils, and the patient care council. For issues related to resource use, like capital requests and new services, the appropriate medical staff representative for the operations council is the medical staff officer usually assigned these duties. For policy and planning, especially strategic planning related to community needs assessment, governance council input from the president of the medical staff is important.

> *The key medical staff leaders are also key decision makers in the council format. All stakeholders are located in the same place.*

The object of integrating physicians and building provider relationships is to improve the care of the patient. The overall corporate mission is to improve the health of the entire community. Achieving improvement requires a whole-systems approach. Managing patients to a value standard is the method of choice for the enlightened health system. Managing patients to a value standard means using proven treatment methods routinely to achieve higher quality outcomes at lower cost.

The progressive medical staff, in partnership with all providers of service, select treatment methods based on "best practices" research (e.g., literature reviews), and expert decision methods (algorithms developed by experts in the field augmented by available research). Best practices are those methods that achieve high-quality outcomes with low resource use. We can define high-quality outcomes as including a low mortality rate compared with an "expected rate" adjusted for severity of illness and a low complication rate (a low morbidity rate compared with an expected rate). Low resource use means low rates of referral, low lab and X-ray usage, short hospital stays, low home health and medication costs, and so on. The highest possible health status and the lowest cost often go hand in hand, as in the case of surgical procedures. It is obvious (and easily documented) that surgical procedures performed smoothly cost far less than those plagued by untoward incidents, accidents, and complications. The shared governance process makes the obtaining of desired outcomes the work of all.

> *Managing to a value standard in shared governance becomes the work of every stakeholder. Outcomes are obtained through the efforts of the team, not just the work of any one member.*

To involve the physicians with the hospital in a partnership rather than a competition requires a change of tactics. Physicians are interested in quality care. Their entire training prepares them to engage in intense discussions on how to achieve better results. Even though their economic incentives are not always aligned with the hospital's, the clinical objectives are the same: excellent patient care and good clinical outcomes. Building on this shared vision, alignment of hospital and physicians is possible. If a method could be found to identify what type of care represents "best practice," if the physicians could be convinced of the superiority of this type of care, and if the hospital systems could be modified to support it, the requirements for partnership would be met.

PHYSICIANS AT THE POINT OF SERVICE

> *When outcomes require a different approach, it is the attachment to our rituals and routines that gets in the way of making any real change.*

Locating the physician at the point of care is critical for successful physician investment in shared governance. If physician opinion is obtained at the provider team level about care, good decisions will result.

An example of a successful process might be resolution of the chart location problem that exists in many hospitals. Because of the validating data in the nursing research literature and a desire to simplify the charting process, nurses have often promoted the idea of moving the vital signs chart to the bedside. There is justification for this. If the person taking the vital signs records the data right away at the bedside, including intake and output (I&O) data, the accuracy of the data is enhanced and the chance for error is reduced. It is a simpler process, has fewer steps, and results in fewer delays. However, most hospitals are still on a "paper chart" system, with change to electronic records still sometimes years away.

Moving the vital signs record to the bedside affects more than the nursing caregivers. Frequently, after the decision to move the record is made, the physicians arrive on the unit to make rounds but cannot find the records since they are not where expected. It is then possible a physician might have to go into a room to see the patient and family without knowing the vital signs and fluid intake and output for the previous night and might have to struggle to obtain the information in the room in front of the family. If the decision to move the record is reevaluated, the physicians and nurses can both provide input, and some modification of the process may result. Even though the problem will ultimately be solved when the electronic medical record becomes standard, in the interim dialogue and accommodation may need to be a part of the documentation management strategy.

PHYSICIANS AND THE CRITICAL PATH

The basic tool currently used for managing patients to a value standard is the clinical protocol, critical pathway, or care path. This protocol is a care plan for a particular diagnosis or problem, based on best practices, research, and algorithms. In the shared governance approach, it is developed at the point of service through engagement of the stakeholders on the individual provider teams. Each path includes multidisciplinary documentation that identifies expected outcomes on a shift-to-shift basis, an associated physician prescription set, a patient information brochure, and a pain control documentation sheet.

> *In systems approaches, problems do not belong to any one individual. If an issue affects the relationship between the partners and their work processes, it is everyone's problem.*

Good documentation sets forth the expected clinical activities, the proper treatments, the expected outcomes, the required labs, and the key decision points.

Deviation from the plan requires reassessment of the patient, with changes in care and treatment aimed at getting the patient back on the path. Documentation "by exception" is increasingly used, meaning that if the desired outcome is achieved, no writing is necessary. If a particular goal is not accomplished or a treatment not provided, documentation is required to identify the variance and to make plans for corrective action.

BECOMING INCLUSIVE

Just getting the hospital staff to begin including physicians in their decision making is usually more difficult than anticipated. Meeting times have to be changed so physicians can attend (meetings before and after regular business hours and at noon are often more acceptable). Physicians are not prepared to function in groups that value and use dialogue and consensus processes. Many have difficulty in understanding and complying with the basic rules of engagement and often use old behaviors to attempt to control or influence outcomes. However, most are very valuable members of their groups and will attend more regularly when they realize there is no other means of influencing decisions in the shared governance approach. New partnership methods of linkage in decision making gradually eliminate the "old" methods (see Exhibit 7-2).

> *In shared governance, the "old" method of deciding is ended. The "new rules" don't permit manipulation of the system in the interests of a single agenda.*

Once shared governance becomes the mode for decision making, the interest of physicians increases and their behavior becomes more consistent (their interest in attending meetings also improves). Collaboration among all the members of caregiving teams and physicians begins to develop, and the locus of control continues to shift toward the point of service.

COMMUNICATION: TRYING TO "RECONNECT"

One of the most visible inclusionary activities in shared governance is the assessment and implementation of new ways of working together. Because the new shared governance structure means that managers and staff council members become very mobile, the old office-based activities and meeting site gatherings

Exhibit 7-2 Operating Objectives for Physicians

- Continually improve quality of care and service
- Improve continuity of care
- Create partnerships
- Increase resource and operations effectiveness
- Increase amount of teamwork and collaboration

become less effective. This is especially true in the emerging multiservice and multisite systems. The creation of the virtual office is going to change the way that people do business and make decisions in the future.

The way to "connect" to exchange information or to come to a decision is no longer just to call a meeting or invite someone to one's office. The establishment of an integrated information network infrastructure and the installation of Lotus Notes and comparable software allow everyone to communicate fluidly not only through e-mail but within whole projects, since users can sit down in any work-space and access their work.

Perhaps the most interesting capability is the "virtual meeting" format that can be implemented by the point-of-service leadership. Any initiator of an idea or champion of an issue can hold a brainstorming session on line. Options include participation by physicians in brainstorming, decision making, and project development—and all this is possible without the physicians' having to leave their offices or attend meetings at inconvenient times.

CRITICAL COMMUNICATION

Communication in a shared governance system is usually less effective than it should be. While every existing tool is used to communicate, often there is poor penetration. Suggested means of getting the messages out include these:

- Newsletter. A physician newsletter should be published every two weeks (if not more frequently).
- Bulletin. An electronic bulletin should be published daily and posted on the units using the e-mail system. Most physicians should receive it electronically.
- Memos and postings. Cork boards in key places like the physician lounge and the entrance to the cafeteria can be used to post information.
- Medical staff meetings. Regular meetings are usually held monthly, and the minutes are reviewed by many other groups as well. Staff members can routinely report changes.

- Minutes. Minutes from unit team meetings should be made available to anyone who has an interest in reading them.
- The information network. Information should be shared weekly to reach those physicians not in attendance.

These usual means of communication do not always overcome the problem of penetration. Additional methods can be pursued:

- Shared points and the agenda from each shared governance meeting can be posted in the physician lounge and published in all the physicians' communication media.
- Cards with contact person phone numbers by specialty can be created and distributed among the physicians.
- Storyboards showing changes being made, their targets, and their progress to date can be created. Eventually, most service areas should have permanent storyboard areas.
- Poster size "checkbook registers" can be posted in all the care areas so physicians can see how the care area money is being spent.
- Unit and special teams can meet with physicians individually and in groups to discuss specific changes. More than one meeting can be held on a specific change.
- Issues and changes and also how they fit into the whole systems should be communicated. The context of an issue or change is as important as the issue or change itself.

Time must be allotted for the suggested "new way to work" systems to help increase penetration of information. In shared governance it is affirmed that a new idea is never communicated enough, and it is worth a great deal of effort to repeat and repeat again the context for any communication.

> *Getting to the underlying causes of conflict is a painful process for all involved. A safe space must be available to confront the issues in a nonjudging but direct manner.*

Results of the "best practices" process should be communicated only through a protocol-tracking system. The results of the protocol application process should show improvements in both cost and quality of care. In the development of protocols based on "best practices," it takes at least a year of reporting, including physician reviews, before a critical mass of support and meaningful data are achieved. Protocol performance must be reported in all the medical staff committees as well as in the patient care and pathway councils. The ideal target for physicians is to manage at least 80 percent of the inpatient business according to value standards, creating a critical mass for faster implementation of value standard tools, protocols, and information systems. Basing all practice standards on best practices will energize more physicians, increasing their participation and improving outcomes.

RESOLVING CONFLICT

Finding and fixing underlying causes of conflict are especially challenging. The political uproar that accompanies reformatting the medical staff creates a terrible distraction and results in an environment bereft of trust for a period of time. Because there are only a few physicians who fully grasp the concepts of shared governance, the discussions of conflict cannot start with causal loop illustrations. They must start at a more elementary point and build to the kind of trusting collaboration that gets into the more painful truths related to underlying causes. Using the work of the "best practice" process as a vehicle to demonstrate, not just propose, benefits is a method of validating whole-systems clinical processes and integrative decision making. Since the "best practices" process offers an opportunity for research and development and causes everyone to feel more open to new ideas, it provides fertile ground for real problem resolution for physicians and others.

GOVERNANCE FOR THE NEW VISION

Governance structures to support the pathways are always slow in being transformed into a truly integrated network model. The management service organization (medical staff organization [MSO]) usually has its own traditional structure, and this structure will affect how the hospital system builds its shared governance structure. Throughout the process, teams of physicians and other partners must work on blending the functional areas

> *The partnership between medical staff and system requires clear points of intersection where the interests of both can be negotiated and integrated.*

of the two organizations based on clinical practice and their business interdependencies.

One team can be assigned the job of designing the way the whole service system should work over time. The process of physician–hospital partnership and integration is linked closely to the assessment of the community needs and to the ultimate structure of the IHN. This team can be a blend of physicians, hospital leaders, MSO leaders, and even community representatives. Discussions must at first center around the needs of the various elements of the network to have a say in decisions affecting the network. Since the recurring issue of control centers around ownership or partnership, the element of unilateral control is removed by creating a model showing the functional relationships of the network members supported through management service agreements that would link the MSO decision processes to that identified in the shared governance system, creating the foundation for real partnership (see Figure 7-6).

In the shared governance structure, a community development team can survey the community of subscribers, prioritize their needs, and use the information for deliberations on how to achieve a truly integrated system. The group need not have "line authority" except that given it by all the members of the emerging network. It is empowered to review the community needs and the network needs and propose changes to determine the organizing and relational priorities for the coming year (or years) for the new partners. Those priorities are then built into the management service agreements between the medical and health system partners. Everyone participates in the setting of service priorities, and each entity can feel comfortable that their particular needs and contributions have been considered.

STRATEGY PRIORITIES

It is the job of the governance council and the MSO board to prioritize strategies for their organizations and to incorporate the recommendations of their work groups (such as the community assessment group mentioned above) into those strategies. It is also their job to see to it that the objectives to be achieved by the strategies are clearly articulated and carried out as agreed to by their organizations. The communication responsibility of these two groups is twofold: they report the strategies to the operations and patient care groups in each of their organizations and to the governance council and the governing board(s). The MSO board reports the strategies to the constituent organizations and physician members.

The MSO management leadership and the operations council focus on resource management in the five resource areas: fiscal, material, human, systems, and sup-

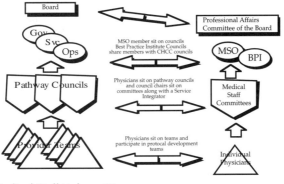

Figure 7-6 Medical Staff Linkage Diagram

port (see Chapters 2 and 5). As the physicians become increasingly integrated, the two separate operations processes will overlap more often. Having members from both systems (medical staff and provider partners) on all councils ensures that the work can be better organized and duplication avoided.

Through the "best practices" process, physicians can interact significantly with the patient care council (all providers). Both are accountable for how clinical work is done. The focus of these groups is the point-of-service connection between what the community needs and what is delivered. These are the groups that look at ways to continuously improve the quality of service delivery by using "best practices" principles in the development of practice standards (see Figure 7-7)

> *Many of the current separate functions of the medical staff will disappear as they become more integrated within the system.*

These network relationships exemplify the kind of functional relationships that hold the network together. There are many other tasks, such as contracting, community assessment, and claims management, that can be more efficiently performed in a joint manner than done separately. Such tasks can be performed anywhere and are sometimes undertaken either by the health system or by the MSO. As long as there is agreement about the level of service to be provided and a group to determine priorities for development, the needs of the network should always be met.

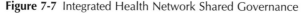

Figure 7-7 Integrated Health Network Shared Governance

Physician integration into the shared governance structure has already begun in many systems. The interfacing MSO should be designed to extend that integration. Each of the main shared governance corporate councils (governance, operations, and patient care) should have physician members, and the pathway and provider team groups at the point of service also should each have physician members. Early on, decisions shift closer to the point of service, and the corporate-level groups should be setting priorities, determining policies, and making any decisions that will have an impact across all service areas. The partnership between the medical staff organization and the system facilitates full continuum planning and decision making by paralleling the health system's work with the MSO and connecting physician-related structures through the application of shared governance concepts (see Figure 7-8).

> *The real struggle for physicians is seeing themselves as a partner in the health system rather than controllers of it.*

The goal of the medical staff and system leaders should be to ensure that all the medical staff committees eventually merge with pathway councils or corporate councils and that the joined yet parallel structures of the health system and MSO become completely merged. The whole system will thus become committed to

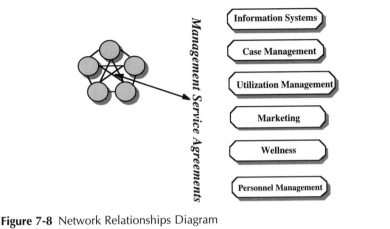

Figure 7-8 Network Relationships Diagram

addressing best practices for the community that they serve together. As this chapter indicates, there are clearly many barriers to overcome to realize this goal, but a careful and phased approach will be likely the most successful one.

SHARED GOVERNANCE AND MANAGED CARE

As in many struggles, the real reasons for conflict are sometimes lost in the turmoil of raging emotions and feelings of the moment. The urge to strike out or retaliate for the painful parts of the change process often overcome the craving for an amicable settlement of the issue. In *Getting to Yes*, Fisher and Ury describe the dangers of position bargaining: "As more attention is paid to personal positions, less attention is devoted to meeting the underlying concerns of the parties. Agreement becomes less likely."[3(p.36)]

Talking about interests, options, and standards offers a basis for getting to an agreement. The principles of shared governance (equity, ownership, accountability, and partnership) reveal themselves through this same type of dialogue. But shared governance provides the option to go a step further than expressing these principles within the limits of a trained negotiating team. Instead, understanding the interests, options, and standards of another stakeholder group becomes the business of everyone in the system. This has extremely important implications for a physician in deciding whether or not to align with a particular system.

A scenario that exemplifies this dynamic is unfolding in one way or another in many health systems. It has to do with the security of livelihood and the quality of work life. It plays out daily through the point-of-service decisions that affect physician interests. When physicians are active collaborators in the processes associated with shared governance, whether it be in councils, provider teams, or at the point of service, the other members of the system begin to understand and appreciate their perspective and concerns.

Suppose, for example, an internist who serves on the patient care council is asked to address a provider team working on the new computer system. This physician has grown comfortable talking openly with multidisciplinary groups of providers with entirely different training and background from her own, and the team has also reached a comfort level and believes the physician to be reasonable and sensitive to her patients' needs. During the dialogue, the physician is asked to describe what her rounds are like. The entire team is shocked at the delays and barriers the physician states she must overcome every single time she makes rounds. Laying the information out on a flipchart, the team might find that the existing systems cause nearly two hours per day of wasted time—time spent waiting for, hunting down, or verifying information. Needless to say, this finding would have enormous implications for the design of a new information system.

> *When an individual projects a unilateral agenda, there is no interest in what is best or right. Instead, there is an effort to achieve a singular goal without broad enough ownership to sustain it.*

How might the shared governance structure affect the physician's role and sense of security? By participating in the shared governance structure, the physician is more likely to know what is going on in the system as well as have an impact on decisions at the point of service. Indeed, substantial benefits—such as information about best practices for a particular diagnosis, a course on managing populations

> *Focusing on the same issues, partners can begin to really work on barriers to their relationship and the effectiveness of their work.*

to a value standard, or case reviews and grand rounds—will be more readily available to this physician (and of course the system will gain from the physician's participation as well). When a new program is designed, for example, the physician is more likely to benefit from it if she was involved in the design process.

In the managed care market, a physician can lose huge chunks of his or her practice through the simple act of signing a contract. As long as the ebb and flow of the market tides continue to pull at physicians, there will be anxiety and concern. Investment in the emerging system offsets the dangers of wrong decisions and ties the physician's success to the success of the whole system.

In the process of implementing shared governance, there are a few simple principles physicians must keep in mind as they integrate with the health system. Shared governance is an accountability-based approach to structuring relationships. Therefore, personal and collective accountability is central to the success of decisions in the system. Physician members must apply the same rules of accountability as everyone if their role and participation in the system is to bear any real fruit. For example, they must

- reach an understanding of commitment to a process and the accountability entailed by it before embarking
- hold everyone accountable for his or her performance in and out of the meeting related to implementing the decision
- never sway from the targets set by the group
- be prepared for a large outlay of energy
- never stop learning
- respect all participants

A FEW QUESTIONS FOR THE PHYSICIAN'S SHARED GOVERNANCE JOURNEY

Implementing shared governance raises some unresolved questions for physicians as they confront the issues of health system integration:

- What benefits do physicians gain from being members of a system instead of independent practitioners?
- Market dynamics and health care economics are powerful and often negative forces that batter physician and health care system alike. Will membership in a "system" protect the physicians or make them more vulnerable? Can the system be protected without harming any individual physician?
- How can the long-term perceptual and cultural conflicts be removed to enhance the value of partnership and begin the long road to the trusting relationships characteristic of shared governance?

WHAT SEEMS TO BE WORKING SO FAR

The evidence for what works for physicians in a shared governance framework is growing. The consistent application of these rules, for example, seems to facilitate the achievement of sustainable outcomes:

- Locate physicians at power points for decision making, then hold them accountable for decisions made there and for defending them to the rest of their medical staff "partners."
- Move point-of-service decisions to the team of caregivers. Decisions are best made when the physician makes rounds with the care team.
- Convert waste time for physicians to productive time. Using communication tools set up in the units, surgical lounge, physician lounge, medical records completion areas, and offices, allow physicians to focus on issues and their role in solution seeking. Tools for automated brainstorming, collecting input from physicians, information sharing for proposals, planning, and solution seeking must be provided.
- Dialogue, dialogue, dialogue—even when it is noisy and painful. Understanding the issues, interests, options, and standards that are important to work effectiveness and relationship building is the first step toward partnership.
- Take the broad view and try to grasp the "whole system" so that each "piece" can be kept in proper perspective.

THE FUTURE FOR PHYSICIAN PARTNERS IN SHARED GOVERNANCE

The term "best practices" has at least three meanings. It is used to define the philosophy of organizing all clinical functions to constantly improve practices of any kind. It is used to describe practices that surpass all other practices commonly used in effectiveness and efficiency. Finally, it is used to refer to the process in which research and development of "best practices" anywhere in the organization are supported. No matter how "best practices" is defined, it can be used to help answer four questions that physicians feel are key:

1. Where do I learn how to manage care in a capitated environment?
2. How can I find out how I am performing compared with my peers?
3. Where can I find the information and the method for managing a capitation budget so I know if I am making money providing services?

4. How can I have input into the creation of the standards against which I will be measured?

In committing resources to help the physicians answer these questions, the system is building partnership. When physicians create protocols designed around "best practices" through their medical staff committee process, they are building a partnership. When physicians are fully invested in working with other providers at the point of service, that too is building partnership. When managing a member population to a value standard becomes the theme for the IHN and those efforts are supported by the "best practices" process, everyone is working as a partner—a fully engaged member of a health system that values his or her membership. The task of creating a structure that builds and sustains partnership lies at the heart of shared governance efforts.

It takes some real visible successes for everyone to feel the kind of trust in the system that will make it sustainable, but the foundations can be strongly laid and ready to support full physician integration into a shared decision-making framework. Such is the intent of the shared governance approach. Perhaps, through this approach the goal of a complaint-free and fully invested physician partnership is not so far-fetched after all.

REFERENCES

1. H. Coeling and J. Wilcox, "Steps to Collaboration," *Nursing Administration Quarterly* 18, no. 4 (1994):44–55.
2. M. Young, S. Rallison, and P. Eckman, "Patients, Physicians, and Professional Knowledge," *Hospitals and Health Services Administration* 40, no. 1 (1995):40–49.
3. R. Fisher and W. Ury, *Getting to Yes: Negotiating Agreement without Giving In*, 2nd ed. (New York: Penguin, 1991), 36.

SUGGESTED READING

Ackoff, R. 1994. *The democratic corporation.* New York: Oxford University Press.
Baker, J. 1995. They may want to take charge, but can physicians really organize? *Journal of Health Care Finance*, 21, no. 3:6–8.
Coeling, H., and J. Wilcox. 1994. Steps to collaboration. *Nursing Administration Quarterly* 18, no. 4:44–55.
Deckard, G. 1995. Physician responses to a managed environment: A perceptual paradox. *Health Care Management Review* 20, no.1:40–46.
Fisher, R., and W. Ury. 1991. *Getting to yes: Negotiating agreement without giving in.* 2nd ed. New York: Penguin.
Gamliel, S., et al. 1995. Will physicians meet the managed care challenge? *Health Affairs* 14:131–142.
Goldsmith, J. 1993. Driving the nitroglycerin truck: The relationship between the hospital and physician. *Healthcare Forum Journal* 36, no. 2:36–40.

Porter-O'Grady, T. 1992. *Implementing shared governance*. Baltimore: Mosby.

Relman, A. 1988. Assessment and accountability: The third revolution in medical care. *New England Journal of Medicine* 319:1220–1222.

Young, M., S. Rallison, and P. Eckman. 1995. Patients, physicians, and professional knowledge. *Hospitals and Health Services Administration* 40, no. 1:40–49.

Zander, K. 1995. *Managing outcomes through collaborative care: Care mapping and case management*. Chicago: American Hospital Publishing.

Chapter 8

Integrating across Organizational Parameters: Linking the System

Tim Porter-O'Grady and Marsha Parker

Life can only be understood looking backward,
but can only be lived looking forward.

Sören Kierkegaard

Constructing an integrated delivery system is virtually equivalent to building a horizontal organizational system. The move to horizontal systems is relatively recent in health care, but a horizontal structure is becoming increasingly essential for appropriate functioning.[1] No health system can have all the facets of service it will need in a subscriber-based approach. Since the health systems are increasingly subscriber driven, connecting the subscribers to the services they need will be the main work of the delivery system (Figure 8-1).

In subscriber systems, comprehensiveness is critical to success.[2] The buyers of services will be looking for a composite of services that address their prevailing concern, which is cost-effectiveness, and subscribers will be looking for breadth of services and satisfaction with care.

Certainly, linkage of all the components of service will be critical to the effectiveness of the organization. Internal alignment serves to facilitate the formation of seamless integration along the continuum of care. The design of the internal structure follows the patient flow and advances patients along the clinical pathway that most effectively meets the patients' needs and operates least expensively.[3]

THE PATIENT PATHWAY

All service structures should follow some pathway that represents the demand for service along the continuum. Patients are not simply looking for good illness

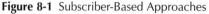

Figure 8-1 Subscriber-Based Approaches

services. Given a choice, they would not seek to become ill at all. Few, with the exception of those with severe mental illness, consciously seek to be ill. Illness is often caused by lifestyle choices—the way one works, interacts, eats, exercises, thinks, and looks. Many of the illnesses experienced in American society result from not living a balanced, active life.

Much of what constitutes health care today relates to sickness care services. The focus of the system on providing sickness services inherently advances sickness unless there is some offsetting factor that reduces dependency on such services. Historically, there has been no interest in or economic benefit from health-driven services. However, in subscriber-based approaches, where cost becomes a central factor, not wasting dollars is increasingly important. There is an overriding need to be judicious in the use of services and the expenditure of dollars,[4] and profits are directly related to the ability to keep as many prepaid dollars as possible and to reduce the use of services that consume a large number of dollars. That means reducing the use of services solely directed to sickness care, where the highest amount of cost is located.

> **Much of what is offered as health care in America is really sickness care. Health is simply not the issue.**

It is in this frame of reference that the need to build new linkages unfolds. As comprehensiveness becomes the critical factor in the delivery of service, linkage to necessary services is accelerated (see Figure 8-2). The ease of access to and use of such services by the subscriber become important to both the provider and the patient. The low cost and the effectiveness of these services become everyone's concern. Anything that does not improve the individual's health and reduce

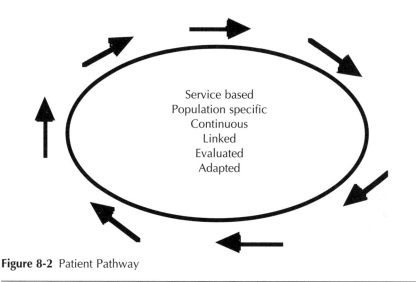

Figure 8-2 Patient Pathway

dependency on the services of the system adds demand and cost to the system. Thus the new focus is on creating health.

NEW REALITIES

The new focus on health has many implications for the service system, and strategies such as these are becoming necessary:

- constructing services that center around managing lives rather than managing disease
- reducing institutional services that require the consumer to come to the provider rather than the provider going to the consumer
- serving the provider of services as if he or she was the customer of services rather than a partner in the provision of services
- identifying and minimizing need rather than intervening and treating after a condition is present
- creating linkages that advance the health status of consumers rather than aid in illness identification and response
- engaging employers in efforts to improve health and thus reducing the health services costs and intensity costs.

- decentralizing services to the buyers' locations, thus making it easier to meet demand early than to simply provide services at the supplier location

Each of these strategies radically changes the approach to the delivery of services, and the traditional physician- and hospital-centered framework must be replaced by a broader community-based framework. In this new framework, the following occurs:

- Providers focus on assisting individuals to delineate risk factors and influences on health status over their lifetime.
- Health screening becomes a fundamental focus of health care rather than an adjunct to treatment.
- Clinical sites are created where subscribers live and work to make access to services as convenient as possible.
- Healthy behaviors and the costs and risks of nonperformance are identified.
- Providers create partnerships with certain members of the subscriber group, who then assume responsibility for the health relationships in the workplace or community setting.
- Primary care networks and providers are linked to ensure quick and convenient access to essential information and services.
- The information system network is used to support information sharing and consumer linkage at all points along the service continuum.

BUILDING THE CONTINUUM OF CARE

The movement toward managed care forces the health system toward linkage along the continuum of care. Payers and buyers of health services simply cannot sustain a focus on price for very long and ensure that viable services are provided to subscribers. The ability to manipulate prices carries the relationship only so far. Currently, pressure exists to drive prices downward without affecting the character of the services or the willingness of health providers to negotiate prices. The suicide level is reached when services promised cannot be delivered at the price promised, and the subscribers do not get what their agents contracted for.

It is early in the price–service cycle.[5] Therefore, providers and buyers are still at some distance from dialogue regarding the balance between cost and appropriate service. Two factors will occur to change this situation dramatically, and neither is far off. First, the price parameters will be stretched to the limit beyond which no health system can go and survive. Secondly, there will be a demand to know what is happening at the service end of the arrangement and whether subscribers are getting what they need. It will be necessary to achieve some service outcomes that will themselves affect the future generation of costs and expansion of interventions.

Long-term success will not depend on the price–service relationship. The value equation shows the importance of three factors: cost, quality, and time (or activity). No one of those factors

> *Focusing on the price of services alone is not a sustainable strategy. The buyer eventually wants to get the outcomes paid for.*

can be applied without an equal effort being directed to the others. This is a hard-learned lesson, but the long-term viability of any managed care and capitated approach depends on its mastery.

It is incumbent upon the leadership in any health organization to be cognizant of this reality and to structure services in a way that anticipates the requisites of the value equation. In the long run, the organization's competitiveness will depend on how well the balance between price sensitivity and service effectiveness has been maintained and how sustainable that balance is.

HORIZONTAL SERVICE DESIGN

An increasingly important goal in health care is to integrate around specific patient populations. These populations are composed of subscribers who represent a specific set of needs. The kind of services offered will depend entirely upon the complexion of the subscriber base. If service viability is to be maintained over the long term, there must be a tight fit between the kind of services offered and the needs of the subscriber population.[6]

> *Providers are now configuring around populations rather than patients. This changes the focus from treating illness to creating health.*

Therefore, the health care organization must be fluid and flexible in its service structure. For every contract obtained, the organization will have to have a service framework available to satisfy the demands of the contract. It is in this context that the continuum of care and appropriate linkages become central to the structure of the health care organization.

Subscriber satisfaction is not going to result simply from excellence in any one component of the delivery system. Also necessary will be a strong connection between providers within the full range of services the subscriber expects. Furthermore, subscribers will not remain satisfied if the services contracted for do not match their expectations or their genuine needs. An inexpensive price tag will not long interest any subscriber whose wants are not met.

> *Health providers need to ensure that the fit between the services provided and the population served is clearly defined.*

Ultimately, it is important to be able to clearly enumerate what is obtained for the price paid. It is equally important to look at what subscribers are getting in other buyer–provider arrangements. If the data show that superior services are being offered at the same or a better price elsewhere, it should come as no surprise that buyers will be interested in switching contracts. Over the long term, the fixation on price will give way to interest in the components of the service framework and the context for service the provider has constructed (see Exhibit 8-1). There are a number of areas buyers will become increasingly interested in knowing more about:

- What are the measures of care that determine the relationship between what is done and the outcomes that are achieved?
- How does the cost per unit of service compare with the cost for like services offered by other providers?
- What is the range of services provided to specific populations?
- How does the provider know the appropriate fit between the character of the subscriber population and the provider's service configuration?
- What are administrative and support costs per subscriber in the provider organization?
- How are "best practices" maintained and improved as a foundation for the clinical routines and activities of the key providers of health services?
- What are the focused service activities that address the health concerns of subscribers and keep them from using more expensive intervention services?

These questions form a framework for considering the interests of buyers. Increasingly the ability to keep people from expending resources is as critical as the kind of resources used. The current focus on lowering the levels of intervention creates a dynamic that is threatening to existing service patterns. It makes

Exhibit 8-1 Capitated Requisites

- Flat sum
- Advance payment
- Defined service set
- Payment amount reflective of the population
- Quality driven
- Contract renegotiation

many of them obsolete and forces the provider organization to match what it does to the health needs of those it serves and what the buyers are willing to pay for.

LINKAGE DEFINES THE SYSTEM

Linkage between components of the delivery system will become increasingly critical to the viability of service provision. Some new thinking about what service provision should look like will be required. Some changes in existing relationships will have to occur. Practice arrangements will need to reflect the different character of clinical connections in the delivery system:

- Gatekeeping roles will be assumed by primary care providers, who will manage entry to the system and direct people along the clinical pathway.
- Many primary care providers will not be physicians, simply because most of the roles will not require the skill set of medical doctors.
- An increasing number of patients will need life management skills rather than illness services, requiring them to acknowledge their risk factors and to deal with them.
- Required but nonowned services will have to be provided under shared risk agreements to ensure all the services needed are available to subscribers.
- Ownership of health activities will be taken over by the subscribers, who will have increasing responsibility for making decisions about what services will and will not be used.
- Nonallopathic methods of treatment that produce significant outcomes will become fully accepted.
- Services will be brought to the workplace so that factors influencing the degree of health risk experienced by subscribers can be quickly and adequately addressed.
- There will be significant cost sharing for health programs, especially those that relate to the reduction of existing health risks over which the subscribers have direct behavioral control.

HORIZONTAL LINKAGE

Horizontal linkage requires virtually every provider to gain the ability to negotiate relationships along the continuum of care. In the past, the marketing or development office would provide most of the services needed to make and finalize the connections and contracts between service entities. It is now necessary for connections and contracts to be fashioned by the point-of-service leadership, with the support of marketing and development. Ownership and stakeholder requirements encourage the parties to any relationship to play the major role in defining it and in building the specifics that will act as a foundation for the relationship. Some specific activities will have to be considered:

- articulating a mutual purpose so that the parties are clear about the reason for the relationship
- clarifying the expectations each has of the relationship and the benefits that will accrue to both
- knowing what real barriers to the relationship exist and making it safe to put them on the table for the parties to address jointly
- identifying the quid pro quo for each party and the outcomes anticipated from the relationship
- negotiating the roles of the two parties so that accountability can be clearly defined and duplication and cross-referencing activities can be kept to a minimum
- addressing the financial obligations associated with each role and the way those will be managed and distributed over the course of the relationship
- developing a continuous evaluation mechanism (including period group review) that looks at the character of the relationship and the outcomes of work over the course of the relationship.

PROVIDER LINKAGE

Internal linkage throughout the service system will be vital to the success of the organization. Building a seamless system of services means that the essential relationships are always supporting the purposes of the services. Therefore, there must be a mechanism to ensure the resolution of conflict and service flow over the life of the relationship. The consumers have a right to expect that the service providers have a mechanism for building their relationships, solving problems, and advancing the work of the health system to the benefit of the consumers.

History, however tells a different story. The "silo" approach to organizational structure created functional and departmental barriers between people and did not foster the development of meaningful and functional relationships between the disciplines. Often one part of the clinical system would work in conflict with other parts of the system. The issues at stake were not always clear, and the problems associated with the immaturity of the relationships began to spill over into the patient–provider relationship. Now, in order to ensure effectiveness, it is critical that the stakeholders form clearly defined relationships that allow them to progress toward mutually defined goals. The process of creating the necessary type of relationships should be guided by the following rules, among others:

> *Linking the providers along the continuum of health care is the critical work of the system's leadership today.*

- Physicians are not outside the relationships necessary to the obtaining of desired outcomes and therefore cannot be treated as customers of the system.
- Physicians and the other disciplines must establish new relationships configured around the contribution of each to the attainment of patient service outcomes.
- The medical staff organization must be formally reconstructed to remove all barriers to the development of relationships with point-of-service providers and problem-solving mechanisms strictly within the point of service.
- The independent entrepreneurial physician practice will no longer be able to thrive in the emerging marketplace. Increasingly multiple practice arrangements will be necessary for success.
- Nurses will play an increasingly large role in building and maintaining the continuum of care and fostering the linkages necessary to fully serve the needs of the subscribers.
- Multidisciplinary group practice arrangements centered around particular patient populations will require equity in decision making and resource sharing.

ORGANIZING AROUND POPULATIONS

Patient populations will form the core of service configurations. As indicated in this book, organizations will configure around the point of patient care and provide services to specified patient populations. The continuum of care will serve as the template for the services provided. Meeting the need for clearly enumerated protocols and cost-moderated activities will demand the investment of all who have a stake in the relationship. Time and energy must be committed to discovering the activities that demonstrate the greatest impact upon the subscribers' health. Identifying those activities and building on them will be the main work of the clinical leadership for some time.

DEFINING LINKAGES

Building a more horizontal organization requires starting from the top down and the bottom up at the same time. The disciplines of visioning and mental modeling are crucial in helping the organization move forward as a whole. Progress depends on breaking down linkages and building them back up. No less important is the context within which processing occurs. The leadership must learn to create overview templates with the necessary flexibility to allow people at the point of service to recreate linkages. It is a noisy, messy enterprise and never very comfortable.

One of the most important things to learn about radical change is that it is more important to build something based on principles and shared goals than to simply eradicate the old barriers. Unfortunately, once the old barriers come tumbling down, so do all the old linkages. All those influences and feelings that give workers some sense of where they stand in the organization, what their value is to the whole, are suddenly gone. Bereft of those guideposts and attachments, workers feel abandoned and "outside the information loop." It is of paramount importance that the vision for the new structure be very widely shared so that workers have the choice to enroll in the new paradigm. In the absence of a vision, informal parallel structures will be built.

> *Service organizations are no longer built from the top down or from the bottom up. Rather, they are constructed from the inside out.*

BUILDING THE VISION

The propagation of a shared vision is not accomplished by the mere construction of the vision, nor by communicating it a dozen times or so. "Building shared understanding of the grand vision is a continuous process of endless dialogue."[7]

If the vision entails the implementation of whole-systems shared governance, most players will not have a clue what that means. Even after years of implementation, not all the definitions will be clear to everyone. What is crystal clear, however, is the need to view health and health care from an entirely different perspective than has been used in the past. The value of using systems thinking is that it offers a much more complete context for observing, learning, and designing for sustainable change.

> *Systems thinking is essential to outlining how the organization functions. From a whole-systems perspective, the contribution and constraints found in any part of the system are clearer to all.*

The learning that happens along the way continuously alters people's viewpoints. What is thought to be true may change radically from one day to the next, depending on what new information or insights have occurred in the meantime. While some may feel the previously held views are invalidated, experience is indicating that each new level of learning refines the old views rather than nullifies them. It is just that the evolution is so rapid that it can appear chaotic. Developing comfort with that chaos is one of the challenges of the new environment. In fact, it is very difficult because so many of the old linkages are gone, whereas the new ones are not yet in place.

So what is a linkage? No doubt everyone involved will be struggling with that question for many years to come, but progress is being made. According to one current view, a linkage consists of

- a set of interrelationships that control behavior and connect elements of a system
- the influences on the dynamics at work in any given situation that are the living parts of the interrelationships
- the drive of the structure itself to develop certain types of interrelationships
- the feelings each individual has in trying to be aware of his or her own personal needs and what the whole organization needs at the same time ("Are my thoughts and actions in tune with the whole?")

At innovative hospitals and health systems, the learning goes on, but linkages are felt, and their absence is noted very quickly when shared governance–oriented reorganizing and restructuring has occurred. As soon as the dismantling of old structure begins, the breakdown in linkage is often revealed by the increasing number of complaints and the feelings of being outside the loop, even among those who were heavily involved in designing the changes.

What is observable in shared governance is the representation of the various perspectives. For example, policies and procedures, memos and minutes, plans and conceptual drawings are all tangible. What may be more important, though, is what can be *felt*. One feels linkage when there is a pressure to behave in some way defined through one's relationships. There is an energy that flows along the linkage that creates a sense of urgency to act. This is often evidenced in the revealing of the distance between where one is and the location of the agreed goal. Reinforcing and the balancing influences have their effect through these linkages. There can never be a change in one element of the system without some exchange of energy with other elements through the linkages.

> *A change in any one part of a system means a shift in every part of the system.*

STRUCTURAL LINKAGES

A typical hospital system in the United States used to be made up of hundreds of cost centers supervised by hundreds of supervisors and managed by 10 or more layers of expert managers and administrators (see Exhibit 8-2). As indicated in previous chapters, there were dozens of vice-presidents and senior vice-presidents, many assistant administrators and directors, several presidents (one of which was also a chief operating officer [COO]), and the chief executive officer (CEO). Decisions were made in a hierarchy of management groups and committees, such as the CEO cabinet, the CEO council, the administrative staff committees, and specialty-specific management groups. It frequently took months to get capital requests through the system. Any major policy change or tactical plan change took even longer. No one manager or director in the system had a picture of the whole, nor was anyone accountable for the success of the whole. Indeed, the senior leader had an incentive to make his or her own facility succeed even if at the cost of harming one of the other facilities in the system. It is not easy to understand what the benefits of this structure were, but there was and still is significant bemoaning of its loss.

In one hospital system, restructuring reduced 214 management positions to a total of 34 management positions and 6 consultant positions. The position of only one person was not touched, and that was the CEO, who was the unswerving champion of the changes then and since. The 34 managers included 30 service leaders (pathway), 2 facility integrators (physical plant), and 2 service integrators

Exhibit 8-2 Management Layers

- Service or team coordinators
- Assistant supervisors
- Supervisors
- Assistant managers
- Managers
- Assistant directors
- Directors
- Assistant administrators
- Associate administrators
- Administrators
- Vice-presidents
- Senior vice-presidents
- President
- COO
- CEO

(administrators). The two service integrators and the consultants answered to the CEO, and the facility integrators answered to the service integrators. The principles used in creating the structure and creating new linkages were these:

- The continuum of care across an individual's lifetime should be the backbone of the living system.
- The shared governance principles of accountability, equity, partnership, and ownership should be the behavioral ideals.
- A shared vision incorporating these principles should be the center of all design efforts.
- The congruence of the structure with all the above must be ensured.
- Support systems need to be designed around the shared goal of "managing the health of the community to a value standard."

Guiding ideas were then spun off of these principles. These ideas have become more and more the rules of action followed by staff working on any problem or project.

NEW VALUES

The range of options can be made congruent with the theme by asking the question, "What value does this add to managing a patient to a value standard?"

Value standards fall into four categories: localness, openness, quality (service), and flexibility. Examples of possible value standards include these:

- Localness. Ninety percent of all decisions should be made at the point of service.
- Openness. Resources such as information belong to everyone. Everyone can be trusted with the information they need to make their decisions.
- Quality. Ideal patient flows (experiences and outcomes) are everyone's accountability.
- Flexibility. None of our structures, systems, policies, or procedures are perfect. All can be changed in the light of new information or ideas.

The gestation period for instilling guiding ideas is not short. It often takes years, not months. One of the service integrators in a transforming hospital carries around a verse from Longfellow's "Psalm of Life":

> Let us, then, be up and doing,
> With a heart for any fate;
> Still achieving, still pursuing,
> Learn to labor and to wait.

The labor spent in instilling guiding ideas and designing the structure based on these ideas is an investment in the future, and while it always has some short-term benefits almost immediately, the larger benefits will take a longer time to arrive.

DELINEATING THE PATHWAYS

Functions are sorted into two categories along the continuum: member service pathways and support service pathways. The pathways function as illustrated in Figure 8-3.

At the outset, the focus of the change leadership is on the corporate organization and does not expand to include the full integrated health network and the service community until later in the process. The pathway design drives the management structure, and the number of service leaders (pathway managers) is determined through agreement to a span-of-control target of more than 100–150 workers per manager.

Decisions regarding the practice, quality, and education issues for the pathways fall within the accountability of the pathway councils. Decisions across pathways are the accountability of the corporate councils (service, operations, and gover-

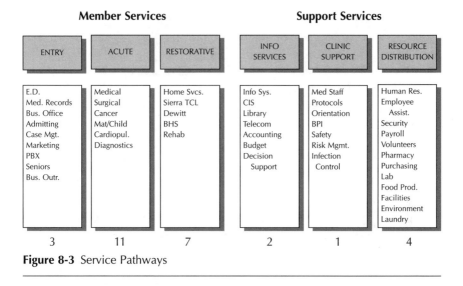

Figure 8-3 Service Pathways

nance). Figures 8-4 and 8-5 show the linkages to the medical staff structure as well as the linkages between councils and provider teams (within each pathway).

The provider team is the core of the service system because it lies at the heart of the point of service. All linkages are designed to directly or indirectly support the functional service areas. The provider is now empowered to make point-of-service decisions and is supported by the structure. The accountability of each of the decision centers of the structure flows from the work needed to sustain and preserve the relationships between the team members and those they serve. In some integrated models, for example, the patient is also a team member and has the same goal—achieving the best outcome possible.

The support area teams (engineering, laundry, grounds, etc.) are called "service teams." Early in the development of the new system, the support pathways are often a step removed from the point of service and are therefore viewed as less critical to the outcomes. This perception of them is at odds with the notion of whole-systems integration, according to which each element is of value to the whole. Such thinking also begins to create pathway boundaries that, while fewer in number, are no less debilitating than the department barriers of the old model. At the inception of shared governance, the focus is on changing the support pathways into process teams that are more fully integrated into the continuum of care activities. In time, what were once identified as separate support structures will disappear.

Figure 8-4 Integrated Pathways

SYSTEMS LINKAGES

A continuum of care cannot be maintained without tools. The information system becomes the center around which the health system revolves. Indeed, information forms the foundation of the sustainability of the future health system (see Figure 8-6). The ability to link professions and information together becomes critical to speed, portability, and technology application. Without an adequate information infrastructure, none of the current teletechnologies can be implemented. There is a need to identify the contributing factors increasing the cost of health care and control them. In a subscriber-based approach, the only way to ensure control is to build an information system that provides immediate and accurate data to those who need it.

> *Information is the lifeblood of the shared governance organization. Indeed, it is the central variable that will determine the organization's sustainability.*

THE NEED FOR INFORMATION

Information, to be effective, must be in a format that meets the needs of those who receive and use it. Most

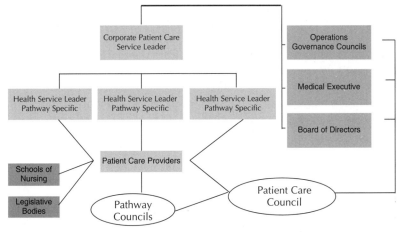

Figure 8-5 The Patient Care Leadership after Integration

information systems reflect the perceptions of the information experts, not necessarily the needs of the users. In the future, user-friendly and provider-driven information structures must be built that tie all the components of the system together in a meaningful way.

Figure 8-6 The Future Shared Governance Community Health System

The horizontal linkages related to building a clinical continuum demand support constructed so as to interface with the clinical process. Further, whatever information systems are built, they must intersect in a way that addresses the organizational system's comprehensive information needs. Some considerations that will have to be addressed are as follows:

- The information system must reflect the patient's health journey or pathway and must track the patient through all the intersections needed in the system.
- The information that is available must be comprehensive. It should include financial, resource, and clinical data in a format that makes service delivery effective and resource issues clear to all the providers.
- Everyone who needs information should have easy access to it, and it should be in a form that allows it to be understood and used.
- Linkage of the various service settings, such as the physician's office, the clinic, the outpatient center, the patient's home, and acute services, by the information system is a basic expectation.
- Clinical performance evaluation along the care continuum is essential to determine clinical effectiveness at all levels of the service system.
- The ability to evaluate and change the parameters of service when the data suggest they need to be changed is increasingly necessary as clinical protocols become more precise and more fully inculcated into the delivery of patient care services.
- Information systems operate at the point of service so that the clinical users can access what is needed and document the activities of clinical work in a way that interfaces well with the other parameters' guiding action.

There is perhaps nothing that will have as great an impact on the design of health services as the development of an integrated, portable, and decentralized information system. The major capital project for most forward-thinking health systems will be a well-designed and integrated health information infrastructure.

PATHWAYS AND INFORMATION

Building pathways that are clinically focused and user specific is an essential task,[8] and structuring them within the context of a well-defined and functioning information system will be critical to long-term success. It is also important for users to be computer literate, since any provider's worklife will be influenced by what the information system provides in the way of support and information about outcomes. Therefore, the development programs of the health system of the future must provide a thorough understanding of computer and information systems.

To begin to understand why some of the system linkages were built, one must keep in mind four system levels at once: events, patterns of behavior, systems, and mental models. All four are interrelated, and a change in one causes change in the others. Systems thinking was in its infancy during the initial development of information systems, and at that time the goal was simply to make sure that the weight of the old manual and paper systems did not impede the burgeoning new systems.

> *Systems linkage tells the members of the organization where the key intersections are and how the system maintains its integrity.*

That meant that, in each case, the kinds of things influencing workers' beliefs and actions should "look" like the new system, leaving as little of the old system as possible in order to break the workers' dependence upon it. Performance evaluation, competency testing, compensation policies and procedures, style of communication, informal rewards, and access to resources (purchase requisitions, etc.) all had to change to reflect the new information infrastructure principles and models.

The effort to incorporate systems notions should begin when the shared governance process is initiated. The implementation process associated with information system development will lag behind the full understanding of the principles and guiding ideas underpinning whole-systems shared governance. For example, compensation management changes will require abundant education of human resource and information management personnel as well as other members of the health system. At the outset, many of the staff will still see the old system operating, which will delay the generation of evidence demonstrating the viability of the new approach to compensation management. Leadership forbearance is especially important during this period of change. Even senior managers can experience this developmental lag and might long for the old system because of its familiarity and stability while they are struggling with the application of a better but uncharted compensation information system.

In the first year, as more of the information infrastructure is implemented within the shared governance model, the new system begins to work better and eventually becomes the accepted means of performance measurement and compensation management.

COMMUNICATION LINKAGES

Deep in the struggle to redesign the shared governance structure to support reengineering, both staff and management come to feel they are on a roller coaster ride while living the changes. No matter how comprehensive, the changes themselves seem to be only superficial evidence of the organization's real shift. The real changes are much deeper—at the heart of the organization. The interdependence of individuals, one relying on another, in times of "noise" is incredibly energizing, whether or not the consequences

> *The major problems in implementing any change can be most frequently attributed to failures in the communication process.*

are positive or negative. Everyone feels the energy of transformation but no one can pin it down or define what it is.

All kinds of lessons are learned about communication while implementing new organizational structures. According to systems thinking, dialogue lies at the foundation of every human enterprise. Without it, little agreement in the organization will be possible. Ruffles of change may appear around the edges, but a critical mass is never attained unless it has been preceded with vast amounts of focused, intense dialogue. New communication linkages must be built and tested against the new patterns of behavior and events unfolding every day. There must also be coherence between what is "talked" and what is "walked" before dialogue gains momentum.

> *Before it can become a "learning organization," any health care organization must ensure its members engage in systems learning.*

One thing that is learned once communication becomes formalized in the infrastructure is that sensitivity to linkages pays big dividends. For example, one learning lab process that can be helpful in building commitment to learning and achieving positive outcomes is called "whole system templating." This process can also be used to help change agents consider linkages and impacts of change while in the design and redesign phases of their work. Whole system templates are brainstormed with mixed groups of stakeholders as a means of helping novice and advanced beginner systems thinkers to look at the broader implications of changes they might be considering.

Templating is not flowcharting or model building but rather the practicing of new disciplines together with colleagues in a defined practice field. All templates result from a "walk through" of some of the linkages identified in health delivery organizations that create general parameters for the practice field. The process itself must be "loose," drawing more from the right side of the brain that houses our capacity to comprehend wholes, patterns, and synthesis. It requires integration rather than analysis, and so concentrates more on relationships and context than a tally of neatly ordered parts.

> *Often visualizing a change helps translate it into a plan that can be implemented.*

The desired outcome of a templating session is greater awareness of the whole. There are only a few basic assumptions used in all templating sessions. One is that all open systems are constantly exchanging energy with their environments and that the exchanges are highly organized but in constant change—a sort of "flowing wholeness."[9] The principle task is to establish a new cycle of learning that connects practice and performance (note that synthesis is an important method for the whole). The goals are:

- to achieve breakthroughs in learning infrastructure
- to help everyone imagine the whole
- to help everyone rethink and recognize his or her own relationship to the whole
- to strive for alignment of vision and mental models

The technique of templating grows through application and is different for every group that attempts it, but the results are usually very positive.

Another helpful exercise is based on an old technique called "focusing," which grew out of Eugene Gendlin's work at the University of Chicago.[10] Roughly, it requires people to sit quietly, focus on an image or idea, and allow feelings to well up. They then ask that feeling to identify itself and judge whether the answer is correct by whether it "feels" right. A feeling-based consensus can sometimes result when a group tries to visualize linkages and their relationships to the whole. The group outcomes are amazingly easy to translate into the practical and concrete designs for new processes and systems. It is as if a road map is laid out in front of a traveler who has been trying to create it one mile at a time.

THE PROCESS OF BUILDING LINKAGES AND TEAMS

The building of linkages is an ideal place to use the template approach. The first step is to select a group of empowered, energetic workers who represent a variety of perspectives. They must be willing to take risks and withstand some "noise" from their coworkers in order to do the "right" thing for the patient population and community they serve. Once that group is organized, some basics must be agreed upon:

- rules of engagement
- rules of brainstorming
- use of the five disciplines of a learning organization
- common problem-solving steps
- definitions of template elements

The rules of engagement are meant to define how the individuals interact within the group setting to maximize the ability of the group to accomplish its work. The group determines what those rules are going to be, but they generally include both the rules of polite society (e.g., do not interrupt others and be on time) as well as rules for handling issues (e.g., be willing to confront issues and be honest and truthful).

The brainstorming rules are intended to create an environment conducive to creative thinking, especially the sort in which one member's thoughts inspire others to have even more creative thoughts. The rules consist of such items as these:

- Have fun.
- All ideas have merit.
- Allow no one person to dominate.
- Encourage all members to participate.
- Try to build on one another's creativity.
- No pagers!

The five disciplines of a learning organization—shared vision, mental models, systems thinking, personal mastery, and team learning—form the foundation for linkage design. They are used to "see" the system and the implications of changes. They channel the group's thinking so that it is productive and the linkages are congruent with the needs the new system is designed to meet.

Common problem-solving steps are discussed in order to develop a common language for talking about change. When one member of the team mentions flowcharting the "as is," the rest of the team will not understand that is the second step in that person's problem-solving technique unless change terminology is discussed and clarified early in the life of the group.

Defining template elements is the way the group begins to narrow the universe of work possible in linkage design. Examples of template elements include the following:

- vision, values, guiding ideas
- structure
- governance
- decision-making loci
- information flows in and out of decision-making loci
- cultural dynamics, such as
  —informal leaders
  —linguistic interpretation
  —traditions or customs
  —how ideas flow through the informal networks
  —changing roles and status
- formal information flows
  —expectations of council and team members regarding verbal communication
  —written communication flows
  —access to information systems
  —design of information systems
- observable signals of empowerment
- culturally determined systems of competence (the understanding of the differences in linkage required by populations of various cultures)

INTERACTIONS IN THE SYSTEM

Anything that influences the relationships between the system components (or any place where there is an exchange of energy) can be used as a template element. These things become the pieces of a jigsaw puzzle. The outside border, like the jigsaw pieces with the straight edge, is made up of the vision and mental models that are shared.

> *All systems support what goes on at their center. The purpose of the structure is to support the service.*

The vision and mental models grow out of the need to do more than deliver inpatient care. The mission of most facilities includes the goal of "improving the health status of the community." This cannot be effectively achieved using the old department structure. The natural barriers to stretching care across the continuum of care are often too tough to break. For example, unit managers usually possess accountability for a unit budget and will rarely risk dealing with issues related to the care of whole patient populations. CEOs and finance officers whose bonuses are based on annual hospital profits are reticent to spend precious dollars on things with no clear short-term benefit.

ORGANIZING AROUND THE PATIENT

In order for the mission of improving health status to be fulfilled, a new "model of response to patient need" is required as the first step. Health is a continuum from birth to death, whereas an illness lasts from onset to cure or death. Old-style hospital systems are built around segmented functions (departments) designed to deliver repetitious tasks within a specialty to all the patients for whom services are ordered in a given day. In the new health system, the services are designed around the movement of each person along the continuum toward the best health status possible. Systems are then organized around the patient (patient-focused care), and the organization is designed around patient populations. Support functions are created as process teams organized around a set of outcomes that support the delivery of services to those populations. In the master path diagram (Figure 8-7), the continuum displays parallel paths toward the best health status possible for individuals and populations. At the system level, this means that the primary care provider (PCP), in partnership with the member, is the manager or facilitator of the master path. The goal is to maintain maximum health, and only a failure of that pathway results in illness or a detour from the pathway.

When a member has some episode that requires more intensive application of resources, the result is a detour from the master path. Detours may require that the member become an inpatient in an acute facility, have surgery in an outpatient surgery center, spend a few weeks in a convalescent facility, or have some other less intensive intervention. In the case of any detour, the goal is to get the person back on the healthy "master path" as soon as possible.

The patient populations or subscribers are broadly described and are basically healthy. Those requiring closer focus are the chronically but not acutely ill population and the acutely ill or injured population, and of course these populations can be further divided. In order to create an operational organization to support the various identified patient populations and to make it easier to manage each

PCP = primary care provider
BHS = best health status

Purpose: to manage the health of the community to a value standard

Figure 8-7 Master Path Diagram

---

population (or individual patient) across the continuum, operational pathways are designed, as shown in Figure 8-8. These pathways initially are just acute care related but expand to include physicians' offices and clinics. Integrating efforts across all points of service is the responsibility of leadership. Each pathway covers all related facilities and services and has one management and governance structure. Corporate service and operations councils with members from all pathways deal with issues affecting all the pathways (see Chapters 4 and 5).

MAKING THE SYSTEM FUNCTIONAL

The service elements within the pathway are organized into a pathway council and point-of-service provider teams. The pathway council has staff members representing perspectives from all the service areas within the pathway. Managers often sit as advisors, but the chairs are providers. Physicians are strongly encouraged to be members of these councils and provider teams rather than critics or distant advisors. The meetings are held at times that make it as convenient as possible for physicians to attend. The groups are multidisciplinary and make all the decisions about how the work is to be

> *Physician membership on councils builds partnerships between stakeholders and ensures that all stakeholders are in the making of decisions that will affect them.*

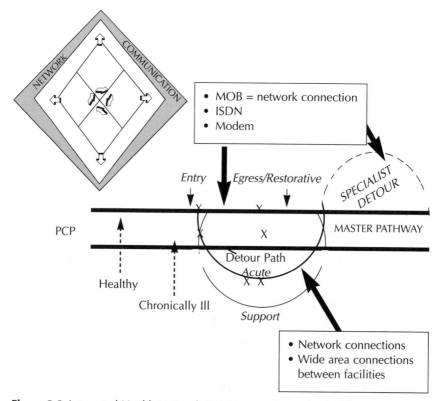

Figure 8-8 Integrated Health Network Core System Components, Phase One

done. The one exception to the rule is the "best practices" process. It should be a part of a support pathway, and its council is made up of "best practices" physicians and providers from other disciplines. The work of this "subpathway" is to generate a "best practices" environment for the whole system and is heavily focused on providing the physicians in the system with the things they need to successfully manage patient populations.

The linkages between the points of service are complex and critical. Not only must the pathways work across facility lines, the provider teams must work and have support across pathway lines (see Exhibit 8-3). Decision making is moved increasingly to the point of service, requiring point-of-service access to the information needed to make informed decisions.

There is no way to put together new provider teams across a whole system and have them all be competent on the first day. Everyone starts out as a novice and

Exhibit 8-3 Continuum of Care Services

Everything must integrate across the system for the purpose of building a seamless continuum of care.

Continuum
- Primary and Family Health
- Cancer Services
- Rehabilitation
- Behavioral Health
- Home Services
- Women's Health
- Community Services
- Acute Services
- Trauma Level 1
- Burn Unit

must stumble a little on the way to competence. It is very important to provide an environment in which the standards are clarified and reclarified and in which the stumbling is viewed as positive learning instead of a reason for termination.

In the pathway design, the template elements are considered one at a time and then expanded as all try to see the way these influences might operate on the components of the system. For instance, the way physicians used to make things happen when they were unhappy was to go to the CEO or to the board of directors. The new linkage requires them to go to the point-of-service team if the issue is a patient care, clinical, or relational issue. The team member who deals with the issue then discusses with the physician how to directly address it.

> *All transformation requires learning from everyone in the system. Indeed, the system becomes a learning organization.*

They come to an agreement about how to proceed and put in measures to ensure successful follow-up. If the concern cuts across pathways, the team member brings the physician to the pathway or corporate council to further refine the solution. Whatever solution is agreed to here is final.

Should the problem require immediate action, the team member and physician can act on the spot or include an empowered chair of the unit or pathway council in the decision making. This allows the "management by committee" barriers to be sidestepped when speed is important. All quick-response decisions are reviewed by the appropriate group to make sure any needed communication linkages are constructed and any education requirements met. The CEO should always refer complaining physicians back to the point of service. Such a response, made in a supportive way, begins the slow and inexorable culture shift. Physicians must always be actively involved in making collaborative decisions in most, if not all, of the pathway councils and provider teams.

All members of the system experience role changes. For the acute facility caregiver, the old role was to complete all assigned tasks according to productivity targets without any untoward patient events. Accomplishment of tasks over a long period usually meant a salary increase, and working occasional extra shifts, mentoring new workers, or taking on special assignments would likely result in an outstanding performance review rating. Historically, there was little or no requirement to fully collaborate with other disciplines, and the outcomes of cases were not carefully tracked. The goal was simply to get tasks done while avoiding unpleasant incidents.

> *Shared governance is not management by committee; if it is, it simply does not work. It is, instead, an accountability-based approach to obtaining effective decisions.*

In the new environment, the requirements are significantly different. Now care providers are accountable for moving each patient through the episode of illness or injury to the best "value outcome" (meaning the best clinical outcome at the least cost). Not only must a caregiver do the kinds of things necessary to achieve the desired outcome whether they are on a traditional worklist or not, the provider must also marshal other resources to expedite recuperation. The new environment has standards for value outcomes that must be met or exceeded, and any variance from these standards must be reviewed by the team so that any problems can be solved.

There are a number of linkages required to enable providers to operate effectively in their new role. Information must be complete and easily accessible. It must include not only the clinical data and the standards but the financial data and the targets. Real-time glimpses of how providers are doing on a given case would be the ideal. Other linkages include connections to the evaluation, compensation, and competency processes, which must all be redesigned to support the new role. The providers must have a loose relationship with the pathway council and feel supported by that council when they find a better way to deliver care.

The availability of resources is critical to the success of the providers. They must have the ability to purchase what they need when they need it to improve outcomes without having to go through a long or convoluted approval process. At some hospitals, for example, a checking account containing $10,000 is disbursed to each care area for staff to spend as they see fit. This is a commitment to empowerment that might average a minimum of $200,000 over a six-month period. The fear initially was that the workers would spend indiscriminately. The opposite has actually occurred. Many provider teams spent less than the allotted amount; they all tracked what they spent, and wonderful, thoughtful things were done to help patients and their families, with no manager intervention or approval required. The results were so encouraging that the same amounts have again been allotted to the staff. There are now more people understanding budget and purchasing in the organization than ever before and making independent decisions at the point of service to help patients reach their best health status.

Manager roles also change significantly. In the old paradigm, the manager directed activities, and all significant decisions had to be made by or approved by the person in control of a department. The managers, in turn, were restricted by the department structure and by facility boundaries. In shared governance, the manager is coach, mentor, teacher, and resource manager. The boundaries between facilities or institutions are gone because the structure

> *Managers may budget dollars, but they rarely spend them; their staff does!*

does away with departments, and the service or pathway manager is accountable for providing whatever the providers need in any pathway across all facilities.

The management group is the hardest group to get to accept their new role because it represents a shift of individual power to the point-of-service teams. The linkages required for this group to move have to do with core values and lots of dialogue. Eventually managers learn to value helping the teams find their own way to the best outcomes instead of making them follow the steps the managers think will lead to the best outcomes.

The issue for whole-systems shared governance leaders very quickly becomes, How big is the whole? With large corporate concerns currently swallowing up health care–related organizations, there is little doubt that building an organization that is fast, fluid, flexible, and horizontal is a good survival tactic. Understanding the linkages within one's own system and the linkages to the global system requires a new awareness. As Kenichi Ohmae points out in his book *The Evolving Global Economy*, "However managers do it, however they get there, building a value system that emphasizes seeing and thinking globally is the bottom line price of admission to today's borderless economy."[11]

The next step after integrating across organizational boundaries may be integrating across zonal boundaries on a much grander scale. Regardless of the requisites for inclusion, there must be a format, a structure, through which relationships can be obtained, facilitated, and sustained. This structure must bring the stakeholders together and provide a format for the work they do. Its parameters must be flexible and fluid in a way that allows for adaptation and dramatic change. In shared governance, a framework is established that moves an organization from vertical to horizontal linkages, fosters inclusive relationships, and provides the parameters for changing the organization's configuration to one that supports a systems view and the intersection of all the elements that make a system successful and sustainable.

REFERENCES

1. A. Barting, "Integrated Delivery Systems: Fact or Fiction," *Healthcare Executive* 10, no. 3 (1995):6–11.
2. T. Porter-O'Grady, "Managing along the Continuum: A New Paradigm for the Clinical Manager," *Nursing Administration Quarterly* 19, no. 3 (1995):1–12.
3. J. Griffith, V. Sahney, and R. Mohr, *Reengineering Healthcare: Building on CQI* (Chicago: Health Administration Press, 1995).
4. D. Cave, "Vertical Integration Models To Prepare Health Systems for Capitation," *Health Care Management Review* 20, no. 1 (1995):26–39.
5. D. Kirkhart, "Shared Care: Improving Health Care, Reducing Costs," *Nursing Management* 26, no. 6 (1995):26–33.
6. J. Beaulieu and D. Berry, *Rural Health Services: A Management Perspective* (Chicago: Health Administration Press, 1994).
7. P. Senge et al., *The Fifth Discipline Fieldbook* (New York: Bantam Doubleday Dell, 1994).
8. S. DeWoody and J. Price, "A Systems Approach to Multidimensional Critical Paths," *Nursing Management* 25, no. 11 (1994):47–51.
9. M. Ferguson, *The Aquarian Conspiracy* (Boston: Houghton Mifflin, 1980), 156.
10. Ferguson, *Aquarian Conspiracy*, 164.
11. K. Ohmae, *The Evolving Global Economy: Making Sense of a New World Order* (Boston: Harvard Business School Press, 1995), 270.

Chapter 9

Information Management for Point-of-Service Decision Making

Marsha Parker, Lynn Neimeth, and Tim Porter-O'Grady

The Age of Technology will make neighbors of strangers, and strangers of neighbors.

Marshall McLuhan

THE NEW INFORMATION INFRASTRUCTURE

Fostering the principles of shared governance (equity, accountability, partnership, and ownership) so that they are applied in daily decision making throughout an organization requires radical new approaches in organizational design.[1] The most critical area needing redesign is the information management system. The components of information management in a shared governance organization are as follows:

- the structure, culture, training, information, and "systemness" embedded in the organization's activities
- the design of information flows between and among decision makers and councils
- philosophical and conceptual modeling congruent with shared governance
- data collection and delivery methodologies (procedural and design agreements that treat information as a dynamic)
- hardware and software applications (putting the right pieces together to enable the flow of information)

THE IMPLICATIONS OF SHARED GOVERNANCE PRINCIPLES AND STRUCTURES FOR INFORMATION MANAGEMENT

The basic principles of shared governance all have a profound impact on the way information is conceptualized and the way systems for managing information are designed.[2] The new design for information management must treat information as a dynamic rather than as a commodity. Or as Margaret Wheatley has said, "The nut of the problem is that we've treated information as a 'thing,' as an inert entity to disseminate."[3] If the flow of information could be viewed as a river, then currently there are only tiny tributaries

> *Information is the new structure for society. It does not simply change what we do; it is defining what we will become.*

flowing from and to the point of service. Only the immediate information contained in the observations of the provider or the paper records of individual patients freely flows at the point of service. Even then access is not unfettered.

The paper records are restricted resources that can be used by only one person at a time, and they never portray things as they are at the moment. Aggregated and trend data are the bulk of the river, and

> *Information is not a thing; it is a dynamic, a living process. It acts more like a river flowing than a machine producing.*

that river flows primarily toward management. There are obstacles like cataracts that narrow the river and obstruct flow. These usually include the information experts, sometimes called analysts, who spend their time aggregating and trending information for others—again, usually managers. The more aggregated the data, the more senior the managers to which it is likely to be available, which means the flow is being further diverted away from the point of service.

One way to illustrate the problem is to view information from the perspective of a point-of-service decision maker. In our example, the point-of-service person, let us call her "Kelly Caregiver," is working in a shared governance organization. She is accountable not only for a daily caseload of patients but for the outcomes of care for those patients' entire experience with the organization. Further, she is accountable, as part of a team council, for the improvement of the outcomes of her patients and many other patients like hers that make up the population served by her work team. Her job does not end there. She is accountable for the way the work is done, for the competence of the workers who provide the services, and for the appropriate use of the information that flows as a result of the work.

Kelly works in an environment that values her equally with every other provider of service in the organization, from the housekeeper to the radiologist to the CEO. Equity is built right into the structure and is enabled by such systems as the compensation management system and the communication system. The principle of partnership

> *The information flow is continuous. It allows everyone to dip into it at any point along it when and where they need information in a format they can use.*

entails that every individual is provided access to the capabilities and resources of every other individual in the organization. Ownership fosters a willingness to offer those capabilities to any other partner because it is the means of supporting the worker, the work, and its outcomes.

INFORMATION AS A RESOURCE

The most important thing Kelly needs in order to fulfill her accountability every day is information, but not information handled in the traditional way. Unfortunately, tradition still rules in the area of communication. Kelly comes to work at 7:00 AM and participates in clinical report, where she receives a flow of information lasting a few seconds or a few minutes about each of her assigned patients. That information contains some clinical indicators of the patients' status and problems. Major procedures pending are sometimes included and sometimes not. Kelly then goes to the many charts and lists used in her service area, checks the pending or open physician prescriptions for medical care, and creates her version of a worklist for the day. That worklist shows the tasks necessary for her to complete for her load of patients within her 12 hours. She measures her success by

> *Information should help the provider make the decision that leads to the best outcome in the most timely fashion. It facilitates the provider's effort to do the right thing the first time, every time.*

whether or not she is able to finish up the task list and handle the inevitable interruptions by the time her shift ends.

The decisions Kelly makes throughout the day have to do with fitting together the tasks on the worklist with the immediate demands of her patients. She has an excellent education and knows the value of assessing and educating her patients. She is always driven by the need to do the right things and feels the pressure of her philosophical ideals, which frequently are at odds with the demands of the day. The kinds of things she must decide are, for example, "What is the most critical thing to do now? Ms. Smith must be ready for surgery in 15 minutes, and Dr. Jones is here demanding to know why his patient did not get the appropriate prep last night." Kelly has a "funny feeling" about Mr. Green but has not had time to get in the room to do an evaluation yet, and two members of her provider team do not understand their assignments. The information required to support the decisions she must make is scattered: a paper chart she needs is in the possession of someone else at the moment; the nurse for Dr. Jones's patient is now at home asleep; the surgery schedule is posted on the wall behind the counter, where everyone is charting; the competency/skills checklists are in the manager's office; and the routine for prepping patients for surgery is on a form back in the unit clerk's area of the nurses station. Gathering the data she needs is a formidable and time-consuming task. Furthermore, the difficulties she faces are not unusual, as every nurse can attest. Imagine the impact on the worklist if Mr. Green suddenly suffers an arrest and Kelly must manage a code. Will others help? Certainly, health care providers always rise to the occasion, regardless of what their workload is. But what happens when the providers Kelly hopes will ride to her rescue need rescuing themselves?

Kelly has had some exposure to systems thinking and realizes, once she is home and rested, that there are underlying causes of several of the problems she typically must deal with. The team members should be better trained and more aware of their roles, two novices should not be scheduled together, there really should be a better way to handle the presurgical patients earlier than following report, and she has no idea if cardiac arrest is common in the particular patient population that includes Mr. Green. Could Mr. Green's arrest

> *Many times the real questions about information are who has the right to access it and how can it be controlled? In truth, however, information should be widely generated, not narrowly controlled.*

have been avoided? Was her decision to quickly prepare Ms. Smith for surgery first an indirect cause of his arrest?

Where could she take all her concerns? Her supervisor? How many times has she complained without anything being done? Maybe she should air her concerns in the staff meeting. That is not for another week, and the meetings usually are not long enough or focused enough to deal with such issues. Maybe if she complained to Dr. Jones about her workload, he could get something done. Of course, she might then be viewed as a complainer. It is really not her job anyway, so maybe she should just keep quiet.[4]

SHIFTING CONTROL

In a shared governance model, the problems do not just go away, but there is a shift in the locus of decision making to the place where the problems occur and the means to uncover sustainable solutions exist.[5] One of the guiding ideas of shared governance is that the bulk of the decision making needs to occur at the place where the work is done.[6] How will Kelly be able to move decision making there? While the answer is not complex, its implementation certainly will be. Kelly needs to bring about radical change in the following five elements before she will be effective in moving 90 percent of the decisions that most concern her to the point of service where she lives and works:

1. structure
2. culture
3. training
4. information
5. systemness

Structure

The shared governance model described in this book begins to put people with a point-of-service perspective into a structure that fosters seamless relationships throughout the system. People at the point-of-service begin to create the work practices, policies, and procedures that have real meaning—real impact.[7] All the old stultifying administratively controlled three-ring binders are done away with, and only those few remaining rules that are fundamental to the integrity of the organization remain. The streamlined administrative framework makes those rules much easier to internalize and use in decision making than the massive books that ostensibly governed behavior in the old system. Like boosting stations, the corporate councils become places to which information flows, is aggregated and made congruent with the needs and decision requirements of the organization, and then is distributed to those who may have need of it.

> **Information should always facilitate decision making. Information should support anyone attempting to make the right decision the first time and every time.**

When Kelly needs decisions made regarding issues in her service area, she has her own multidisciplinary provider team to assist her. If an issue impacts more than just her service area or just her caseload of patients, Kelly can call on her pathway council to help. The object is to bring together the appropriate perspectives and disciplines to make the best possible decisions.[8]

Culture

The culture of the organization must support the empowerment of those providers who are struggling with the changes necessary to optimize their work.[9] Kelly, in our example, must feel confident that the values supporting her are uniformly held by all other members of the organization, including those in the management structure. All the usual checks, authorizations, and controls of the old system are replaced with enablers and empowerments, such as competency- and team-based compensation, peer review, and outcome-based evaluation. The leaders of the organization, as information management role models, must exhibit openness and sharing. They must demonstrate the value of the learning organization. Kelly must be able to quickly and easily access the information that will help her find the right solutions, preferably wherever she happens to be when she needs it. Finally, resources must be put at her disposal to carry out the implementation of her decisions.

> **In any system, it should be very simple for anyone at the point of service to satisfy a patient or family need.**

For instance, if Kelly decides a patient would be much calmer if he knew his family had money for a meal and a motel room for the night, she could access organization funds set aside for such purposes with no need for any authorization (her service's "checkbook"). It should be that simple to facilitate the provision of good service!

Training

Of course, Kelly does not instinctively know that aggregated and trended data for a patient population with Mr. Green's diagnosis might help her create a protocol of care based on "best practices" that would have reduced the chance of Mr. Green's having an arrest at that point in his course of illness. Nor would she automatically know that she could pull up flowcharts of the surgery preparation procedure and find that 6 of the 14 steps are no longer really necessary or that taking the old and new flowcharts to the councils would be an easy way to ensure that changes in procedure occur organizationwide, thereby helping many surgical patients. But these are skills that are easily learned if training and education are made available.

Information

However, even if the structure, culture, and training were in place, there would still be little change in Kelly's daily life without information. It does her no good to know the techniques for reading and utilizing aggregated and trended data if they are exceptionally difficult to get or if she must know ahead of time the specifics or the sources of a report in order to even request it. There must be information, not just data but usable information, available to Kelly when and where she needs it (see Figure 9-1).[10] It is the food for thoughtful processing and decision crafting.

So, is the answer to anticipate what Kelly will need and create tidy routine reports by the cartload every month? That has been the method used in the past to send information to the vicinity

> *At the point of service, information should be both easy to get and easy to use. There is nothing worse than dealing with information that has no meaning or cannot be used.*

of the decision maker. Unfortunately, it may not meet Kelly's need for availability and timeliness. Not many providers will take the time to wade through multiple reports to digest what is in each one and then pull out items from each to put together in a meaningful final form. They will go with their intuitions instead and take the consequences. Something much different is needed.

Technology is no longer the barrier. The only limit is the way information is conceptualized.

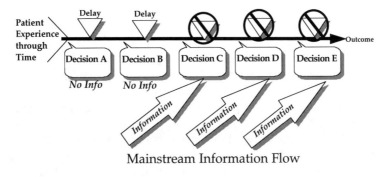

Mainstream Information Flow

Figure 9-1 Effect of Informed Decision Making on Patient Flow

Systemness

Linkages and relationships create systemness.[11] The linkages that are supported in a shared governance environment not only must facilitate the daily work but must lead the organization as a whole to the next level of evolution.[12] Shared governance supports point-of-service decision making and requires that the system be designed to ensure such decision making. User interface and ease are requisites for any data-based process that is intended to support decision making. They are also important for the relationship of the organization to its market and the community. It is not too much to expect every employee in an organization to "think globally and act locally" and to understand that every customer comes from and returns to a place that has contributed significantly to his or her being a customer in the first place.

> *In a shared governance system, all information is directed to supporting the point-of-service decision maker. It is there where the critical day-to-day issues are addressed and where most of the data support should be focused.*

So how does information management "systemness" fit in a shared governance approach? The relationships and linkage of information flows make up the feedback mechanisms of communication, and communication feeds decision making. In a sense, systemness is equivalent to the essential data sharing that tells one part of the system how another is doing and how changes in one place cause changes in the other parts of the system, and it is this systemness that must be recognized and supported to sustain a shared governance approach.

If systemness could be visualized, it might look like a flow of work with decision loops all along it that relate to the patient experience through time. Whether the decisions support a smooth, unobstructed experience for the patient or become sources of delay and frustration depends on the stream of information that drives the decision process (see Figure 9-1).

INFORMATION FLOW AMONG SHARED GOVERNANCE ENTITIES

The shared governance structure comprises the corporate councils, the pathway councils, all the provider and service teams, and all the partners throughout the system, including suppliers, patients, individual staff partners, and physicians. In the old hierarchy, the lower down the person, the more dilute the information. Point-of-service personnel and customers got only what they could gather for themselves and what was immediately available in the provider–customer interaction (e.g., the medical record). The higher up the person, the more condensed the information. In the past, only senior management got aggregated, trended information that reflected the status of

> *In the past, only senior management got aggregated data. The point-of-service person never saw how his or her work affected the whole system or how others affected his or her work.*

the entire organization. The result of this style of information flow was that each employee had no idea how his or her individual efforts affected the overall organizational outcomes—a form of isolation from the tactics and strategies upon which the decisions of the organization should be based.

In the shared governance system, strategic and tactical levels of information are routinely dealt with in all councils and provider team settings. The context for decisions is constantly being created jointly by the point of service and all levels of the structure. Because both formal and informal information exchange is vital, the informal "grapevine" is channeled by making the workings of the councils open to anyone.

Since there are no secrets, the informal networks should carry much more real information than they used to. Not that those incredibly imaginative and inventive individuals that exist in every organization will cease to feed the rumor mill; it is just easier to verify or discredit unsubstantiated stories. The formal information flow is supported by having the membership of each of the corporate councils assigned specific pathways that they are responsible for keeping informed. It is also supported with all the typical tools, such as minutes, newsletters, share points, and bulletins, and everyone in the organization has access to the e-mail system and can have a personal e-mail address.

> **The purpose of all information that flows through the shared governance system is to get the right data in the right form to the right person at the right time.**

The purpose of all information flow in the shared governance decision-making groups is to get the right information to the right point of service at the right time. The corporate councils must ensure that the processes are designed, implemented, and maintained with that goal in mind.

SELF-DIRECTED WORK GROUPS AND INFORMATION MANAGEMENT

When planning how to use self-directed (point-of-service–driven) work groups in the implementation of a major new clinical information system, several values, assumptions, and guiding ideas should be placed on the table. The backdrop for consideration is formed by the principles of shared governance: equity, ownership, accountability, and partnership. Secondary guiding values include openness, "localness," and merit. And the main assumption should be that "any person, given the right information and the knowledge of how to use it, will make a sound decision."[13]

All these elements must be incorporated into the information management philosophy of the organization, and it makes sense to include them in the theme that will form the foundation for those designing any new organization-wide information system.

> **The most difficult challenge for team development is learning how to manage confrontation and conflict.**

The self-directed teams should be put together using a mix of staff (some clinical practitioners and some technical experts) to keep the perspective as broad and "whole systems" as possible. Each team should go through a rigorous training and on-the-job work experience program before the actual system development tasks begin. During development, the team members should familiarize themselves with shared governance principles and structure, shared leadership skills, and the many redesign and reengineering efforts going on throughout the organization.

Training encompasses the topics of project management, systems thinking, systems assessment and design, shared governance principles, collaborative decision making, confrontation, presentation, continuous quality improvement, and basic problem solving. Each team member can then be given projects requiring the utilization of all the skills taught and be coached by other team members as well as by a service leader. The most difficult skills to master are those required for handling confrontation and conflict.

> *Self-directed information teams, like all teams, must learn their "rules of engagement" with each other in relation to the work they do. Outcomes of work cannot be obtained if there isn't a framework to facilitate and sustain them.*

The evolution of the team during the first year involves intense learning, and some of the original members may exit as the team grows. Inevitably, problems bubble to the surface and demand changes in behavior. To the extent that the members can be flexible and adapt to the more sophisticated expectations, they will succeed. If a member cannot adapt, the rest of the team must address the problem and, if necessary, remove the member. This is the toughest side of accountability. It is not okay to accommodate an ineffective or inflexible member. Everyone must be capable of fulfilling his or her accountability. For the team to come to this understanding and then take the necessary action is a sign that it is becoming truly self-directed.[14]

In order to build a team context for their actions, the members usually spend a great deal of time in the early months developing the parameters within which they intend to work. Their activities include writing out the philosophy they will use to do their work, their goals and objectives as individuals and as a team, the rules they will use to deal with one another, and the behaviors they expect from one another. They can choose to coordinate their activities by rotating members into and out of a "coordinator" role. The coordinator is responsible for calling meetings and making sure the timelines are displayed so that any red flags can be picked up right away. The coordinator also has the primary duty of bringing together any team members in conflict and seeing to it that a resolution is reached.

Team-based evaluations can begin with a tool used by service leaders that everyone uses to evaluate everyone else—a 360-degree approach to performance review. The results can be aggregated and shared with the team members. The service leader can then follow up with any coaching or counseling indicated by the results. As the team matures (i.e., as the members become more comfortable with their own skills and with each other), the evaluation process involves more open dialogue within the team itself.

> *Information development teams focus on the format for information generation. How it is used and applied at the point of service is determined in conjunction with the user.*

INFORMATION PROJECT TEAM

A good project team will include both clinical staff and technical staff. The team has a direct relationship to an information management steering committee (or some similar group). Each team member is accountable for the management of a piece of the project; and, of equal importance, each is accountable for his or her work and responsible to the other members. There is a role for a team leader or chair of the group, whose primary responsibilities are to run team meetings and to facilitate the activities. The team can decide that this role be rotated on a variable timeline basis so that all members have their turn. Project team assignments can be completely handled by the team, with input from its advisors, which should include the information systems service integrator, the consulting partner for information, the service leader, and the clinical information system vendor representatives.

> *Sustainable outcomes depend on the ownership of the work designed to produce them. The higher the level of ownership of the work, the more sustainable the outcomes. While this is a simple truth, it is counter to the design of most organizations.*

The team should apply standard project management techniques, such as the development of problem statements, the identification of agreed outcomes, and the measurement of progress toward these outcomes. One of the primary benefits of this approach is that there is a uniform, well-understood process for solving problems. Each project manager is responsible for the development and maintenance of a Gantt chart for identifying barriers to achieving the desired outcomes or other issues that need resolution.[15]

THE TROUBLE WITH VENDOR PARTNERS

The self-directed work team concept is not generally well understood by software vendors, and shared governance or team leaders will have to take the time to explain the basic philosophy. The initial reaction will likely be skepticism based on a strong conviction that a major implementation effort must be supported by a hierarchical structure with "someone in control." Doubts about the concept usually emerge in the first six months, before the perseverance of the project team is able to change the vendors' perceptions of what works.

As the project approaches the completion of system tailoring and the beginning of integration testing, it often becomes apparent that not all of the objectives are being met. More importantly, it often becomes apparent that not all the objectives are clearly defined. When some objectives are not fully achieved, the leadership begins to assume more of the responsibility to ensure that the project schedule is not jeopardized rather than dealing head on with the noisy issue of individual accountability in a self-directed work group.

> *There is much talk of self-directed work teams. There is precious little evidence of belief in them in health care or in their real value to the organization.*

The chief information officer (CIO) can act as facilitator for the team in a series of sessions focused on assessing its strengths and weaknesses as a self-directed work group and determining its next steps. Three key outcomes should result from these sessions:

1. The team should remain a self-directed work group so that it can keep accountability for the work it does.
2. There should be continued emphasis on performance evaluation and continued attention paid to the kind and quality of the relationships between members.

3. The ability of team members to directly confront issues that belong to them and deal with each other honestly and frankly should continuously be developed.

The Clinical Information System project will not be successful if the system implementation stops at the creation of the self-directed work team. The ties between the developmental process and the operational units are key. The team, supplemented by pathway personnel, should engage in building a good information infrastructure. The time commitment of the pathway personnel varies by area, from minimal involvement (e.g., periodic meetings) up to a full slate of activities. The project managers also must work closely with the pathway councils and provider teams as they redesign the work flow to accommodate the new level of automation.

> *In planning for effective information systems, it is important that the users be part of the team. Information should not be designed by the information senders without input from the end users.*

To ensure appropriate linkage, a patient care task force should be involved in the project from the development of the request for proposal through implementation. The plan should be that this group, supplemented by representatives from other groups, will function as a user's group once the system is operational.

THE SUPERUSERS

Another step necessary for moving an entire organization toward automation self-sufficiency is the development of "superusers." These are individuals whose role is to help point-of-service staff identify problems, develop solutions, and answer questions. The superusers will be required to fully understand the work flow in their areas and to possess the information system skills necessary for superior first-line support.

The advantage of a whole-systems involvement process such as shared governance is that the major clinical information system is installed on time and on budget and there is a "whole systems" perspective. Any member of the system can take the initiative to fix a problem when it arises in order to keep the project moving as it should. This approach provides the fast, fluid, and flexible teams of problem solvers and system designers. Whatever unpredictable shifts in the health care marketplace are thrown at the organization, it will have the resources to develop an effective response.

INFORMATION MANAGEMENT PHILOSOPHY

A view widely shared both inside and outside of the health care industry is that the industry comprises data-intensive, autonomous organizations. One common problem with the information transmitted, however, is that it is designed by the senders rather than the receivers. As a result, there is a mishmash of data processes and connections that are poorly integrated and not very effective (see Figure 9-2). Over the course of the past few years, experts have recognized that an important part of the health care business is information management. Organizations that expect to survive as the health care environment undergoes

> *Over the next decade, more than 50 percent of the capital outlays of the health system will be devoted to building a new information infrastructure for health care.*

major transitions must manage information as an asset and leverage it accordingly.

At most health systems, the largest capital investment by far is in the clinical information system. The largest investment of time and energy is in the people who will run and use the system. Information management requires a cultural change—a change in what happens in people's minds as they approach their work. Such a foundational change requires a whole new philosophy.

A well-developed philosophy of information management holds that

- information is truly a shared resource for all members of the integrated health system
- access to information should be uniformly available to all authorized members of the integrated health system
- adequate education that allows the users to take advantage of the system's capabilities must be provided
- members of the integrated health network should be able to use information wherever their workplace is

GOOD INFORMATION MANAGEMENT STRATEGIES

It is widely recognized that a health system's ability to compete and survive in a rapidly changing health care market is highly dependent upon the creation of

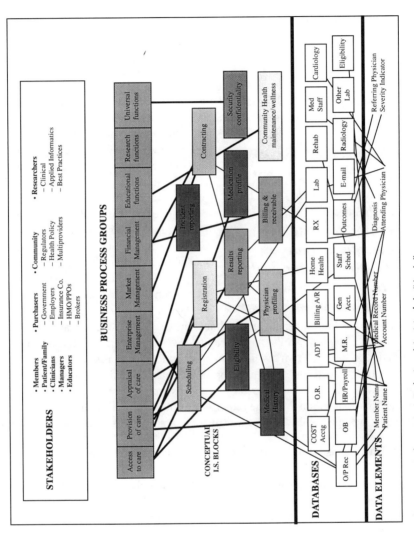

Figure 9-2 Information Relationship Model: "As Is"

information management strategies and the successful implementation of key information systems. Figure 9-3 shows that the information management strategies are in fact tactics with specific outcomes that tie directly back to one or more corporate strategies. The tactics in turn become drivers for specific information system projects that have specific goals as well. There may be a single project (or perhaps multiple projects in various stages of implementation) whose purpose is to support a given information management strategy. The following information management strategies can help enable operational improvements that in turn will improve the value of the services:

- Provide for the integration of all network partners by providing the electronic communication linkages that support the collection and exchange of information.
- Provide a common set of information management tools so that individuals and teams can get the information they need to pursue their goals.
- Bring clinical and financial data to the point of service to support the timely, cost-effective, and high-quality decisions.

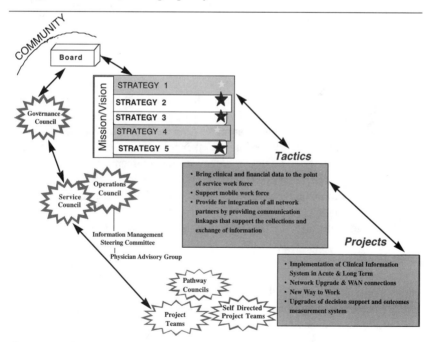

Figure 9-3 The Information Management Cascade

- Provide the information management support that enables the organizations within the integrated health network to evolve into knowledge-based learning organizations at the staff level.
- Provide information management tools that support worker mobility and ensure access to needed information regardless of the workplace location.
- Make it feasible for all service providers to share applicable data about a customer.
- Ensure that the information system protects the "customer" and the user from the complexity of the system and safeguards confidentiality.
- Provide the information management tools that will enable focused diagnosis, treatment, and business decisions to be made.
- Have use of aggregate data along with external databases and comparative data, to pursue opportunities for improvement in practice.

TACTICAL IMPLEMENTATION—SOME SAMPLE PROJECTS

There are several significant projects that symbolize the drama of implementing information-based processes in a health system. One sample strategic and tactical cascade suggests some key information projects for the future of effective health systems:

- Network Upgrade
  This project encompasses a comprehensive data communication network plan that entails rewiring all existing facilities, includes installation of network management tools, and establishes high-speed wide area linkages between facilities. The data communication network provides the infrastructure foundation that will enable all other information system endeavors to move forward. It ties directly to three information management strategies:
  - Provide for the integration of all network partners by providing the electronic communication linkages that support the collection and exchange of information.
  - Provide information management tools that allow mobility of the worker and ensure access to the information he/she needs regardless of the workplace location.
  - Build the information infrastructure that will define the health system of the future and create the mobility necessary to bring health services to the subscriber rather than the subscriber to health services.

VIRTUAL OFFICE: NEW WAYS TO WORK

The success of shared governance is highly dependent upon effective communication. The "new way to work" concept supports new ways of communicating. The concept also enables sharing of work information more quickly and allows widely disparate components to be brought together to form a whole. An integrated set of applications should be created for initial use by the service leadership team, the administrators, and some of the information service pathway self-directed work teams, and a plan should be devised for eventually deploying the tool set throughout the organization. The following applications might be included:

- group scheduling (calendars)
- an improved electronic mail system
- templates that will provide for uniform problem solving
- electronic opinion surveys with prioritization capabilities
- work flow improvements supported by electronic forms
- electronic idea exchange "brainstorming"

The early users of these applications can be characterized as a "mobile" work force. It is imperative that individuals have access to information they need to make decisions and perform their jobs from any location. Therefore, the term "virtual office" is appropriate, and what a "virtual office" approach entails will be described in more detail later in the chapter. Note that this approach is related to the following information management strategies:

- Provide for the integration of all network partners by providing electronic communication linkages that support the collection and exchange of information.
- Provide a common set of information management tools so that individuals and teams can get the information they need to pursue their goals.
- Provide the information management support that enables the organizations within the integrated health network to evolve into knowledge-based learning organizations at the staff level.
- Provide information management tools that support worker mobility and ensure access to needed information regardless of the workplace location.
- Provide information management tools that will enable focused diagnosis, treatment, and business decisions to be made.
- Enable decisions in the shared governance councils and pathways to be made quickly and effectively by providing the tools necessary for thorough deliberation.

CLINICAL INFORMATION SYSTEM

The scope of this project is significant, and the implementation should be planned to last a minimum of three years. The first phase includes the replacement of the registration/admission, discharge and transfer, medical records coding and abstracting, chart deficiency tracking, radiology management, pharmacy, laboratory results reporting, and transcribed report viewing functions and the addition of new functionality for emergency department and automated worklists, order entry, and charge capture throughout the organization. The implementation should occur at all facilities at the same time, including in physicians' offices that currently have access to the existing results reporting system. In subsequent phases, automated documentation (charting and assessments), multidisciplinary care plans, enterprise scheduling, ancillary management, and patient accounting might be added. The clinical information system, which is also further described later in the chapter, is related to these information management strategies:

- Provide for the integration of all network partners by providing the electronic communication linkages that support the collection and exchange of information.
- Provide a common set of information management tools so that individuals and teams can get the information they need to pursue their goals.
- Bring clinical and financial data to the point of service to support timely, cost-effective, and high-quality decisions.
- Provide the information management support that enables the organizations within the integrated health network to evolve into knowledge-based learning organizations at the staff level.
- Provide information management tools that support worker mobility and ensure access to needed information regardless of the workplace location.
- Make it feasible for all service providers to share applicable data about a customer.
- Ensure that the information system protects the "customer" and the user from the complexity of the system and safeguards confidentiality.
- Provide the information management tools that will enable focused diagnosis, treatment, and business decisions to be made.

All of the initiatives mentioned here should be a part of the organization's efforts to build true point-of-service information support. It is simply not possible to build a sustainable provider-driven system without offering the necessary assistance to providers where they live and practice. Furthermore, the empowerment approach simply will not have the infrastructure it needs to sustain point-of-service control and foster good analysis and decision making. A commitment to creating effective information systems indicates the willingness of the organization to build structure to undergird the primary provider–patient relationship and the teams configured around it.

ROLES AND ACCOUNTABILITY

In recognition of the importance of devising information management strategies and implementing information systems that support the strategies (no minor undertaking), an information management steering committee should be established by the operations council. The role of this committee is to:

- develop information management strategies to facilitate managing care to a value standard
- engage in strategic information technology planning for voice, data, and image
- provide implementation oversight for key projects and initiatives
- review opportunities for utilizing information technology to improve value using the Malcolm Baldrige quality management framework or some other national standard

The information management steering committee should be chaired by a physician, if possible, and should include a service integrator, the service pathway leaders, at least two persons from the information services pathway and one person from the system leadership team, the CIO, the chief financial officer (CFO), a representative from the physician groups, and a project manager from the team responsible for implementing the clinical information system.

> *All of the information system development means nothing if it does not enable those at the point of service to make better decisions and to evaluate their outcomes.*

Establishing a physician advisory group is also wise. This can be chaired by the same physician who chairs the information management committee. The role of the physician advisory group is to

- standardize operational information flow for physician users
- champion the use of the clinical information system by the physicians

- participate in the ongoing design and development of the clinical information system (this entails participating in vendor–physician advisory group sessions)
- evaluate recommendations for system modifications and enhancements
- become "superusers" and advocates of the information management systems

Members of the information management steering committee provide a linkage to all three councils. The implications of information management strategy development and strategic information technology planning concern all three councils, whereas implementation oversight and information technology utilization review primarily concern the operations council.

THE CHANGING ROLE OF THE CHIEF INFORMATION OFFICER

The terms "chief" and "officer" connote control and top-down management processes that do not have a place in a shared governance structure. The CIO's new role is to act as a senior advisor for information management and information services throughout the organization. The CIO helps to develop strategies and tactical plans that support a common vision of the "ideal system," and the way of working requires more time be devoted to educating and coaching everyone (not just a few leaders) and openly designing and facilitating information management initiatives (not creating mandates or dictating policies created with limited stakeholder involvement). The education process is not confined to information system staff but encompasses the board, the leadership team, physicians, and the provider teams.

Power in the old model was held by controlling the purse strings for information system acquisitions and the information systems staff. In the shared governance structure, the service integrators have the accountability for the provision of resources, both staff and dollars. This relieves the CIO of having sole accountability for all operational decisions, which provides more time for focusing on strategy development. There are still opportunities to provide expert advice on operational matters, although the actual decision making is done by empowered individuals throughout the organization. The CIO

> *In shared governance, the role of the chief information officer is primarily that of consultant to the system —the entire system, not just the information systems service.*

should be invited to all shared governance council meetings and be highly encouraged to attend the operations council meetings, where tactics are formulated.

The specific responsibilities of the CIO might include these:

- acting as advisor to the clinical information system project
- assisting in the conceptual design of the integrated health network core system
- facilitating "whole systems" thinking and clinical information system template development
- assisting in the design of the learning lab
- facilitating problem-solving sessions
- educating the leadership team, the information systems staff, and the board on information management matters
- participating in redesign teams and system evaluation and selection processes
- developing vendor partnerships and relationships
- exploring telemedicine opportunities

Two of the above items deserve expansion. The first is integrated health network system design, which is covered in detail later in this chapter. The other is the board and the leadership team education.

BOARD SUPPORT FOR THE NEW INFORMATION INFRASTRUCTURE

Specified board meetings should be devoted to understanding and supporting the construction of the information infrastructure. The CIO must act as a bridge between the board and the project team working on the CIS implementation and between them and the information systems service integrator. Creating an interactive learning lab environment is the best method for indicating to the leadership team and the board what the future holds in store and for showing how the information infrastructure fits into an overall design of the integrated health network. The leadership team should format a dress rehearsal for the board meeting. In addition, there needs to be an opportunity to educate the leadership team on board dynamics.

The best way to approach educating the board is to develop a learning lab for them. Storyboards, workstation presentations, hands-on demonstrations, and video presentations are good learning tools. For getting across the nature of the clinical information system, there should be areas set up to illustrate system use from the physician's perspective, the caregiver's perspective, and the patient's perspective. In addition to CIS demonstrations, there should be a workstation available that demonstrates the capability of the new system, a storyboard that provides a snapshot of where the project activities are relative to the schedule, and a description of the work team that is implementing the project.

> *Board support for the new information infrastructure services needs to be gained by involving the board members in the experience of the change through active learning rather than simple presentation.*

Another tool for giving the board a picture of the information systems is a demonstration of the capabilities of the "new way to work" project. A storyboard that describes the data communication network projects, including pictures of the wiring before and after, will allow the board to see the differences. A hands-on presentation built using computer-based training tools might be helpful. The presentation could describe, for example, the merits of the new information processes. Also, a video of the physician interface could be played for the members. Each learning area should be staffed with team members doing demonstrations or answering questions. The physician's perspective area should have tools that show the ease of use of the information system and its potential contribution toward physician inclusion in the organization and should offer a hands-on demonstration of a computer-based training module being developed specifically for physicians.

The impact of a learning lab in terms of increased support from the board can be formidable. In addition to letting the leadership and board learn about the information system efforts, it provides the individuals who are doing the actual system implementation an opportunity to respond to a broad spectrum of impressions and questions from board members. The effect on the entire organization can be very energizing.

In the old model, education of the board on information system matters usually involved a lecture delivered by the CIO and perhaps another senior vice-president. The staff closest to the implementation projects would not have been engaged to participate, and it

> *Every presentation to the board should include the staff upon whom any change will have the greatest impact.*

is unlikely that the entire leadership team would have had an opportunity to see the presentation and participate in refining it for the board. Bringing the stakeholders together creates further investment in and ownership of the challenging process of garnering board support.

INTEGRATED HEALTH NETWORK CORE SYSTEM DESIGN

It becomes clear early in the implementation of patient-based information systems and in the development of an electronic medical record that such a record will be of limited use unless key pieces of information are captured and documented in the physician's office.[16] It should also become clear that an integrated health network needs a more global view of members or enrollees, many of whom are not ill but require health management services (e.g., well-baby checkups, screening exams, etc.). Therefore, the electronic "health" record must span the continuum of care, and the design of the information infrastructure must reflect this level of continuity (see Figure 9-4).

Even though the ideal is an electronic health record, it is not well understood exactly what an electronic health record should be. It is a myth, for example, that adequate health record software can currently be bought and installed. On the other hand, building an electronic health record in-house, without support from vendors, is also problematic. Institutions that have taken this approach have typically spent millions of dollars and achieved only limited functionality. A significant portion of the development cycle is spent on designing the perfect system and never getting anything installed.

> *The day is long past when a system can simply buy an information product and make it fit the needs of the system. The culture of a system drives all design.*

Any successful health system will need to go through a process of creating its own conceptual model of an integrated health record. After all, it is this record that will supply the data that will be fed into the dynamic river of information that will support decision making and enable improvements. The approach taken to developing the information system design should be guided by these rules:

- Develop an "as is" information relationship model (Figure 9-2) and an "ideal" information relationship model (Figure 9-4).

Figure 9-4 Information Relationship Model: "Ideal"

- Develop ideal flows from the perspective of each of these major stakeholders:
  —members (patients)
  —physicians
  —caregivers
- Develop a list of information management needs from an administrative perspective.
- Develop a system integration model (Figure 9-5) and continuum of care models for each layer (Figures 9-6 to 9-12).

A good integrated information model identifies the stakeholders, the primary business processes, the information system conceptual blocks, the databases that support the conceptual blocks, and, at the lowest level, the detailed data elements. The diagram seems fairly straightforward when the focus is on the relationship between a business process and the conceptual information system blocks that support the process. However, at the next level, the complexity of the existing environment is apparent. There are multiple databases that contain the same information. Some of the duplication is within network entities, and some is between entities (e.g., the medical staff organization, the physician's offices, and the pay-

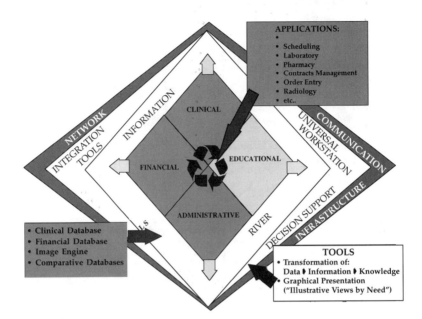

Figure 9-5 System Integration Model

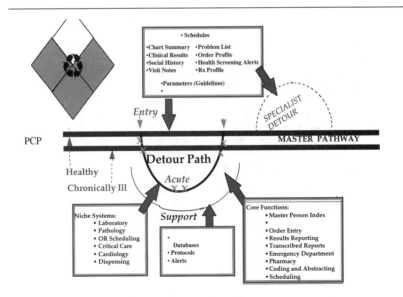

Figure 9-6 Core System Components: Clinical

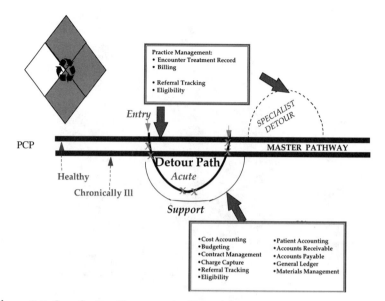

Figure 9-7 Core System Components: Financial

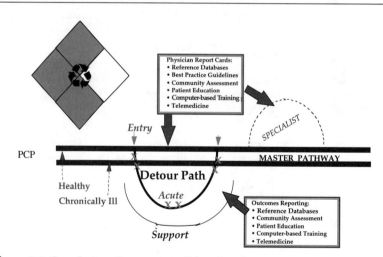

Figure 9-8 Core System Components: Educational

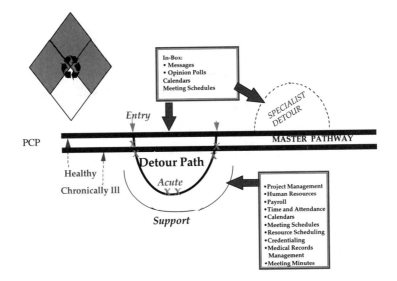

Figure 9-9 Core System Components: Administrative

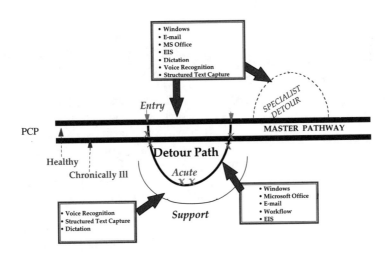

Figure 9-10 Core System Components: Software Components

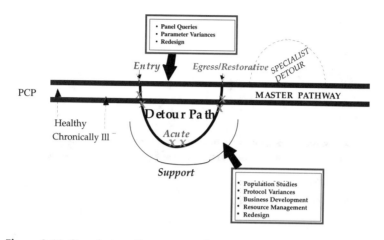

Figure 9-11 Core System Components: Reporting Processes

ers or health plans). It is to be expected that the "data element layer" in an environment with multiple independent or loosely coupled databases would be as complex as a data system in which the data elements are in multiple places and have different definitions.

The "ideal" information relationship model (Figure 9-4) removes the duplicate databases from the picture completely. For example, there is no need for multiple laboratory systems in an integrated health network, or operating room scheduling. The model also contains an "information river," which is a repository for data to flow throughout the system, and an organizational data dictionary, with common data definitions and mapping to the data sources.

> **In an integrated system, the need for data duplication at any level is eliminated forever.**

Without some model of the information relationships, the desired outcomes are unlikely to be achieved, and the complexity that prevailed in the past will grow to the point of causing the entire infrastructure to collapse.

As the ideal flow of information from a member's perspective is developed, it becomes clear that the following goals should be pursued—and that their achievement depends on the existence of a truly integrated information system that allows data to flow freely from the initial intake to wherever they are needed:

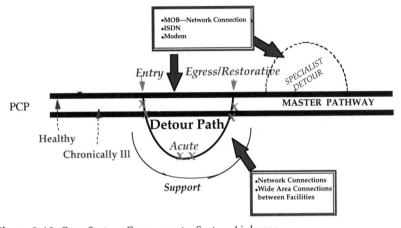

Figure 9-12 Core System Components: System Linkages

- hassle-free care from the time of enrollment:
  —coordinated appointment scheduling
  —data capture at the source (once and only once)
- systemwide identification of the patient and the patient's condition
- orderly, caring, and sensitive service provision
- desired outcomes ("feel better faster")
- restricted access to sensitive data for those who do not have a need to know

Caregiver satisfaction will increase only if the information system achieves the following outcomes:

- convenient access to all necessary information
- access to reference data close to the point of care
- faster turnaround of tests
- accurate tracking of each patient's whereabouts
- process improvements ("saves time")
- desired outcomes
- improved communication between health care team members
- management of a patient population to a value standard

From an administrative perspective, the information system should achieve the following outcomes:

- convenient access to information in support of decision making:
  —financial indicators (e.g., volumes, revenues, contract performance, etc.)
  —comparative information
  —clinical outcomes
- high levels of member, physician, and staff satisfaction
- increased market share

The system integration model diagram depicts the various layers of information technology that are necessary to provide various "views" of information for decision-making purposes:

- The outer layer is the communication layer—the network infrastructure that supports the rapid movement of data, voice, and image throughout the integrated health network.
- The next layer consists of the integration and decision support tools and the conceptual "universal" workstation.
- The information river provides for the combining of information to support the development of multifaceted views. It is commonly referred to as a "repository" or "information warehouse" in today's information technology terminology.
- The center depicts the four functional areas (clinical, financial, administrative, and educational) that are supported by applications that focus on the collection, manipulation, and reporting of data for a specific purpose.

The master path continuum of care model described in Chapter 7 should be used to further define the specific applications that are required to support each of the four functional areas along the continuum of care.

INFORMATION DEVELOPMENT AS EVOLUTION

The design and implementation of the integrated health record and the information management reporting system is an evolutionary process. The first step is to analyze data from external sources to begin to develop population studies. Initially, the reporting across the continuum of care will need to be derived from claims data and external sources.

The ideal information system would allow for "plug and play" pieces that fit together seamlessly with little to no effort, similar to the systems that support banking and automated fund transfers. The reality is that health systems are still

> **Development of effective information systems unfolds over time, each piece relating to another. It cannot be constructed overnight.**

a long way away from achieving seamless integration. It is not financially feasible to replace all of the existing systems within any health system. The new systems must be truly "open" and support industry standards and open system protocols. Proprietary, closed systems are no longer acceptable. Information "islands" are also not acceptable in an integrated health network. Members must be willing to contribute information if they wish to receive information.

Integrated health networks need to partner with vendors who are committed to their success and are willing to partner with other vendors to foster seamless integration. It is a common perception among information management executives and consultants that the majority of vendors today do not truly understand the nature of integrated delivery systems, nor have a clue as to how to redesign the care delivery system. Off-the-shelf hospital information systems have an inherent structure that supports acute care processes (many of these systems are centered around "charge capture," not true clinical care). Considering the ratio of physicians' office visits and ambulatory service visits to acute care hospitalizations, it does seem unlikely that systems with an acute care focus can be adapted for the outpatient setting. Likewise, systems that have been designed and developed for physicians' offices or ambulatory clinics probably do not have the capability to support acute care processes. This should not come as a surprise, since there are relatively few acute care facilities that have a single vendor that provides solutions for all of their information needs. Therefore, why expect there to be a single vendor offering a complete line of software for the emerging and rapidly changing integrated delivery systems? Nonetheless, it is important to maintain a whole-system perspective and select the major components that will benefit the whole rather than a narrowly focused component.

Although it is likely that there will be more integrated system solutions available in the next two to five years, health care organizations must begin to

> **Shared governance depends on the quality and effectiveness of data at the point of service and the ability of the provider and patient to use it.**

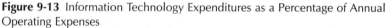

Figure 9-13 Information Technology Expenditures as a Percentage of Annual Operating Expenses

leverage information now to remain viable in today's market. It is going to require a significant investment to obtain the desired results. The service industries that are much further along than health care are investing in information technology (see Figure 9-13). The information infrastructure is the future of health care.

REFERENCES

1. T. Porter-O'Grady and C. Krueger-Wilson, *The Leadership Revolution in Health Care: Altering Systems, Changing Behaviors* (Gaithersburg, MD: Aspen Publishers, 1995).
2. T. Porter-O'Grady, *Implementing Shared Governance* (Baltimore: Mosby, 1992).
3. M. Wheatley, *Leadership and the New Science* (San Francisco: Berrett-Koehler, 1992).
4. J. Begun and K. White, "Altering Nursing's Dominant Logic: Guidelines from Complex Adaptive Systems Theory," *Complexity and Chaos in Nursing* 2, no. 1 (1995):7–14.
5. S. DeWoody and J. Price, "A Systems Approach to Multidimensional Critical Paths," *Nursing Management* 25, no. 11 (1994):47–51.
6. C. Chowaniec, "Democracy and the Living Organization," *At Work* 3, no. 2 (1994):17–19.
7. K. Evans et al., "Whole Systems Shared Governance: A Model for the Integrated Health System," *Journal of Nursing Administration* 25, no. 5 (1995):18–27.
8. J. Byrne, "The Horizontal Corporation," *Business Week*, 20 December 1993, 76–81.
9. J. Kotter and J. Heskett, *Corporate Culture and Performance* (New York: The Free Press, 1992).
10. P. Drucker, "The Information Executives Really Need," *Harvard Business Review* 72, no. 6 (1995):54–63.

11. K. Duncan, *Health Information and Health Reform: The Need for a Health Information System* (San Francisco: Jossey-Bass, 1994).

12. T. Porter-O'Grady, "Whole Systems Shared Governance: Creating the Seamless Organization," *Nursing Economics* 12 (1994):187–195.

13. P. Drucker, *Management* (New York: Harper & Row, 1977).

14. J. Katzenbach and D. Smith, *The Wisdom of Teams* (Boston: McKinsey & Co., 1993).

15. C. Meyer, "How the Right Measures Help Teams Excel," *Harvard Business Review* 72, no. 3 (1994):95–103.

16. J. Tan, "Integrating Health Care with Information Technology," *Health Care Management Review* 19, no. 2 (1994):72–80.

Chapter 10

Building toward Community in Health Care

Tim Porter-O'Grady and Marsha Parker

Loyalty to a petrified notion never broke a chain or freed a human soul.

Mark Twain

HEALTH AND THE COMMUNITY

Implementing shared governance in a health system would accomplish nothing if the health of those served did not improve for the better. The test of any renewal process is its impact on the purposes and work of the organization. Unfortunately, few measures exist yet to determine the relationship between restructuring health care services and community health improvement. However, that does not diminish the need to uncover the relationship.[1]

All the work undertaken at any integrated health network would have no long-term value if it did not address the issue of community health. Achieving the status of preferred health service provider depends on the fit between the populations served and the services offered. Further, patient satisfaction depends on the patients' obtaining health outcomes that can be directly related back to the services provided by the health network. All the shared decision making and seamless structure in the world will be futile if enduring community health is not the main result.[2]

The first step, of course, is to build a service community. That must be the central focus of the renewal and redesign work of shared governance and integration at any health system. The point-of-service design that has been created must support the system's purposes and work. The object is to engage the system at its center and force it to operate in a way that enhances provider–patient relationship.

The service pathways now represent populations of patients, and the service constructs support their needs. All the providers are located in proximity to each other and configured around the patients. Removed from the organization are most if not all of the barriers that impeded their relationships with each other and with the patients. Such are the structural shifts related to implementing shared governance concepts (see Figure 10-1).[3]

> *In the renewal process, there must ultimately be a fit between the changes undertaken within the system and the impact on those it serves.*

The critical issue then becomes, how does the organization, itself growing organizationally more healthy, move more closely to the community in order to build the framework for creating a healthy community?

THE BASICS

Community health cannot be obtained without the community becoming involved in the effort. Allowing a dependent relationship between staff and community members to develop diminishes the members' accountability for their own health. However, for the community to become involved, positive relationships must already exist between providers all along the continuum of care. Therefore, the organization of the system must make possible broad-based relationships between the providers and must sustain those relationships through an effective communication and evaluation system.[4]

> *A health system cannot long sustain a real impact on the health of the community unless the system itself is healthy.*

In newly integrating health systems, beginning parallel and horizontal relationships are being built between physicians and other providers. Linking the physicians together through the clinical network is critical for connecting the physicians to the system (see Chapter 7). Moving physicians to the center of the health care decision process is great, but that does not ensure they will work collaboratively or effectively there. Making it impossible for them to be successful in any other way is an essential management strategy.[5]

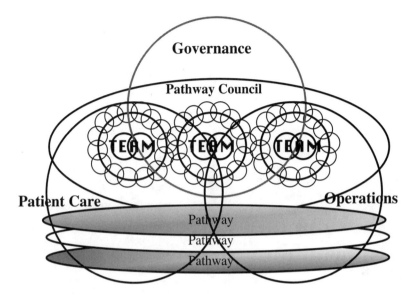

Figure 10-1 Integrating the System: The Whole-Systems Shared Governance Model

---

The need to pull the physicians permanently into a point-of-service partnership demands that every function and element of their practice of medicine be linked to the operating health system and support the partnership. To build a positive partnership between physicians and the health system, the support structure must tie the physicians tightly to the system. This is done, not to "capture" the physicians, but to give them no reason or need to operate outside of the system. In short, management, clinical, and information supports must work in concert to ensure that the physicians never have to go outside the system to get any practice issue addressed.[6]

This approach demands a continuous refinement of the partnership. Achieving a functional partnership does not happen overnight. In fact, it requires a long-term strategy. Such a strategy might well include the following tactics:

- Move the medical service organization the next step into a true committed clinical partnership between the physicians and the system. Make sure that physicians are located at every point where decisions that affect health service are made.

- Incorporate the medical staff problem-solving process into the partnership. This ensures that problems are identified and solved at the point of service. Remove any system or medical staff mechanism that would cause solution seeking to be moved away from the places where problems arise and have their impact.
- Ensure that the elected officers of the medical staff also serve on the organizational shared governance bodies so that physician practice and systems decision making are inexorably joined. This creates a seamless linkage between the organized medical staff and the system to which it is partnered.
- Connect the allied physician group to the information system at all levels, ensuring that all physician support and systems databases are integrated at every level of physician practice—from office management to patient clinical data—for every subscriber in the system.

LINKAGE IS KEY

While linking the physicians is a priority, it is only part of the work. This same kind of linkage must be forged for all the major providers. The nurses must be linked directly to all clinical partners in the system because they manage the patient-based relationships all along the clinical continuum. Pharmacists, therapists, social workers, and others must also be connected to each other along the continuum as a means of assuring the subscriber that all the pieces of the service construct are in place and tracking the subscriber at every level of interaction with the system.[7]

> *The system must support, track, and follow the subscriber through every level of need for the life of his or her relationship.*

High-intensity connectedness ensures that the needs of the subscribers will be fully addressed, the costs associated with service provision will be tracked, the outcomes will be compared and contrasted within the system and between systems, and service value will be continually evaluated. The effectiveness of the health system is determined by the intensity of connectedness at both the provider and the patient level. The patient value stream is therefore emphasized as the core element that drives all others in the system. It is this framework that newly integrating health systems have yet to finalize but upon which they must build future viability.

THE INFORMATION INFRASTRUCTURE

> *In the future, half of all the capital expenditures of a health system will go to find the information infrastructure of the system.*

The future of health care will be intricately intertwined with the development of information technology.[8] Likely half of all future capital resources of any health care organization will be devoted to building its information infrastructure. None of what is currently being constructed at health systems can be sustained without a well-linked information system that operates in a wide variety of areas affecting the community's health.

The effectiveness of services and the linkage of service providers along the continuum depends for the most part on the quality of the information the providers have to manage the clinical relationship. Much of the service network depends on the information system for facilitating work and evaluating effectiveness. Because of the diversity of services and the various locations of the providers, a mechanism is needed to support them and to link them. It is not possible to sustain the decentralized and highly mobile work force in a continuum-based organization without a good information infrastructure.

The problem with most information systems, including those being constructed at integrating health systems, is that few people know what their structure should be and how best to design them to serve the needs of the potential users. The conflict between a vision and the technology needed to realize it is often considerable. Making a truly effective information system requires the joining together of a host of vendors in a cross-platform arrangement whose complexity and cost boggles the imagination.

> *Information must flow smoothly across the continuum, and access to it must be fluid and friendly.*

Further, integrating the various partners to the service arrangement creates all kinds of ownership, use, linkage, and confidentiality issues.[9]

CREATING USEFUL INFORMATION SYSTEMS

Each of these issues must be confronted head on. The importance of good data for a highly decentralized operating and clinical system makes it necessary to ensure the information system is well constructed and useful, and several considerations need to be taken into account when designing the system.

Future components of the information system must be compatible with existing hardware and software and easy to "plug into" the system. Adding some components of the system at later stages will be necessary because of cost considerations and the work related to building the continuum over time.

Information must be designed for the user. It needs to be in a language and a format that allows the user to interpret and apply it instantly. The user should not get information that is valuable to the sender but has no application to his or her work.

It is no longer appropriate for financial information, operational information, and clinical information to be treated as distinct. Each is essential to determining what goes on at the point of service and what resources are needed for the work there. Tightening the relationships between the elements that influence effectiveness becomes one of the major challenges in the design of an information system. Any separation of financial, operational, and service information tends to compartmentalize decision making and reduce its quality.

The data system should be designed by users, not by data management experts. While the guidance and insight provided by the experts are essential to good design, investment in the information system must come from those who use it. If the barriers between information managers and clinical professionals are to ever be broken, both groups must join in the work of designing and evaluating the information system.

In the new paradigm, there is a central role for clinical data on the outcomes of treatment. These data allow sound judgments to be made as early as possible in the care cycle and can be used to adjust clinical processes that are not having the desired effect.

The hardware must be simple and convenient to use. If possible, it must be as portable as the provider is mobile. The more flexible it is, the more likely it will be used appropriately. Further, the more hardware pieces that can fit together or support other pieces, the greater the benefit to the providers. Cable linkages between computers and voice translation to hard data make the system more useful to a wider variety of people.

SUPPORTING THE POINT OF SERVICE

Information is going to be as important to the point-of-service provider as it has been to the finance officer. The medical records function will change dramatically in the new age. Its responsibilities will include helping design the

> *The user must be able to know what to get from the information system. Having information is no good if it isn't used.*

required formats and structures for information and then generating the kind of information the clinical providers need to make their work simple and effective.

The main clinical use of the information technology will be to document clinical events and processes and access and record data in a way that facilitates patient care.[10] The information services need to make sure that providers have easy access to information on all subscribers to the system.

It is no longer appropriate to view financial information as distinct from clinical information. Since the provider is increasingly the locus of control for service decision making, the financial implications of any decision must be available at the point of service. When price parameters are fixed in advance, as they increasingly are, it is important for providers to see how their decisions affect the expense framework for a particular patient and what options might be more cost-effective and service efficient.

CLINICAL SUPPORT

Ongoing compilation of progress indicators regarding a patient's pathway and his or her position on it is also critical to provider decision making. The ability to lay out the critical path and the protocols becomes the foundation for evaluating response of the patient to treatment. Ultimately, of course, information on the outcome for a particular patient should be combined with information on the outcomes of like patients so that the most effective methods of practice can be discerned.

All users should have access wherever they serve patients. The physician in the office should be able to use the data set for his or her purposes with as much ease as the nurse in the field. The more fluid the information network, the more useful it is. The designers should see the network as the primary vehicle for hooking together all the key players along the continuum of care and providing them a platform for communicating with the system, the patients, and each other. Once a patient is within the service system, he or she should be easy to access from any place in the system. The quality of the community-system interface will be dependent almost entirely on the efficacy of the health systems information infrastructure.

REDUCED PROVIDER COMPETITION

All providers are increasingly operating within the same frame of reference. There is less reason in the competitive marketplace for individual providers in the same system to be competing with each other. Physicians in a capitated system are actually supporting each other's practice.[11] Competition for patients and revenue no longer characterizes their relationship. Using the information system to make sure the physicians are connected to each other, to clinical data, and to the patients is now the central work of the information services.

In order to get the physicians deeply invested in the system, it is important to fully connect them to the information structure. Everything linking their individual activities to the information system contributes to their partnership with the organization. For example, it would be ideal if the system allowed the physicians to do billing, patient scheduling, documentation, transcription, and record review from wherever they might be.

INFORMATION FOR EVALUATION

Providers must also be able to evaluate groups of patients and their care over time. The team of providers who serve a defined patient population need to be able to determine what changes in activities or protocols are indicated by the aggregated data regarding that population. Data on care activities and their contribution to the clinical process and to total costs should be available to the team during evaluation. Adjustment of the team's activities, a shift in the team's standards and expectations, or a change in their relationship may entail a change in the database and a reconfiguration of the parameters of care. The system must facilitate this process and ensure that the adjustments can be incorporated when they do not violate other parameters of decision making.[12]

LINKING THE INTERNAL AND EXTERNAL COMMUNITIES

One of the most important uses of information is to link the health system and the community it serves. After all, the ultimate goal of creating a subscriber-based capitated system is to ensure the ongoing health of the community of subscribers while reducing the demand for illness-based, high-cost, high-intensity services. (The assumption is that cost control and service effectiveness are best obtained by decreasing the health system's dependence on such services.)

Simply designing effective treatment protocols and establishing good clinical, operational, information, and financial systems will not accomplish this goal.

These can be viewed as the foundation that must be laid in order to forge connections with the broader community and deal with issues of community health. It is in this context that community health service projects and community health information networks (CHINs) begin to have a defining role to play.

COMMUNITY HEALTH INFORMATION NETWORKS

The use of information technology to construct a database focused on the health of a community and develop the connections to address it is just beginning, and the potential value of CHINs is just now being explored. In order for information to be shared, it must exist, of course, but it also must be available in a useful form. Lack of useability is still an issue today. Ostensibly, CHINs would link health data from a wide range of sources—from public health services to statistical services to competing health systems.[13] The design of the information already existing at a number of these sources makes the linkage of the data feasible.

Most integrating health systems have been committed to building service-based information systems to link providers and operations together. It is expected that these networks will also help link the systems to their communities. However, other community connections must be initiated in order to build a strong health system–community relationship.

> *Information underpins all service relationships. Outcomes cannot be assessed if information is not easily useable by the provider at the point of service.*

An information system must aid in dealing with the health needs and issues that emerge out of the health system–community partnership. There are several guidelines to keep in mind when designing the information system:

- The information system must reflect some level of commitment to the health status of the community. It must be a place where the myriad categories of information can merge so that the community can gain an understanding of its needs.
- Data must be consolidated and reduced to a manageable level. Duplicate and nonessential information must be eliminated so that it does not reduce the usefulness of the data.
- Regardless of the purveyor of the system, the information it generates about the community's health belongs to all the partners. The information must not

be managed or manipulated in a way that obstructs the view of the stake-holders.

- The partners must be involved in designing and structuring the components of the information system so that it fits the needs of the users. For example, all users must have access to all the information generated by the system.
- The information system must empower the partners to meet their obligations. For example, not only will data often reveal a need for action, but they can be crucial in determining what course of action is the best. The information system must provide the kinds of data that are essential for deliberation and decision making.

The development of community initiatives of any kind, including a CHIN, requires a commitment to the equity. As stated previously, equity is based on equality. No matter how large a partner's contribution to the community–health system partnership, it has the right to access whatever is necessary for facilitating its contribution.

> **The information that is generated at the community level must prove itself to be of real value to the community.**

Since care in a continuum-based health system is population based, the group of stakeholders reflects the makeup of the community. Indeed, the community leadership must be involved in decisions on how to respond to the issues brought to light by the health data generated by the CHIN.

Like most community-related activities, decision making regarding health care has political implications. For this reason, the data must be clear, frank, and available. Open data lines facilitate open dialogue. While potential solutions to problems indicated by the data are subject to considerable dialogue and political processing, their effectiveness will be measurably enhanced by the directness and openness of the data generation.

LINKING TO THE POLITICAL STRUCTURE

Linking the information system to local and regional political structure is a challenging yet essential task. It requires dialoguing with the political and bureaucratic leadership as early as possible and linking them to the CHIN. The following guidelines should be kept in mind:

- The community expects its political leaders and structures to help it attain a state of improved health.

- The health systems must maintain direct communication linkages to individual political leaders at the local and regional levels.
- The political leadership should be included in institutional health care planning and policy formation.
- The linkage to the community should reflect the priorities of the political system in areas such as housing and education.
- The health system should become involved with the legislative process through offering testimony, constructing position papers, and engaging in policy development.
- The health system's database should be linked with public and government agency databases as a way of providing comprehensive information regarding the health needs of the community.

Integrated health systems have begun to make the initial linkages necessary to establish a firm foundation for health care information database development. They undoubtedly will continue to recognize that at the center of any effective community–health system relationship will be a well-designed, clearly integrated community health information network.

MAKING THE COMMUNITY CONNECTION

Many of the activities focused on community health depend on ongoing operational and functional linkages between the various health-related service industries.[14] There are a number of principles that pertain to developing these linkages. The following principles should guide the structural activities related to any work undertaken by any partner to the process.

Principle 1: The health system must play the lead role in providing the integration and linkage needed for the creation of healthy community initiatives. Because the focus of the health system is on generating health, it is reasonable to expect that the leadership for creating a healthy community network rests with the health system. The following expectations should flow out from the health system's commitment to creating a healthier community:

- The foundations of partnership are defined as part of the outreach of the health system.
- The responsibility for organizing and integrating healthy community initiative efforts belongs to the health system.
- Focusing on the education and development of the community partners and on the attainment of mutual understanding is essential.

- All the partners should be given an opportunity to be linked to the first activities related to building the community–health system relationship.
- The health system must provide the resources, location, time, and space necessary for the partners to gather.

Principle 2: All partners must be clear as to the vision, content, processes, and expectations of the healthy community initiatives. Without a clear understanding of the constructs and direction of the healthy community initiatives, the role of the partners becomes ambiguous and often skewed. Political and community fears, uncertainty, and lack of trust become accentuated when the contributions of the various partners are vague. Clarifying the significance of each partner's work and the expectations of each partner is an essential first step. Therefore, it is appropriate for these clarifying activities to be performed:

- A retreat for the partners should be utilized as a forum for developing a vision of a healthy community and setting the direction in which the partners should move.
- A facilitating process that includes the following elements should be undertaken:
    —a review of the factors that have led to the current need for an integrated approach to improving community health
    —an articulation of current circumstances and realities affecting community health
    —a delineation of stakeholder contributions to current and future efforts at improving health
    —clarification and articulation of the factors that will likely affect the creation of sustainable healthy community initiatives
- A strategic process directed toward achieving the following should be designed and implemented:
    —an understanding of the priorities and essential components of any healthy community initiative
    —clarification and articulation of the expectations of the partners regarding the improvement of community health
    —a delineation of the functional tasks and activities necessary to create sustainable healthy community initiatives
    —a definition of the strategic initiatives undertaken by the partners for the purpose of creating a model for building a healthy community
    —a commitment by all partners to the vision and direction and defined by them during the leadership retreat

Principle 3: The accountability of and expectations for each of the partners committed to the implementation of a healthy community initiative must be clearly delineated. All the strategic planning in the world will have no value if it cannot be translated into meaningful action. All of the partners to the undertaking should be clear about their role in performing the functions and activities necessary to achieve the desired outcome. A healthy community initiative will be successful only if the partners work to implement fully the components of the process for which they are uniquely accountable. To ensure that ownership of the components will result in the desired outcome, the following will be necessary:

- A governing body whose role is to coordinate, integrate, and facilitate the work of the partners should be created.
- Resources necessary for the activities of the partnership must be provided.
- A method for ensuring that conflicts, uncertainty, lack of clarity, and compliance and performance problems are addressed as soon as they arise must be defined. The goal is to make sure that the partnership is not threatened by the complexity of implementing the initiative.
- The partners must commit to the linkage of the public and private information systems that will provide data to those responsible for implementing and evaluating the healthy community initiative.
- The partners must identify the efficiencies in current health care activities and processes so that they can be corrected.

Principle 4: A mechanism must exist for evaluating the implementation and ongoing operation of the healthy community initiative. Clearly, if there is no way of measuring the changes brought about by the initiative, then its effectiveness will remain unknown—as will any modifications that might improve the initiative. Building evaluation activities into the process is a fundamental obligation of the partners, and the following elements should be considered to be requisite:

- a clear delineation of performance expectations and assignments for each of the partners
- criteria for measuring individual contributions and the linkage between the partners
- regular points of reference when the partners regather to determine individual and collective progress
- a supporting data infrastructure that provides broad-based information on the progress of the partners in integrating activities

- a framework for collective action and a definition of the time parameters within which adjustments and performance changes are to be undertaken
- generation of information regarding the healthy community initiative and communication of it to members of the community in a way that gets them invested in the processes related to their own health and the health of others

Principle 5: There is an ongoing process in place for maintaining a continuing dialogue with the community. Clearly, undertaking an initiative to improve the health of a community does nothing if the members of the community remain unengaged. The leadership should be expected to touch base with every level of the community and every cultural and social enclave.[15] The following tools can help the leaders to reach out effectively:

- an ongoing reporting mechanism for reporting the developmental and initiating activities of the healthy community initiative
- linkage with the press to ensure their investment in publicizing the healthy community initiative
- periodic community or town hall meetings (these can be used as a forum for dialogue and education)
- regular and ongoing generation of information about the health status of the community

These principles should guide the implementation of healthy community activities and partnerships. However, there is plenty of room for individualization. The culture and character of the community and the economic and social conditions that exist will determine which particular approaches and methods should be chosen.

Healthy community initiatives require a commitment to partnership.[16] In fact, building equitable partnerships is the fundamental task of the leadership of a healthy community initiative. It is expected that the health system, which itself undergoes significant changes, will be the place where the integration of the implementation activities begins and is sustained.

At most integrating health systems, building a foundation for a healthy community framework has already

> **Building healthy communities is not simple work. Most health systems know little about the health of the communities in which they reside.**

begun. Elements of the foundation include service pathways, population-based care design, a well-integrated and broad-based health care information system, a learning framework for internal community development, and linkages across the service region. Following are some of the activities that integrating health systems are undertaking to begin to extend their internal change process into the community and to provide initial linkages that will evolve into sustainable relationships.

COMMUNITY PARTNERSHIP ACTIVITIES

At many integrating health systems, the community–health system partnership began as an effort to coalesce fragmented pieces into a more focused system for determining whether the desired impact on community health status is being achieved. The steps that need to be undertaken by the health system leadership include these:

1. Inventory existing efforts within the system.
2. Inventory joint efforts with other agencies or delivery systems.
3. Inventory efforts going on anywhere to assess the health needs of the community (include new software capabilities for healthy community needs assessment).
4. Define "community" and develop population categories.
5. Inventory the resources currently available for the proposed initiative.
6. Inventory the interest of the board and senior management.
7. Inventory the interest of the system staff and medical staff.
8. Inventory the interest of the system partners.
9. Package the information.
10. Find a small group of committed individuals.
11. Plan a proposed system ("We have a dream!").
12. Take the show on the road.
13. Lock down baseline measures and put in place data collection mechanisms for ongoing measurement.
14. Implement the initiative internally and begin a dialogue on implementing it communitywide.
15. Constantly give feedback to all stakeholders.

GETTING STARTED

Most integrated health systems are currently in the "build the system" stage. The kinds of activities helping to focus staff on the community-centered work already ongoing might include

- an executive roundtable to bring together community and hospital system leaders to discuss health care issues
- a "healthy community" task force made up of several local delivery systems to deal with needs and problems such as childhood immunization and teen pregnancy
- a community needs assessment effort
- outreach programs, including prenatal education and diabetes education programs
- roundtable discussions with specific stakeholder groups to uncover health care issues related to specific cultural beliefs and practices and to improve the "cultural competence" of the organization

PARTNERSHIP FOR CHILDREN

Establishing a system of accessible services for children is often a good way to connect a broad cross section of the community with the health system. Young teenagers are having children at an alarming rate in many communities. Most single teenage mothers are very likely to have a second or even third child while very young, are relatively uneducated, and live in deep poverty. In a health system's ZIP code area, a defined percentage of the children live below the poverty level. There may be no fluoride in the water supply, a constant fear of gang violence, and poor air quality. Here is a clear health challenge! These children are the health care consumers of today, and they will continue to be heavy users of health services unless some kind of intervention occurs before their environment causes them to need high-intensity care.

Along with the health system, there are often numerous community and church groups working to improve the lives of the people in the community. Their work is inspiring and impressive. Partnership with them will be necessary to make sure children's needs are incorporated into the health system's community health plan.

A COMMUNITY DREAM

Imagine what it would be like if every health care delivery system and every employer in any market gave back a portion of its profits to improve the health of its community. If each hospital system in the area adopted one ZIP code or clearly defined a service support area and worked on improving the health status of the people in that area, the impact would be incredible. Imagine what could happen if all the agencies currently working in the community pooled their resources and worked toward the same health goals. The overwhelming difficulty of pulling such a diverse variety of political entities together is outweighed only by the outcome if nothing is done.

> *The health care system is a part of the community within which it resides. It has the same obligations of citizenship as anyone who is a member of the local community.*

There is simply no reason why integrating health systems should not provide the leadership needed to structure their relationships with their subscribers and others around the issues of community health. The goal should be to demonstrate a successful outcome with a defined and limited population, which will make the program more appealing to partner agencies and funding sources and allow the effort to become more horizontal.

SHARED GOVERNANCE AND COMMUNITY HEALTH

As noted at the beginning of this book, shared governance is a concept, not a model. In fact, there are many models that apply the principles and practices associated with the concept of shared governance. Whichever one fits the culture and purposes of the organization is the one that should be implemented. However, it is important to keep in mind that the *concept* of shared governance can be applied broadly—for example, to the integration of communities of any size. If a community wants to improve the health of its members, various components will need to be linked in a way that makes for effective joint action. The concept of shared governance is easily adaptable to a community frame of reference and can be used to develop the kind of partnerships between community organizations that will lead to improved health for the entire population.

BROADER NOTIONS OF HEALTH

What has been discussed in this chapter so far forms the foundation for a much broader concept of health and health service and for more intensive

> *Broader notions of health are essential to building toward healthier communities and to creating partnerships between health systems and the communities they serve.*

relationships along a longer continuum within a larger context. Clearly, in order for services provided in a community framework to be sustained, an organizational and systematic structure needs to be in place that gives form to the provision of services. The concept of shared governance can be used to support the enlarged set of organizational relationships entailed by such a structure.

No matter what a health system's size, the accountability of individual providers and groups of providers for the achievement of desired outcomes is essential for the system's effectiveness. In a community context, each health system must have accountability for the improvement of health for the members of the community. Furthermore, the demand for community integration and linkage of health systems throughout the community is no different from the demand for internal linkage within any particular system. Since shared governance is systems thinking applied to organizational relationships, the breadth and depth of the requisite linkages do not change. Only the format of the linkages changes.

> *Shared governance principles require that systems address the whole range of health issues. Therefore, lack of linkage to the community is simply not an option.*

Applying shared governance to a whole community health system (made up of individual health-related organizations) requires linkage at the governance, operations, and service levels. Institutions, services, structures, and resources must be connected in a way that provides a broad-based framework for decision making, service provision, evaluation, and governance. Among the activities associated with each component is the continuing assessment of the fluid boundaries of the shared governance structure and the impact of the social system on the character and the extent of those boundaries. As in all systems, boundaries between components or portions of a community health system need to change when the characteristics of the relationships call for a change.

The application of shared governance to larger systems requires the application of the same principles. If these principles are applied, the integrity and effectiveness of the relationships between the components will

> *The capacity to build toward health in the community is simply a broader view of the system. To do so creates more sustainable relationships.*

undoubtedly be enhanced. The resulting seamless integration around purpose and service, the structural accountability of each of the components, and the linkage between governance, operations, and services will all contribute to the achievement of the ultimate goal—improved health for the members of the community (see Figure 10-2).

ORGANIZING AROUND THE COMMUNITY

The leaders at integrated health systems should see no difference between organizing around a specific patient population and configuring around the entire community. The principles that govern the relationships between components remain essentially the same, although the structures and dynamics may be different. For example, a community health system governance council could

- provide a place where leaders from all the partners in the community health system make decisions about the direction of the system
- establish a mission and objectives for the community health system
- identify priorities and service parameters
- establish policies necessary for consistent behavior throughout the system
- develop strategies and tactics
- deal with integration issues, conflict, and barriers to seamlessness

The governance council could include representatives from all sectors of society, including the private sector, government, and the service agency sector. The governance process would focus on issues that might affect the long-term health of the community. It would truly link, especially at the local level, all of the elements needed to improve people's physical health as well as the social health of the community.

Shared governance at the community level would have the same elements as at the point of service. Breadth does not alter principle.

Guided by the community health system's governance council, the operations council (consisting of community service agency representatives) would deal with operations and resource issues. Its responsibilities would include

- budgeting and allocating resources

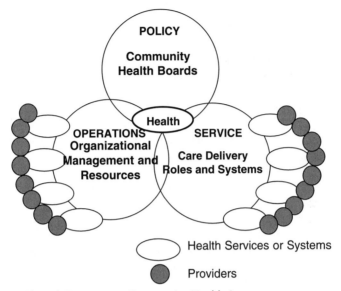

Figure 10-2 Shared Governance Community Health System

- defining the functional accountability and obligations of various components of the system
- defining the support and service structures necessary to integrate the continuum of care
- refining and improving the community information and communication system
- addressing the functional issues of relationship and partnership (those that facilitate or impede the ongoing activities necessary to maintain effective delivery of services within a community health framework)

Here again, the resource accountability of the operations council gets played out in the broad community context. Still, human, fiscal, material support, and systems resource distribution remains its core accountability.

At the service level of the community health system, integration around populations served is just as important as at the systems level. The main difference is that the populations are even more culturally and socially diverse.

The functional linkages and delivery structures still remain the essential core of the relationship between providers and consumers. However, linkage across the community continuum now becomes the framework for the activities of the community consumer services council. Here again, the issues that are deliberated at this level of decision making are those that directly and dramatically affect the achievement and maintenance of health within a community context by and with all those who comprise the community.

COMMUNITY DRIVEN SERVICE

At the community and consumer health services level, decisions that relate to the provision of service unfold within the broader context include

- defining the delivery system, the models, and approaches to the delivery of care
- outlining the linkages of the system along the continuum of care and all of the divisions of service provided within that context
- outlining the delivery mechanisms and the team membership essential to building a multifocal multidisciplinary approach to providing health services
- defining the interdisciplinary relationships, structures, processes, and evaluative activities to determine the successful intersection of disciplinary functions along a health care continuum
- evaluating the effectiveness of services, identifying problems and concerns, moving to solution orientation, outlining responsive and change strategies for adjusting activities, and evaluating the quality of care within the context of outcomes
- redefining and revising the models and approaches to care as the community demands for such changes are required

Here again, the framework remains focused on the point of service, the place where activities that support the outcomes of healthier communities unfold.[16] The intersection between consumers and providers is most intense where the community lives out its life and where the decisions made at the governance level get played out in the activities and functions of the point-of-service providers. Again, within the community context, the seamlessness of the linkages, the representative nature of the governance structure, the framework for decision making, and the point-of-service design work together to create the type of decision making and cooperation most likely to advance the health of the community.

CONCLUSION

The design and implementation of a shared governance approach provides a framework for achieving the broader agenda characteristic of the new health care paradigm.[17] The new paradigm forms the impetus for changing structures and relationships in all health systems. As this book indicates, integrating health systems simply have to take the risk of redefining themselves within the context of the new paradigm—which entails redefining relationships between people, redefining systems, and redefining work.

> *Shared governance reflects the structural requisites of the new age: partnership, equity, accountability, and ownership.*

Certainly, the frameworks identified in this book are preliminary to a set of much broader based frameworks that will be needed. Society is at the cusp of a fundamental change in social relationships driven by the impact of technology. There is risk inherent in creating new kinds of relationships—relationships, in this case, that reflect the interdependence of all people and systems, the need for broad-based horizontal relationships between systems, the desire to re-create communities within the context of the emerging paradigm, and the need to realign the organizational formats in more functional ways.

> *Shared governance represents the effort of systems to configure themselves in ways that engage stakeholders in a collective construction of a preferable future.*

Health care cannot be viewed in the same context it once was. The sickness-driven, event-based delivery of services is no longer adequate to meet society's health needs. In the long term, intervention-oriented health care organizations will not be able to survive. As we build a more effective framework for health care, all the structures, support systems, and relationships that once defined the delivery of health care will come crashing down. The question then becomes, what new structures, support systems, and relationships will emerge to meet health needs in the new social paradigm?

While we are quite clearly at the very beginning of a long and arduous journey, shared governance has already proved capable of creating structures and relationships that reflect the expectations of the emerging age. It clearly has the potential to reengage those individuals in health systems who are undergoing dramatic and even painful changes. Consequently, it also has the potential to play a major role in the new health care paradigm, because in the final analysis it is the energy and commitment of the stakeholders at every level that will sustain the health systems during the protracted but inevitable evolution to come.

REFERENCES

1. J. Champy, *Reengineering Management* (New York: Harper Business, 1995).
2. B. Collora, "Partnerships for Health," *Healthcare Forum* 37, no. 3 (1994):53–72.
3. T. Porter-O'Grady, "Building Partnerships in Health Care: Creating Whole Systems Change," *Nursing and Health Care* 15, no. 1 (1994):34–38.
4. D. Beckham, "The Power of Primary Care," *Healthcare Forum Journal* 37, no. 1 (1994):68–74.
5. R. Coile, "Year 2000 Scenario for Physician-Hospital Organizations," *Topics in Health Care Financing* 20, no. 4 (1994):75–83.
6. J. Goldsmith, "Driving the Nitroglycerin Truck: The Relationship between the Hospital and Physician," *Healthcare Forum Journal* 36, no. 2 (1993):36–40.
7. S. DeWoody and J. Price, "A Systems Approach to Multidimensional Critical Paths," *Nursing Management* 25, no. 11 (1994):47–51.
8. T. Davenport, *Process Innovation: Reengineering Work through Information Technology* (Boston: Harvard Business School Press, 1992).
9. K. Duncan, *Health Information and Health Reform: The Need for a Health Information System* (San Francisco: Jossey-Bass, 1994).
10. S. Carter and M. McKenna, "Nursing's Role in Implementing the Computerized Patient Record," *Seminars for Nurse Managers* 2, no. 2 (1994):96–101.
11. R. Kanter, "Collaborative Advantage: The Art of Alliances," *Harvard Business Review* 72, no. 4 (1994):96–108.
12. M. Bowers, J. Swan, and W. Koehler, "What Attributes Determine Quality and Satisfaction with Health Care Delivery?" *Health Care Management Review* 19, no. 4 (1995):49–55.
13. J. Tan, "Integrating Health Care with Information Technology," *Health Care Management Review* 19, no. 2 (1994):72–80.
14. K. Zander, *Managing Outcomes through Collaborative Care: Care Mapping and Case Management* (Chicago: American Hospital Publishing, 1995).
15. A. Etzioni, *The Spirit of Community* (New York: Crown, 1993).
16. T. Porter-O'Grady, "Managing along the Continuum: A New Paradigm for the Clinical Manager," *Nursing Administration Quarterly* 19, no. 3 (1995):1–12.
17. K. Evans et al., "Whole Systems Shared Governance: A Model for the Integrated Health System," *Journal of Nursing Administration* 25, no. 5 (1995):18–27.

Index